CONSTITUTIONAL RIGHTS AND CONSTITUTIONAL DESIGN

The decisions courts make in constitutional rights cases pervade our political life and touch on our most basic interests and values. The spread of judicial review of legislation around the world means that courts are increasingly called on to settle matters of moral and political controversy, including assisted suicide, data privacy, anti-terrorism measures, marriage, and abortion. But doubts regarding the institutional capacities of courts for deciding such questions are growing. Judges now regularly review social science research to assess whether a law will effectively achieve its aim, and at what cost to other interests. They cite studies and statistical information from psychology, sociology, medicine, and other disciplines in which they are rarely trained. This empirical reasoning proceeds alongside open-ended moral reasoning, with judges employing terms such as equality, liberty, and autonomy, then determining what these require in concrete circumstances. This book shows that courts were not designed for this kind of moral and empirical reasoning. It argues that in comparison to legislatures, the institutional capacities of courts are deficient. Legislatures are better equipped than courts for deliberating and decision-making in regard to the kinds of factual and moral issues that arise in constitutional rights cases. The book concludes by considering the implications of comparative institutional capacity for constitutional design. Is a system of judicial review of legislation something that constitutional framers should choose to adopt? If so, in what form? For countries with systems of judicial review, practical proposals are made to remedy deficiencies in the institutional capacities of courts.

Constitutional Rights and Constitutional Design

Moral and Empirical Reasoning in Judicial Review

Paul Yowell

• HART •
OXFORD • LONDON • NEW YORK • NEW DELHI • SYDNEY

HART PUBLISHING
Bloomsbury Publishing Plc
Kemp House, Chawley Park, Cumnor Hill, Oxford, OX2 9PH, UK

HART PUBLISHING, the Hart/Stag logo, BLOOMSBURY and the Diana logo are trademarks of Bloomsbury Publishing Plc

First published in Great Britain 2018

A catalogue record for this book is available from the British Library.

Library of Congress Cataloging-in-Publication data

Names: Yowell, Paul, 1969- author.

Title: Constitutional rights and constitutional design : moral and empirical reasoning in judicial review / Paul Yowell.

Description: Oxford [UK] ; Portland, Oregon : Hart Publishing, 2018. | Includes bibliographical references and index.

Identifiers: LCCN 2017053830 (print) | LCCN 2017055289 (ebook) | ISBN 9781509913602 (Epub) | ISBN 9781509913596 (hardback : alk. paper)

Subjects: LCSH: Judicial review. | Constitutional courts. | Civil rights. | Judicial ethics. | Judicial review—Moral and ethical aspects.

Classification: LCC K3175 (ebook) | LCC K3175 .Y69 2018 (print) | DDC 347/.012—dc23

LC record available at https://lccn.loc.gov/2017053830

ISBN: HB: 978-1-50991-359-6
ePDF: 978-1-50991-361-9
ePub: 978-1-50991-360-2

Typeset by Compuscript Ltd, Shannon

PREFACE

Some main themes in this book are well illustrated in an important case pending before the US Supreme Court. In *Gill v Whitford*, the claimants have urged the Court to strike down redistricting laws in Wisconsin and impose an alternative to what they regard as illegal gerrymandering. They claim that current laws violate their right to equality under the Fourteenth Amendment. At the hearing the justices discussed a recent study submitted by the claimants and relied on by a lower court, which proposes a formula (termed the 'efficiency gap') for calculating—and expressing mathematically—the degree of partisan advantage that obtains in a given districting scheme. Chief Justice Roberts was reported in the press as saying the study seemed to be 'sociological gobbledygook', while acknowledging this could be due to his educational background. Some commentators claimed Roberts's statement reflected an anti-science attitude. The president of the American Sociological Association wrote an open letter to Roberts, stating that 'social scientists and legal scholars at your alma mater would be disappointed to learn that you attributed your lack of understanding of social science to your Harvard education' and offering to assemble a team of 'renowned sociologists' to teach Roberts and his staff about social science.

Roberts did not claim that the study—or sociology in general—is incomprehensible or meaningless, but he did suggest it could appear that way to the public. If courts strike down an electoral law on the basis of a complex mathematical formula, Roberts worried, the public might suspect that the real motivation is partisan. Justice Breyer evinced a similar concern, asking whether the claims could be explained 'without going into what I agree is pretty good gobbledygook'.

Beyond questions of appearance to the public, the question of judicial training and capacity for understanding social science is a real and serious one. Breyer has written on the importance of scientific evidence in courts while simultaneously warning about problems with judicial competence in using it. It is to his credit that Roberts acknowledged that his educational background (he studied history and then law at Harvard) may not have equipped him to understand the empirical study at issue. It is little to the credit of the president of the ASA that he responded in a disparaging and condescending manner. As this book shows, many judges and scholars have raised concerns about the lack of judicial training to analyse empirical research. The problems are endemic, and even if ad hoc sessions such as the one proposed by the ASA president might ameliorate them in some way, it is doubtful that such training can resolve the larger issues.

Justice Alito raised another issue regarding the empirical evidence in *Gill v Whitford*, noting that the 'efficiency gap' formula is based primarily on a single paper published in 2014. He observed that there is no body of scholarship testing the 2014 paper, which proposed rejecting measures previously used by social scientists. This touches on another theme discussed in this book. I argue that courts should be wary of nullifying laws on the basis of social science research, considering the long-lasting effect of such constitutional judgments alongside the frequency with which social science findings are called into question by later research. With regard to the 'efficiency gap' paper in question, there are now several studies by social scientists and mathematicians criticising aspects of its argument, a number of which were published either shortly before the oral hearing or afterwards. Some of the papers involve complex mathematical analysis.

The central question of this book is whether courts have the institutional capacity needed to decide the empirical and moral issues that play an increasingly large role in constitutional rights cases. The 'efficiency gap' paper in *Gill v Whitford* exemplifies the empirical reasoning that judges are asked to perform. It concerns statistical data regarding distribution of voters and their party alignment, and questions about how drawing lines for electoral districts produces causal effects on electoral outcomes. In the background is the moral reasoning by which courts move from an abstract principle such as 'equal protection of the laws' to a more concrete principle such as 'one-person, one vote', and then to even more specific means for applying that principle to particular electoral schemes. This is the doctrinal question in *Gill v Whitford*, and the case shows how empirical and moral reasoning can become intertwined and bound up in reasoning with a more distinctly legal character. This book does not make sharp demarcations between empirical, moral, and legal reasoning. Any such attempt at categorical definition would leave blurry lines. Nonetheless, the examples and explanations used in this book make clear the difference between text-based legal reasoning and the straightforwardly empirical reasoning and moral reasoning frequently employed in constitutional rights cases.

While I am critical of a number of constitutional decisions for the way in which they have dealt with empirical information, my criticisms do not themselves rely on any detailed analysis of the use of statistics. The errors I ascribe to judges are of the kind that a layman can identify through analysing decisions and underlying sources with awareness of the kinds of mistakes commonly made in dealing with numbers—and which are well explained in non-specialist books such as *Reckoning with Risk: Learning to Live with Uncertainty* (2003) by Gerd Girgerenzer and *The Tiger that Isn't: Seeing Through a World of Numbers* (2007) by Andrew Dilnot, former chair of the UK Statistics Authority, and Michael Blastland. There are other uses of statistics and empirical information by courts that would require more specialised analysis. If the US Supreme Court decides *Gill v Whitford* by relying on the 'efficiency gap' or similar statistical analysis, the rationale of the judgment—and the errors, if any, in the court's reasoning or the underlying study—might be accessible only to specialists or those willing to devote considerable time to complex mathematical problems.

***

I am grateful for permission to borrow from my previously published chapter 'Empirical Research in Rights-Based Review of Legislation', in Peter Huber and Katya Ziegler (eds) *Current Problems in the Protection of Human Rights: Perspectives from Germany and the UK* (Oxford, Hart Publishing, 2013), sections of which appear in modified form in chapter 4.

Many colleagues and friends helped me by reading and commenting on drafts and in other ways. I thank Dominic Burbidge, Fernando Contreras, Donald Drakeman, Donald Hay, Nathaniel Helms, Maris Köpcke Tinturé, Jeff King, Santiago Legarre, Fok-Shuen Leung, Martin Luteran, Kai Möller, Jonathan Price, Grégoire Webber, and David Wiggins. A special debt of gratitude is owed to Cristóbal Orrego and Francisco Urbina. I thank Nick Barber and Richard Ekins, with whom I have been fortunate to collaborate in common research interests and to discuss at length the issues in this book, for many valuable insights. I am profoundly grateful to John Finnis, who helped give shape to several arguments in this book, for his support and guidance through the years. Most important of all, my family has graciously and patiently supported me from the start until the end.

Paul W Yowell
Oriel College
January 2018

CONTENTS

1

Introduction

The decisions courts make in constitutional rights cases pervade our political life and touch on our most basic interests and values. Following the spread of the power of judicial review of legislation around the world, courts are called on to settle issues regarding assisted suicide, data privacy, campaign finance, voting rights, gun control, anti-terrorism measures, marriage, abortion, surrogacy, immigration, and many other matters of deep moral and political controversy. Some critics of judicial review have vigorously argued that entrusting such decisions to courts violates the fundamental democratic principle of equal participation in government. No less vigorously, defenders of judicial review have contended that it is necessary to ensure the survival of a healthy form of democracy that protects the rights of all, including minorities. In this book I focus on a different question. Do courts and judges have the institutional capacity needed to settle the kinds of morally and politically controversial issues that arise in constitutional rights cases?

The power to strike down legislation because it violates abstract moral rights invites judges to engage in broad moral and empirical reasoning over a wide range of questions. For aid in this task, judges increasingly review empirical research to assess whether a law will effectively achieve its aim, and at what cost to other interests, citing studies and statistical information from disciplines such as psychology, sociology, and medicine, and a broad array of non-legal sources. This empirical reasoning proceeds alongside moral reasoning, in which judges employ value-laden terms such as equality, liberty, autonomy, privacy, democracy, and human dignity, determining what those values require in concrete circumstances. I will argue that, no matter how well trained and educated judges are, and no matter how carefully they are selected for office, the institutional setting of a court is lacking in basic capacities for moral and empirical reasoning. The book will also consider proposals to remedy these deficiencies.

We can distinguish inquiries into whether an institution is (i) authorised to exercise a power, (ii) designed for it, and (iii) capable of doing it well. Courts that have the power to review legislation usually have formal constitutional *authorisation* for this, though in some cases they have assumed that power on their own initiative or extended it beyond the formal remit.[1] In whatever way they have

[1] As Alec Stone Sweet observes, constitutional courts 'have shaped and reshaped their own political environments' and 'routinely subvert separation of powers schemes, including elements on which their legitimacy was originally founded': A Stone Sweet, 'Constitutional Courts' in M Rosenfeld and A Sajó, *The Oxford Handbook of Comparative Constitutional Law* (Oxford, Oxford University Press, 2012) 817.

acquired power to enforce abstract moral rights, courts have not been specifically *designed* by constitutional framers to engage in ambitious, open-ended moral reasoning, or to acquire and assess social science and statistical data. As a result, courts generally lack the *institutional capacities* needed to perform these tasks well. In some cases, though, courts have developed processes that help to address these deficiencies.

Most constitutional courts conform broadly to one of two institutional models of judicial review, which I shall call the American and Kelsenian models.[2] Although the term 'constitutional court' can be used in reference to both models, it has a specific sense tied to the latter. In the Kelsenian model the power to adjudicate the constitution is centralised in one constitutional court, and other courts lack this power. Review of legislation by such a constitutional court is generally *abstract*, meaning that the court determines whether legislation is constitutional outside the context of an ordinary legal case. The jurisdiction of a constitutional court is invoked when lower courts refer constitutional questions to it, and in some systems actors in the legislative or executive branches can initiate constitutional cases. In Germany and certain other jurisdictions, constitutional complaints can be initiated by individual citizens. A constitutional court is situated not at the top of the hierarchy of the system of ordinary courts, but outside of that system, and its jurisdiction is only over constitutional issues. The Kelsenian model is so called because of the influence Hans Kelsen had practically in serving on the committee that designed the constitutional court established in Austria in 1919, and theoretically in defending its role and structure.[3] This is the dominant model in Europe, and countries that follow it include Germany, Austria, Italy, Spain, France,[4] and nearly all of the countries that formerly were part of the Soviet bloc. Outside Europe countries with this model include South Africa, Chile, and Colombia.

In the American model, a 'supreme' court has the final say over the constitution and the bill of rights due to its hierarchical superiority within the ordinary court system. The supreme court's primary jurisdiction is over appeals from lower courts, and it decides cases that raise issues of constitutional law as well as non-constitutional law. In this model the supreme court does not have a monopoly on authority to rule on the constitution and rights; this power extends to at least some levels of lower courts.[5] This model originated in the United States, and countries that follow it include Canada, Ireland, and India. Others that partially follow the American model include Greece, Brazil, and Argentina. Some of these countries

[2] Using similar terminology, Stone Sweet observes that the majority trend since World War II has been toward the Kelsenian court: ibid, 816–18.

[3] ibid 819.

[4] The French *Conseil constitutionnel* originally had the power to review legislation only at the pre-enactment phase, but was given a power of *a posteriori* review in 2008. See F Fabbrini, 'Kelsen in Paris: France's Constitutional Reform and the Introduction of a Posteriori Constitutional Review of Legislation' (2008) 9 *German Law Journal* 1297.

[5] In the United States itself the power extends generally to appellate and trial courts in courts in both the state and federal systems.

depart from one distinctive feature of the US system: the limitation of court jurisdiction to actual cases and controversies. Canada, Ireland, India, and Brazil all have some form of reference system that can initiate abstract review for constitutional cases. Nonetheless, in these as well as other countries that follow the American model, judicial review of legislation is generally concrete and case-based.

In the original templates for the two models, there is no provision of institutional capacities for engaging in the kind of broad moral and empirical reasoning common in modern constitutional rights adjudication. In the US, the Supreme Court has always had the basic institutional structure of a common law appellate court. It has no dedicated facilities for acquiring and assessing empirical research, and justices thus rely on the evidential record developed in the trial court or submitted for the first time on appeal in briefs. This is sometimes supplemented by research they undertake personally and on their own initiative. Justices are not openly selected on the basis of their moral or political judgement or beliefs, but rather their legal expertise and judicial experience. Their educational and professional backgrounds fall within a narrow range, and they are usually drawn from a few elite schools.[6] Outside the US, where law is not an undergraduate degree, the formal education of justices on supreme courts may be exclusively legal education. In the US and elsewhere there can be a divergence between the official, public discussion of the qualifications of nominees, and the behind-the-scenes assessment of their moral and political judgement and views on controversial issues. But the need of the system to profess political neutrality is indicative of an institutional structure oriented toward legal expertise, and is also linked to the notion that constitutional law is justiciable in the same way as ordinary law. In the American model even judges in first-instance trial courts are considered competent to adjudicate constitutional rights and determine whether statutes are constitutional.

In contrast to the more legalistic conception of judicial review in the American model, Kelsen conceived of a constitutional court as having both an overtly political function and legislative power, albeit that of a 'negative legislator'; and he designed its institutional structure accordingly.[7] Judicial review would be centralised in the constitutional court, and it would be abstract rather than concrete. The court's personnel would ideally be drawn from the top ranks of the legal academy, and parliamentary bodies would be involved in the appointment process. However, Kelsen thought the court's political and legislative function should be limited to control of structural provisions in the constitution, for example, the division of powers between central and regional governments or between administrative and judicial bodies.[8] He rejected the suggestion that a constitutional court

[6] For example, all current members of the US Supreme Court were educated at Harvard or Yale law schools.

[7] H Kelsen, 'On the Nature and Development of Constitutional Adjudication' in L Vinx (ed), *The Guardian of the Constitution: Hans Kelsen and Carl Schmitt on the Limits of Constitutional Law* (Cambridge, Cambridge University Press, 2015) 47.

[8] Kelsen, 'On the Nature and Development of Constitutional Adjudication' in *Guardian of the Constitution* 47–48.

should have the power to enforce abstract moral rights. He considered vague terms such as 'liberty', 'freedom', 'equality' and 'justice' to be an invocation of 'natural law',[9] lacking in legal content and providing no determinate guidance to a judge.[10] Thus, adopting a bill of rights would give a constitutional court an unacceptable amount of political power.[11] Nonetheless, almost every country that has followed the Kelsenian model has adopted a bill of rights, and advocates of constitutional courts often closely link having such a court to the idea of constitutional rights. As Alec Stone Sweet has noted, theorists have usually 'politely ignored' this contradiction with Kelsen's model and his warnings about adopting vague moral standards in a constitution.[12]

One explanation for this contradiction is that almost all constitutional courts on the Kelsenian model were adopted in the aftermath of authoritarian regimes. Germany, Italy, Spain, and Portugal created constitutional courts in the course of adopting new constitutions following the fascist regimes that had governed them during World War II. A second wave of constitutional courts was created in central and eastern Europe after the fall of the Berlin wall and the Soviet Empire. Countries that have adopted constitutional courts have generally done so at a moment of distrust toward the political system itself, which was new, immature, and susceptible to the influence of residual members who had supported the prior authoritarian regime.[13] Thus constitutional framers wanted an institution to safeguard democratic procedures, and to protect basic rights from the kinds of abuses experienced under fascism and communism.[14] For a number of reasons they found the Kelsenian model of a constitutional court amenable for this purpose.[15] They added to Kelsen's model a bill of rights. But they usually did not equip courts to engage in the broad moral and empirical reasoning needed for accurate, informed decision-making across the wide range of moral and political controversies that come before constitutional courts today.

This book will consider the American and Kelsenian models in further detail, as part of a discussion of proposals to reform the institutional capacities of courts. I will argue that the Kelsenian model is generally superior to the American model with regard to capacities for moral and empirical reasoning. Nevertheless, both models are lacking in certain key institutional capacities when compared to legislatures. Others have argued that courts are institutionally well placed to decide cases about abstract moral rights because they are independent and not subject to majoritarian pressures and the corrupting effects of electoral processes.

[9] ibid 58.
[10] ibid 59.
[11] ibid 61.
[12] Stone Sweet, 'Constitutional Courts' in *Oxford Handbook of Comparative Constitutional Law* 819.
[13] See S Issacharoff, *Fragile Democracies: Contested Power in the Era of Constitutional Courts* (Cambridge, Cambridge University Press, 2015).
[14] Stone Sweet, 'Constitutional Courts' in *Oxford Handbook of Comparative Constitutional Law* 820–22.
[15] ibid.

In chapter five, I consider the counter-majoritarian argument for judicial review of legislation. Even if we assume that legislatures are inherently biased against minorities—a claim I will dispute—it still does not follow that decisions about abstract moral rights should be entrusted to courts. For courts, too, might be poor at deciding such cases, if for different reasons. If the police are prone to corruption and cannot be entrusted to investigate crimes, we should not on that account assign criminal investigation to the fire brigade. Questions about the allocation of power among institutions need to be answered in the light of an analysis of comparative institutional capacities.[16] Such an analysis can also inform discussions over the reform of existing practices of judicial review of legislation.

I. Removing the Blindfold

In artistic renderings of Justice the blindfold covering her eyes represents a certain ideal about how judges deliberate and decide cases. Seeing only the admissible evidence pertaining to the legal question in dispute, judges are blind to other realities about the accused or parties. Their deliberation is not influenced by the identity of the parties or the larger consequences of imposing the judgment required by law. That is so, whether the consequences are for the person on trial or the surrounding society. Judges are enabled to ignore such consequences in good conscience, even to let the heavens fall (*fiat justia ruat caelum*), because the law is an objective measure, laid down previously by an authority distinct from the court. The scales and the blindfold are the reason Justice is entrusted with a sword: her power is not of her own initiative. Reflection on this ideal of Justice blindfolded, in comparison to the situation of judges in constitutional rights adjudication, is a way to begin thinking about whether courts are rightly structured for that responsibility, and whether they have the appropriate capacities. Courts are institutionally structured around the central premise of the blindfold ideal—that the law provides clear, specific direction.

Constitutional rights, because they are formulated in vague and abstract moral language, provide little or no direction for deciding individual cases. Cases are usually resolved not by any specific constitutional text or rule laid down in the past, but by a court's present determination of what is appropriate. Precedent in previous constitutional cases may have some influence, but often it provides only a broad framework for review in which courts exercise fresh judgement. The broad moral and empirical reasoning that judges employ is different in kind from the interpretative techniques employed by courts in ordinary legal reasoning. In constitutional rights cases, many expect that judges should, in effect, remove

[16] See NW Barber, 'Prelude to the Separation of Powers' (2001) 60 *Cambridge Law Journal* 59.

the blindfold, and inform themselves as far as possible about all the facts and moral arguments surrounding a case, and all the consequences for society as a whole of deciding it one way or another. Judges are still expected to show no favouritism to the parties; however, it is not centrally the individual party that stands before the bar of justice, but rather the policy or rule being challenged as unconstitutional. The moral reasoning in many constitutional cases is broad and open-ended, touching on the meaning and demands of values of liberty or autonomy, equality, or procedural fairness. Balancing tests and the proportionality inquiry, the most frequent methods of constitutional rights adjudication, combine moral and empirical reasoning in an inquiry into whether a law's overall benefit to a state is worth the burden it imposes on individual interests. There is a growing phenomenon, especially in the US but spreading elsewhere, of judges conducting their own empirical research. Increasingly, judges go online to investigate empirical research outside the formal record, privately in their chambers or with the assistance of law clerks.[17] The Supreme Court's citation of non-legal sources has increased dramatically in recent decades.[18]

All this is in contrast to the role of the judge in ordinary legal cases, where rules of pleading, procedure, and evidence tightly constrain the issues to be decided, the evidence that can be considered, and the burden of proof to be satisfied. The statutes and other legal norms that guide judges' substantive decisions vary in their degree of specificity, but they provide clearer legal direction than constitutional rights. As HLA Hart observed,

> [T]he life of the law consists to a very large extent in the guidance both of officials and private individuals by determinate rules which, unlike the applications of variable standards, do not require from them a fresh judgment from case to case.[19]

There remains significant room for moral reasoning in various aspects of ordinary legal cases, and more or less loose approaches to interpreting the law; but this is surrounded by constraints on every side.

The limited, constrained nature of judicial reasoning in Western legal systems is, according to Tony Honoré, a legacy of the legal culture of Rome.[20] The Greeks had failed to demarcate a canon of arguments proper to legal discourse,[21] and for them any argument was 'grist to the mill: in particular arguments *ad hominem*, that one's opponent was a scoundrel or that one had oneself performed notable services to the city; and arguments which appeal directly to religious principles or to political considerations'.[22] Roman legal discourse was not limited solely to

[17] See A Larsen, 'Confronting Supreme Court Fact Finding' (2012) *Virginia Law Review* 1255.

[18] F Schauer and V Wise, 'Nonlegal Information and the Delegalization of Law' (2000) 29 *The Journal of Legal Studies* 495; F Schauer, 'The Dilemma of Ignorance: Pga Tour, Inc. V Casey Martin' (2001) *The Supreme Court Review* 267.

[19] HLA Hart, *The Concept of Law*, 2nd edn (Oxford, Oxford University Press, 2012) 135.

[20] AM Honoré, 'Legal Reasoning in Rome and Today' (1973) 4 *Cambrian Law Review* 58, 64.

[21] ibid.

[22] ibid.

acknowledged legal sources of authority, but it was constrained by strong conventions regarding use of non-legal sources. Such open arguments had to be neutral between persons (not conceived *ad hominem*) and systems (appeals to utility, equity, nature, etc had to be based on generally accepted values).[23] Moreover, 'open arguments must ultimately give way to rules':

> [I]n the last resort the argument that the decision proposed is inconsistent with a rule compelling the contrary decision, must be accepted. This in turn entails that the arbiters of society are in the last resort legislators.[24]

These constraints, Honoré argues, gave rise to the impartiality between persons that is crucial to our legal culture: the 'essence of the Roman gift to modern western civilization' is 'the existence of a canon of unacceptable legal arguments'.[25] Among his examples is the canon restricting the extent to which sociological and statistical arguments can properly be addressed to a court.[26] However, observing the scene in 1973, Honoré notes that in 'certain countries, such as the U.S.A., attempts are being made to destroy the separateness of legal discourse,' by making legal issues into questions in which 'every sort of political and moral consideration is relevant'.[27]

The most influential proponent of the use of moral reasoning by judges, Ronald Dworkin, awards an especially prominent place to political, moral, and philosophical considerations in constitutional rights adjudication. Constitutions include a number of abstract rights, he says, with some of 'near limitless abstraction'.[28]

> [T]he Bill of Rights therefore seems to give judges almost incredible power. Our legal culture insists that judges—and finally the justices of the Supreme Court—have the last word about the proper interpretation of the Constitution. Since the great clauses command simply that government show equal concern and respect for the basic liberties—without specifying in further detail what that means and requires—it falls to judges to declare what equal concern really does require and what the basic liberties really are. *But that means that judges must answer intractable, controversial, and profound questions of political morality that philosophers, statesmen, and citizens have debated for many centuries, with no prospect of agreement.* (emphasis added)[29]

John Rawls, similarly, argues that the Supreme Court has authority to settle controversial questions of political morality and remove them from public debate, in its role as an exemplar of public reason.[30] Dworkin has done more than Rawls and most theorists to confront the questions of institutional capacity that are

[23] ibid 65.
[24] ibid.
[25] ibid 64.
[26] ibid 66.
[27] ibid 66.
[28] R Dworkin, *Freedom's Law: The Moral Reading of the American Constitution* (New York, Oxford University Press, 1999) 73.
[29] ibid 74.
[30] J Rawls, *Political Liberalism* (New York, Columbia University Press, 2005) 237.

implicated when such extensive power is given to courts. Unlike many theorists, Dworkin argues that courts lack the institutional capacities needed to handle social science and statistical information.[31] His theory of rights as trumps is designed to avoid the need for this, as chapter three will discuss, but I argue that it fails to do so.

The trend toward morally weighted constitutional decision-making endorsed by Dworkin and Rawls, which Honoré perceived to be accelerating in the 1970s, had begun earlier in the US. In 1932 US Supreme Court Justice Louis Brandeis observed:

> In the cases which now come before us *there is seldom any dispute as to the interpretation of any provision*. The controversy is usually over the *application* to existing conditions of some well-recognized constitutional limitation. This is strikingly true of cases under the due process clause when the question is whether a statute is *unreasonable, arbitrary, or capricious* [and] of cases under the equal protection clause when the question is whether there is any reasonable basis for the classification made by a statute. (emphasis added)[32]

The distinction Brandeis draws between *interpretation* and *application* tracks the difference I observed above between: (i) judging a case by a specific, objective measure laid down *in the past*; and (ii) using a broad standard that requires a fresh judgment *at the time of the trial*. There are many borderline cases between (i) and (ii), but that should not be taken to erase the distinction between the types of decisions, or Brandeis's distinction between *interpretation* and *application*. The half-light of dawn does not eliminate the distinction between night and day. Most constitutional rights adjudication falls into category (ii), as further explanations in this book will demonstrate. Jeremy Waldron has observed that

> constitutional constraints do not operate mechanically, but work instead by vesting a power of decision in some person or body of persons (a court), whose job it is to determine *as a matter of judgment* whether conduct that is contemplated (say, by the legislature) at t_2 violates a constraint adopted at t_1.[33]

As Brandeis describes its task, the Court makes open-ended judgments about whether a statute is 'unreasonable, arbitrary or capricious'.

Chapter four explains Brandeis's own part in establishing the modern approach to judicial review of legislation, through his 'Brandeis brief' in *Muller v Oregon* (1908) (when he was a practising lawyer),[34] which in the US and elsewhere is the label used for briefs in constitutional cases that present empirical research for assessing laws under balancing and proportionality tests. I will show, however, that this technique actually originated in *Lochner v New York* (1905).[35]

[31] R Dworkin, 'Social Sciences and Constitutional Rights—the Consequences of Uncertainty' (1977) 6 *Journal of Law and Education* 3.

[32] *Burnet v Coronado Oil & Gas Co* 285 US 393, 410 (1932).

[33] J Waldron, *Law and Disagreement* (Oxford, Oxford University Press, 1999) 262.

[34] *Muller v Oregon* 208 US 412 (1908).

[35] *Lochner v New York* 198 US 45 (1905).

The claimant in that case succeeded in persuading the Supreme Court to strike down a law setting working-hours limits by presenting a statistics-filled brief arguing that the law would not effectively achieve its purported health aims. This was the first successful use of this technique in a major constitutional case. Against the myth that associates *Lochner* with formalist adjudication, I show that *Lochner* is the paradigm case for modern balancing and proportionality review.

II. Scope of the Argument

Judicial use of empirical and moral reasoning extends beyond proportionality and balancing tests, and indeed it extends beyond constitutional rights and constitutional law. This book does not address every dimension of this phenomenon. I focus on the adjudication of abstract constitutional rights in judicial review of legislation, and in particular on cases that assess the content of substantive law to determine whether it is consistent with rights. The reason for this focus is that this class of cases brings into sharp relief the need to compare the institutional capacities of courts and legislatures. The result of a judgment striking down a law on the grounds that its substantive content violates an abstract moral right is to settle the issue and remove it from the political arena and the legislature's purview. To justify such a constitutional arrangement there must be grounds for being confident that courts have the necessary institutional capacities and are a proper forum for making such decisions. I will argue that we lack such grounds.

Within the class of cases specified on the adjudication of abstract moral rights, I give special attention to the proportionality inquiry, for a number of reasons. The first is its widespread use. The most common method worldwide for adjudicating constitutional rights goes under the label of 'proportionality'; in courts across Europe and many other countries one finds the familiar structure of a multi-part test by which judges scrutinise a law with regard to the law's suitability for achieving a legitimate aim, whether the law is necessary (in the sense of using the least restrictive means), and whether the law achieves an appropriate *balance* between the burdens it imposes and the value of the aim. The US is exceptional in neither using the label 'proportionality' nor overtly employing the familiar multi-part tests. Yet, I will show in chapter two that the prominent and pervasive balancing tests in US constitutional rights adjudication are based on the same fundamental structure of inquiring into whether a law is necessary for achieving an aim and whether it strikes the right balance between collective and individual interests.

Another reason for focusing on proportionality and balancing tests is their Janus-faced appearance. Proportionality is sometimes presented as a kind of limited, technical reasoning that constrains judicial discretion, and which does not seek to supplant legislative prerogatives in law-making. I will argue that while there are certain features of proportionality that channel judicial reasoning, its basic structure invites broad moral and empirical reasoning that is open to the same considerations as legislative reasoning. The same is true of US balancing approaches, where the different tiers of scrutiny ('strict' and 'intermediate' scrutiny, etc) provide a degree of constraint but leave a wide scope for judicial discretion. My account of the origins of proportionality and balancing review and *Lochner* in chapter four will show that the use of empirical research in proportionality and balancing cases was baked in from the start, and is an integral part of the method.

Another concern about proportionality and balancing tests is that they entail a conception of rights as *limited* and *defeasible*, the result of which is that the right recedes from view once it has served to invoke the proportionality test. The court's responsibility is generally not to *interpret* the right by giving it a substantive meaning, but to determine whether the interference with a right is justified. This feature of rights adjudication under proportionality and balancing helps to explain the broad reach of these techniques, and it is partially responsible for the widely expansive power that constitutional and supreme courts exercise over many areas of political controversy.

Lastly, the predominance of proportionality and balancing tests in day-to-day constitutional rights adjudication leads to a gulf between how constitutional rights operate in practice and a number of theories of rights and of constitutional interpretation. In chapter three, I address the relationship between proportionality and Dworkin's account of rights as trumps, which is the most prominent theory of rights in legal philosophy and usually considered the main alternative to proportionality.

There is a growing literature that is critical of the proportionality inquiry,[36] but I do not pursue that topic in this book. Rather, my aim is to analyse closely the operation of the proportionality test and the questions its operation raises with regard to the institutional capacities of courts to adjudicate abstract moral rights.

III. Recovering Montesquieu

Mauro Cappelletti, the leading comparative constitutional law scholar of his generation, was, despite a few misgivings, an enthusiastic proponent of the new constitutionalism that arose after World War II. The central component of the

[36] See, eg, F Urbina, *A Critique of Proportionality and Balancing* (Cambridge, Cambridge University Press, 2017); F Urbina, 'Is it Really that Easy? A Critique of Proportionality and "Balancing as Reasoning"' (2014) 27 *Canadian Journal of Law and Jurisprudence* 167; FJ Urbina, 'A Critique of Proportionality' (2012) 57 *American Journal of Jurisprudence* 49; B Miller, 'Proportionality's Blind Spot: "Neutrality" and Political Philosophy' and G Huscroft, 'Proportionality and the Relevance of Interpretation' in G Huscroft, BW Miller and G Webber, *Proportionality and the Rule of Law: Rights, Justification, Reasoning* (Cambridge, Cambridge University Press, 2014); G Webber, 'Proportionality and Absolute Rights' in V Jackson and M Tushnet (eds), *Proportionality: New Frontiers, New Challenges* (Cambridge, Cambridge University Press, 2016).

new approach was the judicial enforcement of abstract moral rights. Cappelletti saw in this a repudiation of Montesquieu's view of separation of powers, which entailed the primacy of statute law and of Parliament.[37] Rejecting concerns, such as Kelsen's, that adopting vague moral rights represents an embrace of natural law that threatens the legislature's role, Cappelletti wrote:

> Does this development mark the revival of a new 'natural law?' Many have said so. I would go farther and say that modern constitutionalism, with its basic ingredients—a civil-libertarian bill of rights and judicial enforcement of it—is the only realistic attempt to implement natural law values in our real world. In this sense, our epoch, if any, is the epoch of natural law. More accurately, however, I would say that modern constitutionalism is the attempt to overcome the plurimillenary contrast between natural and positive law, the contrast, that is, between an immutable, unwritten higher law rooted in nature or reason, and a passing law written by a particular legislator of a given place and time. The modern constitutions, their bills of rights, and judicial review are the elements of a 'positive higher law' made binding and enforceable: they represent a synthesis of a sort—a Hegelian synthesis as it were—of legal positivism and natural law. They reflect the most sophisticated attempt ever designed to 'positize' values without however, either absolutizing such values or relinquishing them to the mutable whims of passing majorities.[38]

This captures well the circumstances of modern adjudication of constitutional rights, as well as the noble—if not utopian—aspirations that have motivated its adoption. As Cappelletti said elsewhere:

> After the sad experiences of the first half of this century, there arose in Europe the need to put a check upon the legislature itself, for it had become evident that even legislation could be the source of great abuses. Hence Europeans, and non-Europeans as well, embarked on the path taken by the Americans so long before. Higher law was to be expressed in constitutions that were difficult to amend. The judiciary, or a part of it, was to be the instrument for assuring conformity to this higher law. The Old World moved from legal to constitutional justice.[39]

But even if we grant this as a desirable constitutional ideal, Cappelletti overestimates the institutional capacities of judges to fulfil it. In another passage, he is overly sceptical of the ability of legislatures to engage with the 'higher law rooted in nature or reason':

> Judicial review is in essence an endeavor to judge positive law in the light of ultimate values. It is the means by which human aspirations, as expressed in constitutional absolutes, are 'concretized' into a living constitution. In the past, states have existed and prospered without benefit of judicial review, and many will probably continue to do so in the future. They deprive themselves, however, of the sobering and ennobling experience

[37] M Cappelletti, 'Repudiating Montesquieu? The Expansion and Legitmacy of Constitutional Justice' (1985) 35 *Catholic University Law Review* 1.

[38] ibid 31–32.

[39] M Cappelletti, 'Judicial Review in Comparative Perspective' (1970) *California Law Review* 1017.

> that befalls those who check their acts against their principles and strive in performing the former never to lose sight of the latter.[40]

Constitutional theory goes wrong from the start when it assumes that judicial review is the singular means of concretising ultimate values, or of checking acts against principles. And this is compounded when there is no exploration of the judiciary's capacity for undertaking this task.

In chapters four to six, I engage in a detailed analysis of the relative institutional capacities of courts and legislatures, which challenges several of the assumptions and conclusions of the above passages. If, as Cappelletti thought, the modern approach to adjudication of rights is a repudiation of Montesquieu, my aim is to recover Montesquieu, in the sense of engaging in the kind of detailed examination of institutional capacities that underlay his theory of the separation of powers. In the concluding chapter seven, I argue that legislative supremacy remains a legitimate option for constitutional framers, though not the only one. This does not entail a rejection of a 'higher law rooted in nature or reason'; rather, legislation itself can be the appropriate way of concretising 'ultimate values' into specific legal rights. If judicial review of legislation is chosen as a means for protecting such values, framers need to reform constitutional courts to provide them with the capacities needed to fulfil the high task that Cappelletti envisions for them.

[40] M Cappelletti and JC Adams, 'Judicial Review of Legislation: European Antecedents and Adaptations' (1966) 79 *Harvard Law Review* 1207.

2

The Adjudication of Constitutional Rights

In the case of *Carter v Canada* (2012),[1] the claimants argued that a provision in Canada's Criminal Code that prohibits assisting someone to commit suicide violated their constitutional rights under the Charter of Rights and Freedoms. The trial, conducted by Justice Lynn Smith, a trial court judge in British Columbia, lasted several weeks. Most of the time was devoted to testimony from medical doctors, scientists, and ethicists. The evidence included 36 binders of written submissions and over 100 affidavits. It touched on many disputed questions of ethics—such as whether it is ever morally permissible to intend to cause death—and of empirical fact. A key factual issue was the extent to which a regulatory system permitting assisted suicide is likely to lead to pressure on the aged and vulnerable to end their lives, and whether safeguards against this are likely to be complied with. Justice Smith made an empirical finding that such rules are not likely to lead to undue pressure on the elderly and vulnerable in Canada, and proceeded to hold the law unconstitutional. The Canadian Supreme Court affirmed Smith's decision and, without fully reconsidering the evidence regarding likelihood of abuse, upheld her empirical finding on this point.[2] It is noteworthy that in the two decades before *Carter* the Canadian Parliament debated several times whether to amend the law on assisted suicide. At least nine bills proposing to legalise the practice failed to pass, including one in 2010 that Parliament rejected by a vote of 228 to 59.[3]

Carter provides a good test case for considering whether courts have the proper institutional capacities and structures for deciding moral and empirical questions in constitutional cases. This chapter explains the background to modern constitutional rights adjudication and analyses the differences between constitutional and ordinary rights. I explain how the vague wording of constitutional rights invites broad techniques of application, in particular the balancing and proportionality tests that in recent decades have come to dominate constitutional rights adjudication. These techniques, in turn, invite general moral and empirical

[1] *Carter v Canada (Attorney General)* 2012 BCSC 886, 287 CCC (3d) 1.

[2] *Carter v Canada (Attorney General)* 2015 SCC 5, [2015] 1 SCR 331.

[3] See B Chan and M Somerville, 'Converting the "Right to Life" to the "Right to Physician-Assisted Suicide and Euthanasia": An Analysis of Carter v Canada (Attorney General), Supreme Court of Canada' (2016) 24 *Medical Law Review* 143, 154–55.

reasoning about society's need for a law and its anticipated consequences—reasoning which, I contend, resembles legislative deliberation. *Carter* exemplifies these trends in adjudication, in particular the technique of proportionality. Its reasoning will be considered in more detail in section II below.

I. Constitutional Rights and Ordinary Legal Rights

Constitutional rights and human rights are typically formulated in abstract moral language that is significantly more vague than ordinary, non-constitutional law. (The terminology of both *constitutional* and *human* rights will be used in this book, interchangeably to some degree, though the focus will be on constitutional rights and their enforcement in domestic courts.) The operative terms are often 'liberty' or 'freedom'; 'equality' or 'equal protection'; 'human dignity', and the like. The subject matter of constitutional rights embraces expression, religion, association, privacy or 'private and family life',[4] and—in some later rights instruments—voting, marriage, property, operation of a business, treatment of employees, academic freedom and more.[5] It might be thought that such vague, morally-laden terms and the wide scope of subject matter necessarily confer broad power on courts over moral and political questions. Dworkin implies this when he argues that because the 'great clauses' of the Constitution fail to specify what equality requires and what the basic liberties really are, 'that means that judges must answer intractable, controversial, and profound questions of political morality'.[6] While vague language swings open the door to broad methods of application and to responses like Dworkin's, it is also possible to take a narrower approach. Some judges and theorists have advocated narrow interpretive techniques even for broadly worded clauses, though these are generally out of favour today.[7]

Another feature of constitutional rights that shapes adjudicative approaches is that, in the understanding of most judges, constitutional rights can be justifiably interfered with or infringed. This approach is also connected to the vagueness of rights, because many infer from their broad scope that constitutional rights contain unexpressed, built-in limitations. That conclusion, and the way it is applied by courts in constitutional rights cases, marks a subtle but crucial difference from the rights created by ordinary law, such as the specified duties and powers in the law of crime, contract and property. These express firm, relatively precise requirements regarding relationships between persons, specifying the acts and forbearances

[4] See ECHR, arts 8–11.

[5] See European Charter of Fundamental Rights, arts 39, 9, 17, 16, 31, 13.

[6] R Dworkin, *Freedom's Law: The Moral Reading of the American Constitution* (New York, Oxford University Press, 1999).

[7] See the discussion of Justice Black's theory of absolute rights below in section III. In section VIII I argue that originalism, although it is often described as a narrow, textual method of interpretation, is not usually practised as such.

required by law in particular situations. Courts *interpret* these rights, resolving disputes about their application to certain situations, in a way that is formally structured around protecting the right and stating its meaning. Constitutional rights are in most cases not interpreted in the same way. Invoking a constitutional right gives the court a platform for evaluating a law alleged to violate the right; the point of adjudication is not to *interpret* the constitutional right but to evaluate the law in question. This can be seen most clearly in the proportionality inquiry, which starts from the premise that it is frequently justifiable to infringe, or to interfere with, a constitutional right.

Since the proportionality inquiry is the dominant method of constitutional rights adjudication today, this chapter focuses on it. I will explain in some detail the significance of the concept of a right (entailed by proportionality) as something that can be justifiably infringed, how this differs from the concept of an ordinary legal right, and the consequences of this approach for judicial review of legislation. One consequence is that the proportionality inquiry casts a wide net, entailing an expansive supervisory role for courts over legislative enactments. I will also address balancing tests in the US and show that they entail a similar conception of rights and supervisory role for courts. Lastly, I will consider other methods of constitutional rights adjudication that also involve broad moral and empirical reasoning on matters of political controversy.

My account of constitutional rights is in relation to how they are in fact treated by courts; it is neither a claim about the a priori nature of constitutional rights nor a claim about conceptual necessity. It is possible to treat constitutional rights like ordinary rights, and this chapter will show that this occasionally happens, particularly with regard to the narrow class of absolute rights.

II. Proportionality in Practice

In most countries the proportionality inquiry follows the two-stage process exemplified in the jurisprudence of the European Court of Human Rights (ECtHR), a paradigm widely followed by national constitutional courts. In the first stage the court determines whether a law (or other state action) infringes or interferes with a right ('restrict', 'limit' and 'engage' are some of the other terms used to express this idea).[8] In the second stage the court, applying a three- or four-part test whose

[8] The following two cases from Canada and Strasbourg illustrate this conception of rights and an interpretative methodology similar to that followed in many other jurisdictions: *Sauvé v Canada* [2002] 3 SCR 519 [7] ('To justify the *infringement* of a Charter right under s. 1, the government must show that the *infringement* achieves a constitutionally valid purpose or objective, and that the chosen means are reasonable and demonstrably justified') (emphasis added); *Mayeka v Belgium* (Application no 13178/03) (2008) 46 EHRR 23 ('The Court reiterates that an *infringement* of an individual's right to respect for his or her private and family life will violate Art. 8 unless it is "in accordance with the law", pursues one or more [legitimate aims] and is "necessary in a democratic society", in other words,

elements are considered below, asks whether the interference is justified in virtue of being proportionate to the aim or value of the law. This process entails a concept of limited, prima facie rights, as distinct from a concept of absolute or non-defeasible rights. This prima facie concept of rights finds some support in the way that rights are formulated in the European Convention on Human Rights (ECHR) as well as many national constitutions. Several of the most commonly invoked ECHR rights—to freedom of expression, religion, conscience, private and family life, and assembly—have limitation clauses providing that the exercise of the right can be restricted as 'necessary in a democratic society' for protecting certain public interests (safety, health, morals, etc) or the rights and freedoms of others. As a gloss for all these criteria that justify infringing a right, the ECtHR uses the phrase 'pressing social need'.[9] On this approach, a prima facie right is defeated by a pressing social need.

Courts decide whether the interference with a constitutional right is justified by asking the following four questions or some subset or combination of them:

(1) *Legitimacy*: does the measure pursue a legitimate aim?
(2) *Suitability* (or rationality): are the means chosen by the legislature suitable for the intended purpose?
(3) *Necessity* (or minimal impairment): are other less restrictive means capable of achieving the aim of the measure?
(4) *Balancing*: does the measure strike an appropriate balance between the state interest[10] and the burden on the individual right (or interest protected by the right)?

The proportionality inquiry—by which I mean the two-stage process just described and the use of some form of the above multi-part test[11]—is used not only by the ECtHR but by the Court of Justice of the European Union and courts in Canada, Germany, and many other legal systems.[12] Grégoire Webber aptly calls this 'the received approach' to constitutional rights adjudication.[13]

proportionate to the pursued objectives. The question before the Court is whether the interference was justified under para. 2 of Art. 8 of the Convention') (emphasis added).

[9] eg, *ADT v United Kingdom* (Application no 35765/97) (2001) 31 EHRR 33 [31].

[10] The idea of the governmental interest in step (4) is expressed in various ways in different jurisdictions: state, community or societal interest; public or social need, etc.

[11] Although this is a common way of reciting the test, it will be seen below that steps (1) or (2) are sometimes omitted, and steps (3) and (4) are frequently conflated into a single test. For a discussion of different formulations of these tests see F Urbina, *A Critique of Proportionality and Balancing* (Cambridge, Cambridge University Press, 2017) 4–9.

[12] In Canada the leading case is *R v Oakes* [1986] 1 SCR 103. See also C-84/94 *United Kingdom v Council* [1996] 3 CMLR 671 [57]; H Keller and AS Sweet (eds), *A Europe of Rights: The Impact of the ECHR on National Legal Systems* (Oxford, Oxford University Press, 2008) 151, 152 (Germany); 425, 436–37 (Spain); 438–39 (Italy); D Grimm, 'Proportionality in Canadian and German Constitutional Jurisprudence' (2007) 57 *University of Toronto Law Journal* 383. See generally E Ellis (ed), *The Principle of Proportionality in the Laws of Europe* (Oxford, Hart Publishing, 1999).

[13] See GCN Webber, *The Negotiable Constitution: On the Limitation of Rights* (Cambridge, Cambridge University Press, 2009) 65, 116–45.

The operation of the proportionality test is illustrated well in the Canadian Supreme Court's opinion *Carter v Canada*,[14] mentioned above in the introduction. The claimant who challenged the law prohibiting assisted suicide had Lou Gehrig's disease (ALS)[15] and wanted to gain a right to be assisted in suicide by a physician at the point when her condition would be expected to deteriorate. In the first part of the two-stage process of the received approach, the Supreme Court held that the law 'engaged' the claimant's Charter right to life (because it 'might force her to take her life earlier than she otherwise would if she had access to a physician-assisted death'[16]), and her right to 'liberty and security of the person' (because this includes a right of autonomy in medical decision-making).[17] The Court then moved to the second stage to determine whether Canada had provided a sufficiently strong justification for this 'infringement' of the claimant's rights; in other words, whether the limitation on the rights was proportionate to the law's objective.[18] The Court held that the law had an appropriate objective (step (1) of the standard test),[19] which was not to preserve life generally,[20] but to 'protect the vulnerable from being induced to commit suicide at a time of weakness'.[21] The Court also found that there was a 'rational connection' (step (2)) between the law's absolute prohibition on assisted suicide and the law's object.[22] The Court then asked whether 'the limit on the right is reasonably tailored to the objective', a question which in most proportionality cases is the heart of the analysis.[23]

The Court states the same idea in several different formulations, and it is instructive to consider them: 'The inquiry into minimal impairment asks "whether there are less harmful means of achieving the legislative goal"'; 'The analysis at this stage is meant to ensure that the deprivation of Charter rights is confined to what is reasonably necessary to achieve the state's object';[24] 'The question in this case comes down to whether the absolute prohibition on physician-assisted dying, with its heavy impact on the claimants' [rights] to life, liberty and security of the person, is the least drastic means of achieving the legislative objective.'[25] It is clear that the Court's focus is on whether the legislative means are *reasonable*.

[14] *Carter* [2015] 1 SCR 331.

[15] Amyotrophic lateral sclerosis, a fatal neurodegenerative disorder that causes progressive deterioration of muscles.

[16] *Carter* [2015] 1 SCR 331, para 30.

[17] Canadian Charter of Rights and Freedoms, s 7.

[18] *Carter* [2015] 1 SCR 331, paras 95–97.

[19] The Court sought to identify a 'pressing and substantial' object, in keeping with a minor difference between courts that ask for a 'legitimate' aim and Canadian cases that pitch the standard higher at step (1).

[20] For criticism of the Court's refusal to accept this more general aim, see B Chan and M Somerville, 'Converting the "Right to Life" to the "Right to Physician-Assisted Suicide and Euthanasia": An Analysis of Carter v Canada (Attorney General), Supreme Court of Canada' (2016) 24 *Med Law Rev* 143, 159.

[21] *Carter* [2015] 1 SCR 331, para 101.

[22] ibid para 100.

[23] ibid para 102.

[24] ibid.

[25] ibid para 103.

The Court did not include a separate step (4) for balancing, but in assessing minimal impairment the Court included elements of weighing and of balancing the effects on the individual against the interests of society.

The Court concluded that the law did not meet the test of minimal impairment, thereby affirming the trial court's decision that Parliament could enact a regulatory regime that would permit people to seek assisted suicide without exposing the vulnerable to abuse and error, and rejecting Canada's contention that the risks of such a permissive regime 'could not adequately be addressed through the use of safeguards'.[26]

The opinion gestures twice toward the notion of deference, observing that the question of assisted suicide 'involves complex issues of social policy and a number of competing societal values', and that 'Parliament faces a difficult task in addressing this issue; it must weigh and balance the perspective of those who might be at risk in a permissive regime against that of those who seek assistance in dying.'[27] Accordingly, the Court stated that it owed a high degree of deference toward Parliament, and said that '[p]roportionality does not require perfection,'[28] only that the limits on a right are 'reasonable'. Even these gestures toward deference reinforce the expansiveness of the inquiry, for the *reasonableness* that the Court demands is of the all-things-considered kind, and the Court undertakes to engage in the same weighing and balancing of interests it says Parliament must address. Every consideration that Parliament should take notice of in adopting the law is also relevant for the Court, and the amount and range of evidence that the trial court considered is indicative of this.

Fifty-seven witnesses testified in the trial court from a variety of backgrounds: medical doctors, university professors, palliative care specialists, and ethicists. The court received evidence from professional medical associations in Canada, the US, the UK, and New Zealand, and reviewed, inter alia, the regulatory regimes of Belgium, the Netherlands and the US state of Oregon, where assisted suicide is legal, and the experience of patients and doctors under them. There are about 50 pages on empirical evidence in the trial judge's opinion, which runs to about 150 single-spaced pages. The Supreme Court's account shows the range of issues considered at the trial:

> In assessing minimal impairment, the trial judge heard evidence from scientists, medical practitioners, and others who were familiar with end-of-life decision-making in Canada and abroad. She also heard extensive evidence from each of the jurisdictions where physician-assisted dying is legal or regulated. In the trial judge's view, an absolute prohibition would have been necessary if the evidence showed that physicians were unable to reliably assess competence, voluntariness, and non-ambivalence in patients; that physicians fail to understand or apply the informed consent requirement for medical

[26] ibid.

[27] ibid para 98.

[28] ibid para 97 (citing *Saskatchewan (Human Rights Commission) v Whatcott* 2013 SCC 11, [2013] 1 SCR 467, at para 78).

> treatment; or if the evidence from permissive jurisdictions showed abuse of patients, carelessness, callousness, or a slippery slope, leading to the casual termination of life.
>
> The trial judge, however, expressly rejected these possibilities. After reviewing the evidence, she concluded that a permissive regime with properly designed and administered safeguards was capable of protecting vulnerable people from abuse and error. While there are risks, to be sure, a carefully designed and managed system is capable of adequately addressing them …
>
> The trial judge found that it was feasible for properly qualified and experienced physicians to reliably assess patient competence and voluntariness, and that coercion, undue influence, and ambivalence could all be reliably assessed as part of that process …[29]

The Supreme Court applied a deferential standard of review, stating that it would overturn the trial court's findings of fact only on a showing of 'palpable and overriding error'.[30] The task of assessing the momentous and complex factual questions surrounding the question of the legality of assisted suicide thus falls not to the Canadian Parliament, and not even to the Supreme Court, but to a single trial judge. (In chapter four, section V, I discuss this point further and criticise how Smith J handled the empirical evidence.) Even if the Supreme Court were to assume more responsibility for fact-finding by adopting a standard of review less deferential to the trial judge, the initial responsibility to hear the evidence and find the facts would remain with the trial court (in common law systems; the approach in civil law systems differs). Moreover, to decide whether Parliament had chosen means reasonably tailored to its goal, the trial judge had the responsibility of making determinations on questions regarding the moral permissibility of causing death, other end-of-life ethical questions, and all relevant questions of morality and policy. This is the kind of moral and empirical reasoning that the proportionality test invites.

I have noted above that in proportionality cases courts treat constitutional rights differently than ordinary legal rights. For the latter, decisions are framed around interpreting the meaning of a legal right and ensuring that the right is protected or given force. The different approach to constitutional rights can be in seen in *Carter*. In striking down the law prohibiting assisted suicide, the Supreme Court did not conclude that individuals have a *right* to be assisted in suicide. That might seem to be the logical consequence of striking down the law, but it is not. The Court did not *interpret* the right to life or to liberty and security of person to imply a *right* to assistance in suicide or even *permission* for such assistance to occur. Instead, the Court held that the law against assisted suicide *engaged* and *infringed*[31] the claimants' Charter rights (to life, and to liberty and security of persons),

[29] *Carter* [2015] 1 SCR 331, paras 104–106.

[30] ibid paras 108, 109.

[31] 'In order *to justify the infringement* of the appellants' s. 7 rights under s. 1 of the *Charter*, Canada must show that the law has a pressing and substantial object and that the means chosen are proportional to that object'. : ibid para 94.

and that in this particular case Canada had not submitted evidence justifying the limitation on the right as proportionate. This conclusion rested on multiple contingent factors, several of which are included in the above quotation (eg the capability and of physicians to comply with a permissive regime, while avoiding 'carelessness, callousness, or a slippery slope, leading to the casual termination of life'),[32] and the conclusion depended on the empirical evidence regarding each factor.[33] A finding in favour of Canada on any of these factors could have resulted in a holding that the law's infringement of the claimants' rights was justified.

Some courts reviewing laws against assisted suicide have held precisely that. In *Pretty v United Kingdom* (2002), the ECtHR held that the UK's law against assisted suicide infringed the claimant's right to private and family life, but that the infringement was justified.[34] In another context, the ECtHR held in *VgT v Switzerland* (2009) that a law prohibiting an animal rights group from purchasing advertisement on radio or television violated the right to freedom of expression.[35] But when an animal rights group sued the UK regarding a similar law a few years later, the ECtHR held that the law did not violate the right to freedom of expression in *Animal Defenders v UK* (2013).[36] There is no *logical* inconsistency between these two outcomes, because the first case did not hold that there is a *right* to purchase political advertisements on radio or television. Both cases held that the law in question *infringed* the right to freedom of expression; in the first case the ECtHR held the infringement was not justified and in the second case the Court held that the infringement was justified. There was no material difference between the laws of the two states, but there was a difference in the arguments and evidence submitted by the respective governments of Switzerland and the UK in support of their laws, and such differences could explain the different outcomes.

What these cases demonstrate is that by conceiving of constitutional rights as being subject to justified infringement, the focus of constitutional adjudication is shifted away from interpreting the right itself to on overall evaluation of the law claimed to violate the right. The significance of this conception of rights will be considered further below, after an analysis of the US approach to such matters.

III. Proportionality in the US?

In the US, courts do not generally use the term 'proportionality', but they use balancing tests that ask similar questions to those in the four-step European

32 *Carter* [2015] 1 SCR 331, para 104.

33 In several instances the evidence was conflicting or rested on single study, and in other instances the judge noted the lack of a study on crucial points. See ch 4, section V.

34 *Pretty v United Kingdom* (2346/02) [2002] ECHR 423 (29 April 2002).

35 *Verein Gegen Tierfabriken Schweiz (VgT) v Switzerland* (Application no 32772/02) (30 June 2009).

36 *Animal Defenders International v The United Kingdom* (Application no 48876/08) (2013) 57 EHRR 21.

proportionality inquiry. A court's analysis in cases on constitutional rights usually begins with identifying what level of 'scrutiny' to apply when it is claimed that a law violates a constitutional right.

Standard textbook analysis identifies three basic levels in a framework commonly known as 'tiered scrutiny':[37]

(1) *strict scrutiny* requires that a governmental measure be narrowly tailored and advance a compelling state interest;
(2) *intermediate scrutiny* requires that a measure substantially promote an important state interest;
(3) *minimal scrutiny* (or rational basis review) requires a measure to be rationally related to a legitimate state aim.

The foundation for this framework can be traced to *United States v Carolene Products Co* (1938),[38] which signalled a departure from the US Supreme Court's practice during the 30-year period after *Lochner v New York* (1905)[39] of frequently applying intense scrutiny to laws regarding workplace regulation, wages, and other economic matters. The Court upheld the consumer-protection law in *Carolene Products* because it had a 'rational basis', but suggested, in the famous footnote 4 of that decision, that it would more intensively review legislation that affected core constitutional rights or showed prejudice against 'discrete and insular minorities'.[40]

The rational basis review of *Carolene Products* is today the default for regulation regarding workplace, trade, and economic matters, and for most regulation not affecting an enumerated or fundamental constitutional right. This type of review excludes balancing of means and ends as well as any close inquiry into the empirical basis for a measure; courts defer to legislative findings of fact, or to the absence of explicit fact-finding if a set of facts to support the measure can be rationally supposed to exist. The test resembles the first two steps of the European proportionality inquiry, (1) legitimacy and (2) suitability. A governmental measure will be upheld if it has a legitimate aim and suitable ('rationally related') means. It is rare for courts to conclude that a governmental measure lacks a rational basis.

The third and most important level, strict scrutiny, was crystallised in the late 1950s and 60s. In a 1957 decision holding that a college professor did not have to answer questions from a state attorney general about the alleged subversive tendencies of his teaching, the Court held that '[p]olitical power must abstain from intrusion into this activity of freedom … except for reasons that are exigent and obviously compelling'.[41] Justice Brennan linked the phrase 'compelling state interest' with 'narrow tailoring'—an expression for analysis that considered

[37] See, eg, E Chemerinsky, *Constitutional Law: Principles and Policies*, 4th edn (Walters Kluwer, 2011) 687–95.

[38] *United States v Carolene Products Co* 304 US 144 (1938).

[39] *Lochner v New York* 198 US 45 (1905).

[40] ibid.

[41] *Sweezy v New Hampshire* 354 US 234, 262 (1957) (Frankfurter J concurring).

less restrictive alternatives—in *Sherbert v Verner*, a 1963 case on free exercise of religion.[42] Linking these tests together proved a durable framework, which the Court adopted in many doctrinal areas in the ensuing years, during which the label 'strict scrutiny' was adopted.

Led by Justice Brennan, the Court applied strict scrutiny with vigour in the 1960s in cases involving civil liberties and equal protection, striking down most laws considered under that standard.[43] The standard applies to most cases brought pursuant to the First Amendment, including cases concerning restrictions on the content of expression, freedom of association, and certain categories of religious liberty claims.[44] Strict scrutiny has also been applied to an open-ended category of rights not textually specified in the Constitution but held by the Court to be 'fundamental', including the right to travel, the right to marry, the right of parents to direct their children's upbringing, and the right to bodily integrity.[45] In the context of challenges based on the 14th Amendment's right to equal protection under the laws, strict scrutiny applies to 'suspect classifications'—chiefly those based on race, national origin, and similar criteria.

In 1972, Gerald Gunther observed that the standard was '"strict" in theory, fatal in fact',[46] a phrase that has been used by US academics to indicate the small chance of a law surviving once a court determines that it falls under this standard. Recent research has shown, however, that courts apply the test in such a way that many laws are upheld; of 447 cases studied over a 13-year period, 30 per cent of laws survived review under the strict scrutiny standard.[47] Justice Breyer has argued the standard should not be applied 'mechanically'. Rather, a judge should evaluate 'the nature of the potentially justifying "compelling interests," the degree to which the statute furthers that interest, the nature and effectiveness of possible alternatives'; and, in light of this, determine whether the statute harms interests 'out of proportion' to the benefits it provides.[48]

Intermediate scrutiny is a category less clearly demarcated than strict scrutiny. In some areas the Supreme Court has indicated a need for a level of scrutiny between rational basis review and strict scrutiny. In *Craig v Boren*[49] the Court adopted an intermediate level of scrutiny for Equal Protection Clause challenges

[42] *Sherbert v Verner* 374 US 398 (1963).

[43] SA Siegel, 'The Origin of the Compelling State Interest Test and Strict Scrutiny' (2006) 48 *American Journal of Legal History* 355, 359–60.

[44] A Winkler, 'Fatal in Theory and Strict in Fact: An Empirical Analysis of Strict Scrutiny in the Federal Courts' (2006) 59 *Vanderbilt Law Review* 793, 797.

[45] ibid.

[46] G Gunther, 'The Supreme Court, 1971 Term—Foreword: In Search of Evolving Doctrine on a Changing Court: A Model for a Newer Equal Protection' (1972) 86 *Harvard Law Review* 1, 8.

[47] Winkler, 'Fatal in Theory and Strict in Fact'. Although the Supreme Court upheld only one of 12 measures challenged under strict scrutiny from 1990 to 2002, district and appellate courts upheld a much higher percentage of measures: ibid 796.

[48] *Brown v Entertainment Merchants Association* 564 US 786; 131 SCt 2729, 2766 (2011) (internal citations omitted) (Breyer J dissenting).

[49] *Craig v Boren* 429 US 190 (1976).

to classifications based on gender. The Court has applied intermediate scrutiny to classifications based on illegitimacy[50] and in some First Amendment cases, including challenges to regulation of commercial speech,[51] expressive conduct,[52] and content-neutral regulations of the time, place, or manner of speech.[53]

Both strict and intermediate scrutiny involve an inquiry into whether the means adopted in governmental measures are appropriately tailored in view of the value of the aim or state interest. In strict scrutiny, courts ask whether there are less restrictive alternatives in determining whether the governmental measure is 'narrowly tailored'—similarly to the necessity component of the European proportionality inquiry, which is sometimes phrased in terms of 'minimal impairment'. In intermediate scrutiny courts ask whether there is a reasonable relationship between the means and end of government action, but without the strict requirement for narrow tailoring.

In the US, courts do not ordinarily use the language of justified infringements of rights, but their occasional use of that language helps to show that the concept of rights assumed in the tiered scrutiny framework fundamentally resembles the other jurisdictions surveyed in section I above. In 1961 the US Supreme Court held in *CPUSA v Subversive Activities Control Board* that 'compulsory disclosure of the names of an organization's members may in certain instances *infringe* constitutionally protected rights of association' (emphasis added).[54] The Court's explanation of 'infringe' reveals a view that closely resembles other jurisdictions that more commonly refer to the notion of a justified infringement of rights:

> But to say [that a right is infringed] is only to recognize one of the points of reference from which analysis must begin. To state that individual liberties may be affected is *to establish the condition for, not to arrive at the conclusion of, constitutional decision.* Against the impediments which particular governmental regulation causes to entire freedom of individual action, there must be weighed *the value to the public of the end which the regulation may achieve.* (emphasis added)[55]

The Court ultimately decided that the value of the end (national security) outweighed the infringement of the right, thus treating the right in question as a prima facie right. Previous cases had reflected a similar conception of rights,[56] but the statement in *CPUSA* occurs at a significant juncture, when the court was crystallising the strict scrutiny standard. In previous decades, the Court had sometimes treated the First Amendment in an absolute manner, and at other times

[50] *Reed v Campbell* 476 US 852 (1986).

[51] *Virginia State Pharmacy Board v Virginia Citizens Consumer Council* 425 US 748 (1976); *Central Hudson Gas & Electric Corp v Public Service Commission* 447 US 557 (1980).

[52] *United States v O'Brien* 391 US 367 (1968).

[53] *Ladue v Gilleo* 512 US 43 (1994).

[54] *Communist Party of the United States v Subversive Activities Control Bd* 367 US 1, 90–91 (1961) (United States).

[55] ibid.

[56] In *Schneider v State* 308 US 147, 161 (1939), the Court referred to legislation that 'abridges' a right and reflected on the conditions that would justify that.

applied a more free-standing approach to balancing that characterised the *Lochner* era (before *Carolene Products*).[57]

The view of constitutional rights as absolute had been most forcefully advanced by Justice Hugo Black. In his 1960 James Madison lecture, he argued against the view that 'a right may be abridged where its exercise would cause so much injury to the public that this injury would outweigh the injury to the individual who is deprived of the right'.[58] He contended for a view of constitutional rights as 'absolute', and emphasised this in his opinions on freedom of speech under the First Amendment. This did not mean that any law touching on expression in any way was unconstitutional. For Black the interpreter's task was to state meaning of 'freedom of speech' in the First Amendment. In his view, it excluded any limitations on the *content* of speech but allowed for restrictions on time and place of speech, and imposed a need to draw a conceptual line between *speech* and *conduct* (which he thought was not protected). He sometimes voted to uphold laws restricting expression on these bases. Thus Black thought that it was the Court's task to *define* a constitutional right, and, having done so, to enforce it absolutely, that is without balancing against general interests:

> The great danger of the judiciary balancing process is that in times of emergency and stress it gives Government the power to do what it thinks necessary to protect itself, regardless of the rights of individuals. If the need is great, the right of Government can always be said to outweigh the rights of the individual. If 'balancing' is accepted as the test, it would be hard for any conscientious judge to hold otherwise in times of dire need.[59]

In the *CPUSA* case Black dissented, rejecting the majority's holding regarding the method for applying the First Amendment—the notion that the Communist Party's constitutional right could be justifiably infringed—as well as its conclusion. He would have struck down the law that prohibited the Party from advocating revolutionary ideas.[60] By the end of the 1960s, the view of constitutional rights as absolute had been decisively rejected, and in the following decades the balancing tests of the tiered scrutiny framework would become as pervasive in US constitutional rights adjudication as the proportionality inquiry in Europe.[61]

IV. Absolute and Prima Facie Rights

As can be seen from the preceding description of proportionality in practice, in the US and other jurisdictions the rhetoric surrounding constitutional and human

[57] See P Yowell, 'Proportionality in US Constitutional Law' in L Lazarus et al (eds), *Reasoning Rights: Comparative Judicial Engagement* (Oxford, Hart Publishing, 2014).

[58] HL Black, 'The Bill of Rights' (1960) 35 *New York University Law Review* 866.

[59] ibid, 878.

[60] ibid.

[61] See TA Aleinikoff, 'Constitutional Law in the Age of Balancing' (1986) 96 *Yale Law Journal* 943.

rights does not match the reality of how these rights are adjudicated. The human rights set forth in the ECHR and similar instruments are said to embody moral principles that stand above the domestic law of any country. Bills of rights in many national constitutions can be traced to such international instruments, and are usually given a higher rank in the legal hierarchy than ordinary legislation; this ranking is what empowers judges to review legislation for consistency with human or constitutional rights. The law of human and constitutional rights is often considered to have a greater moral worth than ordinary statutory law, and, in many eyes, 'human rights law' and 'human rights lawyers' have an elevated status. This is reflected in the common saying that human and constitutional rights cannot be put up for vote.

In practice, however, these rights are usually applied by courts through proportionality and balancing tests, on the basis of an assumption that it is frequently justifiable to infringe the right in question. If a court concludes that the interests of the general welfare outweigh the individual's interest in the right, it holds that the infringement of or interference with the right is legally justified. Such language indicates that the paradigm of judicial reasoning at work in constitutional rights cases is different from cases involving the interpretation of ordinary legal rights. Paradoxically, ordinary legal rights are treated as *stronger* than constitutional rights in this sense: they are not defeasible by the general interest. If you have a right to fish in the local river, having fulfilled the statutory conditions for obtaining a fishing licence, authorities concerned about overfishing cannot take away your licence on the ground that infringing your right is necessary for the sake of the general welfare. The relevant lawmaker can change the law, but until that point your right to fish is legally non-defeasible.

There are a handful of human and constitutional rights that are considered to be absolute, and thus not subject to being infringed for the sake of the general welfare. The classic example of an absolute right is the right not to be tortured.[62] Torture must be defined, however, and there are cases in which it is unclear whether a given act amounts to torture. If the police threaten to torture a suspect, and then elicit a confession without actually torturing him, is this torture?[63] When courts rule on such questions they interpret the right in the traditional sense; they help to flesh out the meaning of the words of an authoritative legal text, in a way that informs or binds judges in later cases. In cases alleging violation of this right, courts do not ask whether an infringement of the right against torture can be justified, and neither do they apply a proportionality or balancing test. There are a handful of other absolute rights, including the right not to be held in slavery and, at least arguably, certain procedural rights.

[62] UDHR, art 3; ECHR, art 3. See *Saadi v Italy* (Application no 37201/06) (2008) 47 EHRR 17, [127].

[63] Yes, according to the Strasbourg court in *Gafgen v Germany* (Application no 22987/05) [2008] ECHR 565.

The clarity of the moral issues involved in the few—but vital—absolute rights is a large part of what gives a sense of moral urgency to the enterprise of constitutional and human rights generally. Most of the rights in constitutional bills of rights and international human rights instruments, however, lack this absolute character. They are typically expressed in the form 'A has a right to X', where X is an abstract noun or subject-matter, such as life, equality, human dignity, privacy, or freedom of expression. Such *two-term* expressions can be contrasted to the *three-term* structure of absolute rights, which involve a relationship between one right-holder, A, an act-description, Φ, and B, who holds a duty correlative to A's right. So, A has a right not to be tortured by B; B has a duty not to torture A. Hohfeld sets out different kinds of three-term jural relationships in his well-known classification of rights into claim rights, liberties, powers, and immunities.[64] Such a three-term relationship (or ordered set of such relationships) characterises not only absolute human or constitutional rights, but also most of the legal rights in ordinary legislation and common law.

And those ordinary legal rights have a non-defeasible character similar to absolute constitutional or human rights. The exercise of an ordinary legal right is not limited by such considerations as the needs of the general welfare (*cf* the fishing licence example above). Your right to be paid a salary under a contract cannot be defeated by your employer's argument that the general interest of the firm (and hence the long-run interests of its employees) will be advanced by suspending payment of salaries for one month, while the firm deals with an urgent cash-flow problem. The same would be true if the firm suspends paying employees in order to meet tax obligations.

Ordinary legal rights are not absolute in the same sense as the right against torture. If the firm you work for files for bankruptcy, then your right to recover back salary could be cancelled under the specific terms of bankruptcy law. This is not a case in which courts are called simply to balance your prima facie right to be paid your salary against a more general interest, but rather one in which courts apply a specific scheme (expressed in a complex set of three-term, Hohfeldian rights) authorised by the legislature for prioritising the payment of firms' creditors. What both absolute and ordinary rights have in common is they are not defeasible simply by the argument that there is a general societal interest that outweighs them.

In any given case one or more elements of the three-term structure of an absolute or ordinary legal right might require interpretation. And some rights are expressly conditioned by terms regarding fairness or reasonableness, while others might be subject to external conditions arising from a narrow set of public policy concerns. Nevertheless, the task of interpreting an ordinary legal right, including the application of considerations of reasonableness or fairness in the concrete circumstances of the individual case, involves a much more technical and constrained kind of

[64] WN Hohfeld, 'Fundamental Legal Conceptions as Applied in Judicial Reasoning' (1917) 26 *Yale Law Journal* 710.

reasoning than balancing and proportionality cases do. (The technical nature of ordinary judicial reasoning will be considered in chapter five, section I.)

V. Rights, Proportionality and Utilitarianism

In its focus on weighing individual interests against society's general welfare, the proportionality inquiry takes on a partially utilitarian cast. John Stuart Mill had shown the implications of utilitarianism for the notion of individual rights: 'All persons are deemed to have a right to equal treatment *except when some recognised social expediency requires the reverse*'.[65] The claim that individual rights can be sacrificed for the sake of society's overall benefit is what motivated Dworkin to propound his theory of rights as trumps as an 'anti-utilitarian' conception of rights (with Mill in mind), which will be considered in chapter three.

In the proportionality inquiry, as in Mill's conception of a right, so long as society's general interest (read: 'social expediency') is great enough, then the right in question is overridden. Proportionality's concern with assessing the efficacy of legislative measures and balancing that against anticipated side effects is not, in itself, utilitarian. All theories of practical reasoning should allow for weighing the bad consequences of action against anticipated benefits.[66] But in classical utilitarianism such a calculation of consequences is the ultimate measure for evaluating every action.[67] Utilitarianism recognises no absolute rights. The proportionality inquiry does not necessarily entail the adoption of this feature of utilitarianism. Defenders of proportionality, and those who use it in practice, can accept that certain absolute rights exist outside the proportionality inquiry and are not subject to it. But *within* the proportionality inquiry rights are treated in Millian fashion: a rights-holder enjoys his right unless 'social expediency requires the reverse'.

VI. Rights as Interests

The upshot of the received approach to constitutional rights adjudication is that consideration of the particular right on which a case is based is subsumed under the proportionality or balancing inquiry. When a court is asking whether interference with a right is proportionate, or applying a technique such as strict scrutiny, it is not seeking to define or interpret the right itself. The usual methods of textual

[65] JS Mill, *Utilitarianism* (1861), Roger Crisp (ed) (Oxford, Oxford University Press, 1998) 5.36 (lines 33–35).

[66] J Finnis, *Natural Law and Natural Rights* (Oxford, Oxford University Press, 2011) 111–18.

[67] I presume here that rule utilitarianism collapses into act utilitarianism.

interpretation are not in play. Having served to invoke the proportionality or balancing inquiry, the right largely drops out of the analysis.

The proportionality inquiry assumes centre stage, with the purpose of providing a framework for evaluating the law alleged to infringe a right. It might be thought that the particular right somehow anchors the balancing step, because the value of the right is weighed against the state's interest in the legislation that interferes with the right (for example, the value of freedom of expression is weighed against national security in a case involving subversive speech). But when courts state that they are weighing an individual's 'right' against a state interest, this reveals that it is simply a prima facie right subordinated to the supposed need of the general welfare. Perhaps because this seems odd or morally problematic, courts often speak of weighing an individual's 'interest' (instead of 'right') against the state interest.[68] Here again the abstract right drops out, leaving only a concrete interest protected by the right, the value of which is to be decided by the court in the circumstances of the individual case.

It is sometimes claimed that the nature of the right determines the 'intensity' with which courts should apply the proportionality inquiry: the more important or fundamental the right, the higher the intensity of review.[69] While this claim accurately reflects the sliding-scale approach to the value of rights discussed above, the intensity of scrutiny is not determined by the abstract category of the right, but by the particular individual interest claimed to be protected under the rubric of the right. The right to freedom of expression is a 'fundamental' right, but the intensity of review is determined by the particular expression in question. Regulation of political speech is normally subject to high-intensity review,[70] whereas commercial speech receives medium scrutiny and indecent or pornographic speech receives a lower level of scrutiny. To take an example, in *Miss Behavin' v Belfast City Council*[71] each member of the UK House of Lords agreed (or assumed) that the denial of an operating licence to a shop purveying pornographic materials constituted an interference with the claimant's right to freedom of expression under art 10 of the ECHR, but proceeded to describe the value of that right in dismissive terms.[72] Baroness Hale's speech is an example of how some judges determine what value to place on a rights-protected interest:

> My Lords, there are far more important human rights in this world than the right to sell pornographic literature and images in the backstreets of Belfast City Centre.

[68] eg, *Dickson v United Kingdom* (Application no 44362/04) (2008) 46 EHRR 41 [71].

[69] See J Rivers, 'Proportionality and Variable Intensity of Review' (2006) 65(1) *Cambridge Law Journal* 174.

[70] *Animal Defenders International v The United Kingdom* (Application no 48876/08) (2013) 57 EHRR 21, para 102.

[71] *Miss Behavin' v Belfast City Council* [2007] UKHL 19.

[72] Lord Hoffmann states: 'The right to vend pornography is not the most important right of free expression in a democratic society ... If the local authority exercises that power rationally and in accordance with the purposes of the statute, it would require very unusual facts for it to amount to a disproportionate restriction on Convention rights': [2007] UKHL 19, para 16.

> Pornography comes well below celebrity gossip in the hierarchy of speech which deserves the protection of the law. Far too often it entails the sexual exploitation and degradation of women for the titillation of men. ... There were good reasons for refusing to license establishments in this street and even better ones for refusing this particular company a licence. The suggestion that this is a disproportionate limitation on the company's right to freedom of expression is to my mind completely untenable.[73]

A number of proponents of the proportionality inquiry acknowledge that it entails a concept of rights as mere interests. Matthias Kumm says that 'a rights-holder does not have very much in virtue of his having a right'[74] and that it 'does not imply that he holds a position that gives him any kind of priority over competing considerations'.[75] Kai Möller adds that rights have no 'special normative force' and 'operate on the same plane as ... policy considerations'.[76] David Beatty writes that proportionality renders the concept of rights 'almost irrelevant' and makes it liable to 'disappear' except as 'rhetorical flourish'.[77] He candidly acknowledges that the proportionality inquiry is not an interpretative method,[78] and argues that when employing the proportionality inquiry, judges decide according to 'an evaluation of all the relevant interests in a case' and that 'everyone's interests are better served when courts base their decisions on a close and careful evaluation of the facts than when they spend most of their energy trying to divine answers from the words of the text'.[79]

Because proportionality and balancing tests treat rights as mere interests to be weighed against countervailing state interests, then there is no limit in principle to the reach of rights-based judicial review of legislation. Any law can be challenged so long as it can be plausibly said to 'interfere' with any of broad liberties or principles encompassed under bills of rights. It is possible for courts to rule out categorically a claimed interest as not falling within the ambit of a right, and this happens on rare occasions. For example, in the US a very narrowly defined category of obscenity is held not to come within First Amendment protection.[80] The Canadian Supreme Court originally held that someone's claimed interest in being assisted in suicide did not come within the ambit of section 7 of the Charter (life, liberty and security of person),[81] but this was overruled in *Carter*. The decision

[73] ibid para 38.

[74] M Kumm, 'Institutionalising Socratic Contestation: The Rationalist Human Rights Paradigm, Legitimate Authority and the Point of Judicial Review' (2007) 1 *European Journal of Legal Studies* 1.

[75] M Kumm, 'The Idea of Socratic Contestation and the Right to Justification: The Point of Rights-Based Proportionality Review' (2010) 4 *Law & Ethics of Human Rights* 140, 150.

[76] K Möller, 'Proportionality and Rights Inflation' in G Huscroft et al, *Proportionality and the Rule of Law: Rights, Justification, Reasoning* (Cambridge, Cambridge University Press, 2014) 156.

[77] D Beatty, *The Ultimate Rule of Law* (Oxford, Oxford University Press, 2005) 57.

[78] ibid.

[79] ibid.

[80] See *Miller v California* 413 US 15 (1973).

[81] *Rodriguez v British Columbia (Attorney General)* [1993] 3 SCR 519. The Irish Supreme Court also found that there is no right to assisted suicide, and refused to entertain a proportionality-based claim for this under broad rights in the Irish Constitution: *Fleming v Ireland* [2013] IESC 19.

in *Carter* represents the overwhelming trend of cases globally, the overall effect of which is that rights-based judicial review of legislation covers an extremely wide subject matter.

Möller argues that the underlying logic of the modern, proportionality-centred approach to constitutional rights is that rights are grounded in the value of personal autonomy, and that that all 'autonomy interests should be protected as rights, and this includes interests in engaging in trivial and even immoral activities.'[82] Möller acknowledges that this result is 'intuitively implausible' and entails that there is a 'right to murder'.[83] It is easy to justify laws that infringe the right to murder, he argues, but it is important to recognise this as a right, thus allowing individuals to demand from the state the reasons that justify the infringement.[84] The final result, in Möller's account, is that the cataloguing of various individual rights is unnecessary, as all of them could logically be replaced by a single right to autonomy, applied through the proportionality test.[85] The right secures no outcome, however, as everything will depend on how a court weighs the relevant interests in a given case. Möller's account of constitutional rights has been criticised for failing to appreciate the moral significance and force of rights.[86] Nonetheless, on a descriptive level, the account tracks the modern trend in constitutional rights adjudication worldwide.

VII. Moral and Empirical Reasoning

As shown immediately above, when constitutional rights are conceived as interests, there is a vast expansion of the jurisdiction of constitutional courts. This section analyses the kinds of reasoning used in constitutional rights cases. Many theorists and judges acknowledge that proportionality and balancing tests involve broad reasoning about policy and require judges to settle controversial issues. Some, however, have presented these tests as involving a more constrained or technical kind of reasoning.

Some theorists contend that the proportionality test provides judges with a framework that structures and directs their decision-making and restrains their discretion. Detailed descriptions of the test with four sequential steps—(1) legitimate aim, (2) suitability, (3) necessity, and (4) balancing—might give the impression of a structured, technical exercise. But that is misleading. The question of a legitimate aim is usually worked through in perfunctory fashion, with the court briefly remarking on the goal of the law and approving its legitimacy. The rare

[82] Möller, 'Proportionality and Rights Inflation', above n 76, 155.
[83] ibid 155, 164.
[84] ibid 164.
[85] K Möller, *The Global Model of Constitutional Rights* (Oxford, Oxford University Press, 2012) 178.
[86] See G Webber, 'On the Loss of Rights' in Huscroft et al, above n 76.

cases in which a court finds the aim of a law to be illegitimate do not exhibit restraint but, rather, the opposite. To reject the legislature's aim as illegitimate is a bold decision by a court, rooted in an understanding of political morality. Step (2), which considers the suitability of legislative means, is also treated perfunctorily in most cases—if at all. It is very uncommon for courts to find that the legislature's chosen means are wholly unsuited to promote the legislative aim. The question, moreover, is logically subsumed under step (3): if the means are necessary then they are also suitable.

Since steps (1) and (2) play little role in most cases, almost all of a court's reasoning in the proportionality test is around steps (3) and (4). Moreover, it is common for courts either to address just (3) or (4), or to conflate them into a single test.[87] Indeed the 'necessity' test is logically similar to the 'balancing' test. It is possible to find a space between them by treating step (3), necessity, as a narrow inquiry that inquires whether there is an alternative that would achieve the legislative aim *fully and completely*, without evaluating the chosen means or their relationship to the end. Courts occasionally treat step (3) in such a narrow, technical way.[88] More commonly, however, courts either pass over a distinct necessity test and proceed straight to a balancing test, or treat step (3) as including an element of balancing the means and the ends. By this I mean that the court, in considering whether there is a less restrictive alternative, asks not whether there is an alternative that would achieve 100 per cent of the legislative end, but whether there are means that would achieve the legislative end to an appropriate degree, considering the effect of the means. We saw an example of this above in the *Carter* case. Julian Rivers reflects such an approach in his formulation of the necessity test: '[I]s the act the least intrusive means of achieving *the desired level of realisation of the aim*?'[89] The ECtHR has drawn a formal equivalence between the concepts of necessity and balancing:

> [T]he Court recalls that not only must a measure depriving a person of his property pursue, on the facts as well as in principle, a legitimate aim 'in the public interest', but there must also be *a reasonable relationship of proportionality between the means employed and the aim sought to be realised.* This latter requirement [may be] expressed in other terms by the notion of the 'fair balance' that must be struck between the demands of the general interest of the community and the requirements of the protection of the individual's fundamental rights ... The requisite balance will not be found if the person concerned has had to bear 'an individual and excessive burden'.[90]

[87] A review of Canadian cases found that over a ten-year period, 'In every instance in which the minimal impairment test was passed, the proportionality test was passed. In every instance that the minimal impairment test was failed, the proportionality test was either failed or not considered': LE Trakman et al, 'R. v. Oakes 1986–1997: Back to the Drawing Board' (1998) 36 *Osgoode Hall Law Journal* 83, 103.

[88] eg, *Beit Sourik Village Council v Israel and Israeli Defence Force Commander in the West Bank*, Final Decision, HCJ 2056/04, ILDC 16 (IL 2004).

[89] J Rivers, 'Proportionality and Variable Intensity of Review' (2006) 65 *Cambridge Law Journal* 174, 181.

[90] *Lithgow v United Kingdom* (Application no 9006/80) (1986) 8 EHRR 329 [120].

On this approach, the inquiry into the relationship of legislative ends and means (step (3)) mirrors the test for the balance of community interests and individual rights (step (4)). If a court concludes that the law in question imposes (i) an 'excessive burden' on an individual's interest (or right), this is equivalent to concluding that the means employed were (ii) unnecessarily restrictive, (iii) not 'reasonable', or (iv) not proportionate. All four concepts are interchangeable. Thus, the various formulations with which courts describe steps (3) and (4)[91] of the proportionality inquiry can be encapsulated in a single, simple question: has the legislature chosen means that unreasonably impair an individual's interest? The question reflects the judicial inquiry in most proportionality cases, and indicates its broad nature.

Another way in which some theorists have presented proportionality as a technical exercise is by proposing to use a formula through which courts can assign precise, mathematical values to the individual and general interests in a case. The most influential theorist who takes this approach is Robert Alexy. His Weight Formula[92] involves assessing the concrete *intensity* of interference with an individual interest on a triadic scale of *light*, *moderate*, and *serious*, and also assessing the concrete *importance* of a policy goal on the same triadic scale. The formula also includes elements for the abstract weight of the right or policy at issue and the epistemic likelihood for a result to occur, and it places all these elements within an equation yielding a numerical quotient. The law is to be upheld if the quotient is equal to or less than 1, and struck down if it is greater than 1.[93] Richard Posner has proposed a formula for resolving free speech cases that resembles Alexy's in some respects. However, instead of using a finite, triadic scale, Posner assigns a general numerical value to harms and benefits that allows for any degree of gradation.[94]

Alexy's and Posner's approach rests on the philosophical premise that there is a single value that can be used to *commensurate* all relevant interests in a constitutional case. For Posner, the commensurating value is wealth (or units of currency),[95] and for Alexy it is social 'importance' judged from the point of view

[91] Compare the various formulations in *Carter*, above at section II.

[92] Alexy's Weight Formula represents all the factors at issue in constitutional rights cases:

$$W_{i,j} = \frac{I_i \, W_i \, R_i}{I_j \, W_j \, R_j}$$

See R Alexy, 'On Balancing and Subsumption. A Structural Comparison' (2003) 16 *Ratio Juris* 433.

[93] ibid.

[94] Richard Posner argues provides a formula for cases involving the right to free speech, arguing that it should be banned if and only if

$$pH/(1 + d)^n + O \geq B - A$$

where H is the harm (or costs) of the regulated speech, p is the probability that the harm will occur (a number between 0 and 1); d is 'the rate at which future costs or benefits are discounted to the present'; n is 'the number of years (or other unit of the time)' between the occurrence of the speech and when the harm is likely to materialise; O is the offensiveness of the speech; B is the benefit of prohibited speech; and A is the administrative cost of sorting harmful from beneficial speech. See R Posner, *Frontiers of Legal Theory* (Cambridge, MA, Harvard University Press, 2001) 62–68.

[95] ibid.

of the constitution.[96] Thus, adopting the formula approach depends on rejecting the claim made by many moral philosophers that moral values are incommensurable. Francisco Urbina has ably defended the incommensurability thesis in this context, and has compellingly argued that this thesis should lead to the rejection of Alexy's Weight Formula and similar approaches that depend on commensuration of value.[97] I agree with Urbina's criticism but will not purse the details here. One reason is that there is little evidence courts actually follow such a formulaic approach to proportionality and balancing cases, and abundant evidence to the contrary.

Courts that employ proportionality and balancing tests typically address a range of interests and values, making no attempt to bring them into any systematic relationship, much less a mathematical or numerical one. The Canadian Supreme Court has said that it would be 'dangerously misleading' to consider the proportionality test to be 'rigid and technical'; though some litigants perceive it as formalistic, 'it plays an immeasurably richer role, one of great magnitude and sophistication'.[98] It should bring 'together the fundamental values and aspirations of Canadian society', by activating Charter rights and 'permitting only such reasonable limits as a free and democratic society may have occasion to place upon them'.[99] The US Supreme Court has said that in deciding whether constitutional rights can be 'abridged' (ie infringed or interfered with) 'the delicate and difficult task falls upon the courts to weigh the circumstances and to appraise the substantiality of the reasons advanced in support of the regulation of the free enjoyment of rights'.[100] Proportionality involves, according to the ECtHR, holistic assessment of not only the reasonableness of legislative decision-making but also the motivations behind it:

> In carrying out its scrutiny of the impugned interference, the Court has to ascertain whether the respondent State exercised its discretion reasonably, carefully and in good faith. It must also look at the interference complained of in the light of the case as a whole and determine whether it was 'proportionate to the legitimate aim pursued' and whether the reasons adduced by the national authorities to justify it are 'relevant and sufficient'.

These and many other cases show that judges understand their role under balancing and proportionality tests as embracing a range of basic values and broadly reasoning about which policy is appropriate and how it should be implemented.

Such a view is echoed by prominent defenders of the proportionality inquiry such as Matthias Kumm:

> Assessing the justification of rights infringements is, at least in the many cases where the constitution provides no specific further guidance, *largely an exercise of general practical*

[96] Alexy, 'On Balancing and Subsumption', above n 92, 42.

[97] F Urbina, *A Critique of Proportionality and Balancing* (Cambridge, Cambridge University Press, 2017) Ch 3.

[98] *R v Keegstra* [1990] 3 SCR 697, 735–36.

[99] ibid.

[100] *Schneider v State* 308 US 147, 161 (1939).

> *reasoning, without many of the constraining features that otherwise characterise legal reasoning.* (emphasis added)[101]

Kumm argues that the practical reasoning involved in proportionality cases requires judges to make their own, independent evaluations, and to reject legislative decisions insofar as they fall short of what justice requires. 'At the level of evaluating the relative importance of the general interest in relation to the liberty interest at stake, the weights can be assigned and priorities established *as required by the correct substantive theory of justice*' (emphasis added).[102] As Urbina has pointed out, defenders of proportionality and balancing in constitutional rights adjudication face a dilemma.[103] Insofar as these tests are characterised as technical, providing specific guidance to courts and constraining their reasoning, they are liable to leave out considerations that are important in making decisions about human rights. Kumm and Möller insist that proportionality is broad enough to accommodate any moral consideration relevant to human rights.[104] This broad approach amounts to what Urbina calls 'unconstrained moral reasoning'.[105] This represents the general position that courts have adopted.

In addition to moral reasoning, courts applying proportionality and balancing tests engage in empirical reasoning. Because proportionality concerns the efficacy of means and the nature and acceptability of side-effects, questions about empirical causality are built into it, in various respects. The Canadian Supreme Court has said that proportionality 'is by its very nature a fact-specific inquiry':

> In determining proportionality, [a court] must determine the actual connection between the objective and *what the law will in fact achieve*; the actual degree to which it impairs the right; and whether the actual benefit which the law is calculated to achieve outweighs the actual seriousness of the limitation of the right. In short, [this] is an exercise based on the facts of the law at issue and the proof offered of its justification, not on abstractions. (emphasis added)[106]

Here 'actual' signifies a concern with facts, actualities. The ECtHR holds that national authorities must show 'that they based their decisions on an acceptable assessment of the relevant facts' in order to demonstrate conformity with the principle of proportionality.[107] The US Supreme Court has stated that 'underlying

[101] M Kumm, 'Political Liberalism and the Structure of Rights: On the Place and Limits of the Proportionality Requirement' in G Pavlakos, *Law, Rights and Discourse: The Legal Philosophy of Robert Alexy* (Oxford, Hart Publishing, 2007) 140.

[102] ibid.

[103] See F Urbina, *A Critique of Proportionality and Balancing* (Cambridge, Cambridge University Press, 2017) 131–36.

[104] See ibid.

[105] See ibid. Urbina argues that while this approach has some advantages, it also has severe drawbacks; he identifies a number of problems judges encounter if they must exercise unconstrained moral reasoning, and shows how specific legal direction can overcome these problems. See also F Urbina, 'A Critique of Proportionality' (2012) 57 *American Journal of Jurisprudence* 49.

[106] *RJR-MacDonald, Inc v Canada* [1994] 1 SCR 311 [133].

[107] *Makhmudov v Russia* (2008) 46 EHRR 37 [65].

questions of fact may condition the constitutionality of legislation', and the Court must verify the existence of the facts.[108] In cases involving a rights-based challenge to the constitutionality of legislation, courts regularly assess the results of research in economics, psychology, sociology, medicine, and other fields, especially when assessing the strength of the state's interest in legislation but also for other aspects of the proportionality test. Examples of this will be discussed in chapter four.

VIII. Other Adjudicative Methods

While proportionality and balancing are the methods of adjudication used in the large majority of constitutional right cases, there are other methods or approaches that involve broad moral and empirical reasoning. These include various interpretative approaches which stress that judges should base decisions not on the textual meaning of a constitutional provision or the intent of drafters, but instead on principles of justice or fairness not directly manifested in the constitutional text. Sometimes the constitution is characterised as a 'living' document or compared to a 'living tree'. This is meant to emphasise its flexibility in reflecting or incorporating society's changing views on questions of political morality. On other views a constitution includes principles that are *unwritten* yet justiciable, and some hold that judges are authorised to rely on natural law (for example, Chief Justice Beverly McLachlin of the Canadian Supreme Court).[109]

There is a vast literature on these and other broad theories of constitutional interpretation, and this is not the place to attempt to catalogue or explain them, or to discuss criticisms.[110] What these approaches have in common is that: (i) they reject the proposition that constitutional interpretation should be limited

[108] *O'Gorman & Young Inc v Hartford Fire Ins Co* 282 US 251, 257 (1930).

[109] McLachlin characterises herself as 'modern natural law proponent' in the sense of accepting that 'there are there are certain fundamental norms that no nation should transgress', the identification of which presupposes 'the existence of some kind of natural order'. She states: 'The contemporary concept of unwritten constitutional principles can be seen as a modern reincarnation of the ancient doctrines of natural law': B McLachlin, 'Unwritten Constitutional Principles: What is Going On?' (Lord Cooke of Thorndon Lecture, Victoria University of Wellington Law School, 1 December 2005) <www.victoria.ac.nz/law/centres/nzcpl/publications/nz-journal-of-public-and-international-law/previous-issues/volume-42,-december-2006/mclachlin.pdf>. McLachlin states that unlike ancient doctrines, her account 'does not fasten on theology as the source of the unwritten principles', and that their content is determined by examining 'history, values and culture of the nation, viewed in its constitutional context'. For Thomas Aquinas, however, natural law can be described (using McLachlin's terms) as 'fundamental norms' corresponding to a 'natural order'; although their ultimate source is theistic they are grasped and understood through natural reason rather than reliance on theology or revelation. See *Summa Theologica* I–II, question 95.

[110] For a consequences-based argument that judges should confine their role to interpreting clear, non-ambiguous constitutional provisions and otherwise defer to the legislature, see A Vermeule, *Judging Under Uncertainty: An Institutional Theory of Legal Interpretation* (Cambridge, Mass, Harvard University Press, 2006).

to clear, text-based rules; and (ii) they embrace either moral reasoning or empirical reasoning, or both. Although theories for adjudicating and interpreting constitutional rights are presented and justified in many different ways, almost all of the commonly followed theories involve the potential for a court to reject a legislature's decision on the ground that the legislature failed to judge correctly on some matter of political morality (including reaching a correct balance of good and bad effects of legislation) or of empirical fact.

Originalism, a method of interpreting constitutional rights used mainly in the US, proposes to limit interpretation to discerning the textual meaning of constitutional provisions or the original intent of their authors, and it might be thought that this is a way of avoiding broad moral and empirical reasoning by courts. Justice Scalia recommended originalism on the grounds that it promotes judicial restraint and deference to the legislature and the democratic process, and that it accords with the courts' proper role as interpreters of law rather than makers of it.[111] But in his hands and those of other practitioners, originalism frequently culminates in the application of a balancing test.

Most proponents of originalism today reject Justice Black's view that the task of the interpreter is to fix a clear meaning of the constitutional right and apply it without considering whether some governmental interest requires limiting the right. In opinions that use originalist methods, reasoning based on text and history is sometimes used to decide whether a claimed interest falls within the scope of a constitutional right—for example, an interest in possessing a gun for self-defence (*Heller v District of Columbia*),[112] or using corporate funds to advertise in support of a political candidate (*Citizens United v Federal Election Commission*).[113] Originalist methods may also be used to set limits to what legislatures can do in relation to a right—for example, barring legislatures from using campaign finance restrictions to promote equality of power between individuals and groups (*Buckley v Valeo*).[114] Even in this more historical mode, the abstract moral language of constitutional rights creates an open door for judges to have recourse to political opinions, either overtly or surreptitiously.[115] And it draws courts into historical research that stretches their capacities in ways analogous to research into general empirical facts; such research employs sources rather different from legal enactments and texts, and courts have repeatedly made mistakes identified by scholars who have investigated the record.[116]

Once the initial historical work is done, judges relying on originalism often proceed to apply a balancing test, via an established category within the tiered scrutiny

[111] See A Scalia, *A Matter of Interpretation* (Princeton, Princeton University Press, 1998) 10.
[112] *Heller v District of Columbia* 554 US 570 (2008).
[113] *Citizens United v Federal Election Commission* 558 US 310 (2010).
[114] *Buckley v Valeo* 424 US 1 (1976).
[115] See F Cross, *The Failed Promise of Originalism* (Palo Alto, Stanford University Press, 2013).
[116] See D Drakeman, *Church, State, and Original Intent* (Cambridge, Cambridge University Press, 2010) 11–12 & ch 4.

framework or sometimes in a looser way. At this stage the moral reasoning—that is, the assessment of the reasonableness of the legislature's means—entailed in a balancing test is in play. For example, in *Citizens United* the Court said the government must prove that a law furthers 'a compelling interest and is narrowly tailored to achieve that interest'.[117] Many such opinions turn on an assessment of the empirical evidence in support of the government's interest. In at least four landmark cases decided during his last years on the Court, Justice Scalia wrote or joined majority opinions striking down laws in which some form of balancing or rational basis test was used, in which a crucial issue was empirical. In *Heller*, it was whether legalising handguns would lead to their criminal use; in *Citizens United* it was whether indirect corporate expenditures in support of political candidates (as opposed to direct contributions) would lead to political corruption; in *Shelby v Holbrook*,[118] which struck down portions of the Voting Rights Act of 1965, it was whether the conditions regarding racial discrimination in affected states had changed since the Act was adopted; in *Brown v Entertainment Merchants Association*,[119] it was the effects on youths of playing violent video games. In each of these cases there were dissenting opinions arguing at length, and citing extensive empirical evidence, that the legislature had acted reasonably in enacting or maintaining the law. In *Brown*, Scalia himself relied on his review of empirical evidence to reject a submission by the state of California in support of the law; his analysis is considered below in chapter four. Thus, even the Court's leading proponent of originalism applied the method in cases that turn on moral and empirical reasoning used to second-guess legislative judgments.

If originalism is open to moral and empirical reasoning in this way, then more broadly conceived methods of interpretation will likely encroach even more into the realm of legislative judgement. Judges speaking extra-judicially sometimes acknowledge this. As Justice Kenny of the Irish Supreme Court wrote, 'Judges have become legislators and have the advantage that they do not have to face an opposition'.[120] Justice McLachlin, who presided as Chief Justice in *Carter v Canada*, said in a speech to a judiciary conference 14 years earlier, that although resolving disputes is still the 'primary and most fundamental task' of the judiciary, courts also have a responsibility to change the law, and not only in minor ways:

> In the latter part of the twentieth century, the lawmaking role of the judge has dramatically expanded. Judicial lawmaking is no longer always confined to small, incremental changes. Increasingly, it is invading the domain of social policy, once perceived as the exclusive right of Parliament and the legislatures.[121]

[117] *Citizens United*, above n 113, 573.

[118] *Shelby v Holbrook* 570 US 2 (2013).

[119] *Brown v Entertainment Merchants Association* 564 US 786 (2011).

[120] J Kenny, 'The Advantages of a Written Constitution Incorporating A Bill of Rights' (1979) 30 *Northern Ireland Legal Quarterly* 189, 196.

[121] Remarks of the Right Honourable Beverley McLachlin, PC, Chief Justice of Canada, to the The Fourth Worldwide Common Law Judiciary Conference (5 May 2001) <www.scc-csc.ca/judges-juges/spe-dis/bm-2001-05-05-eng.aspx>.

This involves making 'difficult choices' about 'policy questions', which are polycentric in that they demand foresight of the consequences of pulling one strand of a 'complex web'.[122] Such choices require access to empirical information, and courts must strike 'the balance between the conflicting values which most closely conforms to justice as society, taken as a whole, sees it'.[123]

McLachlin acknowledges that this new lawmaking task raises serious questions about the institutional capacity of courts: 'There is a very real question whether courts, which lack resources for gathering and collating information and opinion available to the legislatures, are the best institutions to decide complex social policy questions.'[124] She contends, however, that this judicial lawmaking role has been imposed on judges, and that courts can overcome institutional weaknesses because the judicial office is inherently impartial:

> But that question [of institutional competence] is increasingly moot. The reality, at least in Canada, is that judges are being required to decide these questions, no matter how difficult it may be. … In their final form, judgments on social policy questions are often not all that different from legislation. It is the process by which the judgments are arrived at that distinguishes them. Legislation is often the product of compromise or conflict between various political factions, each faction pushing its own agenda. The judicial arena does not, and should not, provide simply another forum for the same kind of contests. Judges must maintain the appearance and reality of impartiality. It is impartiality that distinguishes us from the other branches of government, and impartiality that gives us our legitimacy. … Judges are not politicians. Nor are they advocates. Judges are, quite simply, impartial decision-makers.[125]

No close observer of modern judicial review of legislation believes that judges are impartial in this way when they adjudicate constitutional rights.[126] There is, however, a more basic flaw in McLachlin's argument. Even if judges conscientiously adhere to the ideal of impartiality, this cannot overcome institutional deficiencies with regard to the capacity for acquiring information and engaging in the moral reasoning that shapes policy and lawmaking choices. This chapter has demonstrated the ways in which vague rights language and broad adjudicative methods open the door to moral and empirical reasoning in constitutional rights cases. Chapters four to six will consider examples of the many important moral

[122] ibid.
[123] ibid.
[124] ibid.
[125] ibid.
[126] What Andrei Marmor said of the US could be applied to Canada and many other jurisdictions: 'Any reasonably informed observer of U.S. constitutional cases would have to admit that most of the important constitutional decisions of the Supreme Court are reached on (so-called) ideological grounds. The justices' moral, political, sometimes even religious, convictions tend to influence, not to say determine, the outcome of their decisions on constitutional matters, though, of course, rarely the public reasons given for them. The reasons are always cast in legal terms and phrased as legalistically as possible': A Marmor, 'Randomized Judicial Review' (April 2015), USC Law Legal Studies Paper No 15-8, available at SSRN: <https://ssrn.com/abstract=2568725>.

and factual issues that courts decide, and argue that the judicial capacity in this area is substantially inferior to legislative capacity. Among the cases that will be analysed in detail is *Carter v Canada*. I will argue that both the trial court and the Canadian Supreme Court made numerous missteps in their empirical reasoning (see chapter four, section V). If McLachlin is correct in claiming that courts are 'required to decide these [difficult] questions', then it must also be admitted that constitutional framers have not equipped courts with the institutional capacities needed to perform that task competently.

IX. Conclusion

Courts gained the power to enforce constitutional rights against the legislature as a result of the widespread perception that such rights should be inviolable. Paradoxically, in the now-standard methods of adjudicating constitutional rights, they are defined by precisely by their violability. The starting point in a constitutional rights case is that a right has been infringed, interfered with, or abridged, and this opens up an inquiry into whether such interference is balanced or proportionate. The balancing and proportionality tests used to resolve the vast majority of constitutional cases are elaborately phrased in terms of 'strict scrutiny', 'compelling state interest', 'narrow tailoring' and 'less restrictive alternatives'. When closely examined, these tests, in their essence, involve asking whether the legislature has chosen means that do not unreasonably burden individual interests, in light of the value of the legislative goal—or in short, whether the law is reasonable. To make this assessment, courts need to engage in the same kinds of moral and empirical reasoning that legislatures would employ in deciding whether to adopt the law. An analysis of comparative institutional capacity is the subject of chapters four to six. But first, in chapter three, I will consider Dworkin's theory of rights as trumps. I do so because it appears to reject the balancing approach as well as the prima facie conception of rights that has been described in this chapter, and thus to eliminate the need for a court to rely on empirical reasoning in assessing the reasonableness of the means that the legislature has chosen.

3

Are Rights Trumps?

The most influential theory of constitutional rights is Ronald Dworkin's account of rights as trumps. It is also the most widely discussed alternative to the concept of rights assumed in the proportionality inquiry. As shown in chapter two, proportionality and balancing tests treat rights as prima facie rights, which can be justifiably infringed for the sake of the general interests of society. This results in a similar position to John Stuart Mill's utilitarian view of rights, in which individual rights are sacrificed for the sake of social expediency. With Mill as one target and the US Supreme Court's use of balancing tests as another, Dworkin calls his conception of rights 'anti-utilitarian', and he rejects the model of rights that calls for balancing individual rights against the demands of society at large. He argues that individual rights are *trumps against* the general welfare.

In his early work, Dworkin proposes two distinct theories of rights as trumps. The first, which I call the *shielded-interest* theory and analyse in section I, takes rights to be important values that must be protected against utilitarian justifications for laws; hence Dworkin terms it 'anti-utilitarian'. I show that, on close inspection, the shielded-interest theory ultimately collapses into a form of balancing. In the *filtered-preference* theory, which is discussed in section II, rights do not trump utilitarian justifications generally but only certain *external* preferences people have for how goods and opportunities should be distributed to others, which result in corrupted justifications for law. Dworkin depicts legislative deliberation as a mechanical process in which legislatures maximise utility by aggregating all of society's preferences and translating them into law. Courts are assigned the task of filtering out external preferences by determining which laws are motivated by them, and striking down those laws.

A lesser known feature of Dworkin's theory of rights, which I discuss in section III, is that it addresses the argument that courts lack the institutional capacities needed to adjudicate rights. Dworkin is unusual among defenders of judicial review of legislation in recognising that it is a fundamental problem for courts to rely on statistically-based social science research in constitutional rights cases. With astute observations on the nature of such evidence, he argues that relying on statistics to make causal judgments lies outside the normal competence of courts. He further contends that social science is not a proper ground for constitutional law because it relies on observations of behavioural patterns that can undergo rapid transformation.[1] In his view, the adjudication of rights should not depend on 'numbers'.[2] Since his theory of rights is not information-based, Dworkin thinks his theory obviates the need to compare the capacities of courts and legislatures to deal with scientific research. This contrasts with the approach of courts that rely on proportionality to adjudicate rights and say that proportionality is in its nature a fact-specific inquiry.

In section IV, I consider modifications Dworkin made to his theory of rights in later work. I argue that, in the end, he fails to provide an adequate alternative to the treatment of rights in the proportionality test. The theory of rights as trumps does not dispense with a need for comparative analysis of institutional capacities. Moreover, the theory gives a distorted view of legislative deliberation, which becomes an obstacle to a proper comparative analysis of institutional capacity. Since legislatures, on his view, are simply concerned with maximising utility or advancing the general welfare, they are inherently the foe of rights. Courts are the forum of principle—or rights—and constitutional rights are vindicated only when courts strike down legislative action. I will argue (initially in this chapter, and more fully in chapter five) that Dworkin's view of the legislative process—which is built into his theory of rights—is reductive and flawed. We should reject the theory of rights as trumps in favour of a view that sees rights as an integral part of the general welfare, and sees legislatures as having the capacity to promote and protect rights.

I. The Shielded-Interest Theory

In the Introduction to *Taking Rights Seriously*, Dworkin calls individual rights 'political trumps held by individuals'[3] and gives this general definition:

> Individuals have rights when, for some reason, a collective goal is not a sufficient justification for denying them what they wish, as individuals, to have or to do, or not a sufficient justification for imposing some loss or injury on them.[4]

Dworkin argues that rights function as trumps against any type of collective goal or conception of the common good. The arguments in *Taking Rights Seriously*, however, discuss collective justifications for laws almost entirely in terms of utilitarianism. The idea of rights defended there is, he says, 'parasitic on the dominant idea of utilitarianism, which is the idea of a collective goal of the community as

[1] R Dworkin, 'Social Sciences and Constitutional Rights—the Consequences of Uncertainty' (1977) 6 *Journal of Law and Education* 3, 6, 12.

[2] ibid 8.

[3] Ronald Dworkin, *Taking Rights Seriously* (Cambridge, Mass, Harvard University Press, 1978) xi.

[4] ibid.

a whole.'[5] Thus Dworkin begins by accepting as a working postulate a definition of the general welfare in utilitarian terms. Although Dworkin calls his theory of rights 'anti-utilitarian', it accommodates and privileges basic utilitarian principles by conceiving of the general welfare as an aggregation of interests or preferences to be satisfied, and by assuming that it is possible to advance the general welfare of the whole by imposing loss or injuries on some.

Rights 'trump' utilitarian justifications for laws in two different ways in Dworkin's work. In the first, *the shielded-interest theory*, rights form a protective barrier around certain important individual interests and shield them against utilitarian arguments. Dworkin originally propounded the shielded-interest theory in the 1970 essay 'Taking Rights Seriously,'[6] later the title chapter of his 1977 book. Here Dworkin does not argue for the existence of any particular rights; he assumes but does not defend the thesis that people have 'fundamental' moral rights against the state, and explores the consequences of conceding that such rights exist.[7] A right is fundamental if it is necessary to protect a person's 'dignity, or his standing as equally entitled to concern and respect, or some other personal value of like consequence.'[8]

In several places Dworkin describes the claim to a right in this form: A has a right to X (where X is some opportunity, resource, or liberty) even if denying X to A would further the general interest.[9] The 'even if' in the formulation is crucial: the hypothetical conflict with society's general welfare is what gives intelligibility to the claim of a right.[10] This definition sets up an intrinsic opposition between rights and the general welfare. Rights are vindicated or protected when some measure that would promote the general welfare is defeated.

In Dworkin's claims about the trumping power of rights, the bark is stronger than the bite. He says that he rejects the balancing model of rights, which 'recommends striking a balance between the rights of the individual and the demands of society at large'.[11] Though that model is 'established in our political and judicial rhetoric', Dworkin contends it is 'false' and that the 'heart of the error' is the balancing metaphor.[12] But in fact the shielded-interest theory resembles balancing

[5] ibid.

[6] The essay was originally published in the *New York Review of Books*.

[7] ibid 184–85. See also xii–xiii.

[8] ibid 199.

[9] ibid 91, 169, 192, 364. '[A] claim of political right is a claim to a trump over the general welfare for the account of a particular individual. When someone claims a right of free speech, for example he claims that it would be wrong for the state to prohibit him from speaking on some matter *even if the general welfare would be improved* by preventing him from speaking' (emphasis added): *Taking Rights Seriously* 364.

[10] 'The hypothetical nature of the claim is important. We emphasize the special injustice of torture, for example when we speak of a right against torture, because we claim that torture would be wrong *even if it were in the general interest*' (emphasis added): *Taking Rights Seriously* 364.

[11] ibid 197–98.

[12] ibid 198–99.

and proportionality tests used under the received approach to human rights. Dworkin acknowledges that the state can legitimately curtail the exercise of even a fundamental right in order to prevent substantial harm to others or society.[13] The shielded-interest theory only rejects *sheer* balancing: the proposition that a right is overcome whenever the considerations that support a proposed law tip the balance toward the general welfare, however slightly. In his review of *Taking Rights Seriously*, Joseph Raz said that Dworkin's arguments amount to two truisms: that rights matter and that they may defeat other considerations. He observed that 'almost always Dworkin sounds as if he meant to say something much more far-reaching'; however, '[n]owhere does he say clearly and unambiguously anything more than that rights have some weight however little and may override considerations which aren't themselves rights'.[14]

Responding to Raz's critique, Dworkin offers only a minor adjustment. He claims it would be 'pointless' to say that A has a right *merely because* A's interest in X is stronger than B's (for example when A has a strong preference for pistachio ice cream and B has a mild preference for vanilla).[15] That would 'inflate the number of rights grotesquely, and so make the appeal to a right banal';[16] a right must outweigh 'some collective justification that normally provides a full justification for the decision'.[17] Dworkin's view can thus be contrasted to Möller, who supports 'rights inflation' and argues that rights extend to trivial and immoral activities (see chapter two, section VI). Dworkin, however, assents to Raz's characterisation of the basic logic of his theory, stating: 'No alleged right is a right (on my account) unless it overrides *at least a marginal case* of collective justification' (emphasis added).[18] This is not essentially different from how Raz formulated his position: that rights have *some* weight and *may* override other considerations. Dworkin makes no detailed attempt to describe the strength or weight that rights have in withstanding collective justifications and acknowledges that 'some rights are more important than others', meaning that they resist some collective justifications more forcefully than others.[19] Thus, the logic of Dworkin's shielded-interest theory is consistent with balancing tests. In a sense, the theory of rights as trumps is a balancing test. The invocation of 'A's right to X' is simply a rhetorical tool for indicating (in an indeterminate way) that there must be a sufficiently weighty justification for denying X to A. This is the same basic logic as in the proportionality inquiry.

[13] ibid 200–204.
[14] Joseph Raz, 'Professor Dworkin's Theory of Rights' (1978) 26 *Political Studies* 123, 126.
[15] *Taking Rights Seriously* 365.
[16] ibid 365.
[17] ibid.
[18] ibid 366.
[19] ibid.

II. The Filtered-Preference Theory

Dworkin originally developed his second theory of rights as trumps—which I call the filtered-preference theory—in a series of essays in 1976 and 1977.[20] Unlike the shielded-interest theory, the filtered-preference theory does not assume the existence of rights that have a special weight. It is a method of deriving rights as part of a basic theory of political justification and identifying their content. Rights are conceived as the result of refining utilitarian justifications by excluding certain types of preferences. This can be pictured as a filtering process; hence 'filtered-preference theory'. The essay that outlines this theory in its most general form is 'What Rights Do We Have?' in *Taking Rights Seriously*, which concerns the relationship between liberty and equality.

Dworkin begins by arguing that liberty can legitimately be constrained only on the basis of certain limited types of argument, and he gives the following 'crude typology' of political justifications.[21] Arguments of *principle* constrain liberty in order to prevent distinct injury to an individual. Arguments of policy seek to realise a state of affairs in which the community as a whole, not just certain individuals, will be better off as the result of a constraint on liberty.[22] There are two basic types of arguments of policy. *Utilitarian* policy arguments hold that the community is better off when citizens as a whole have more of what they want (even if some have less). *Ideal* policy arguments, in contrast, are those that seek to bring the community closer to some objectively true ideal, whether or not citizens desire the improvement.[23] These ideal arguments, according to Dworkin, conflict with the liberal conception of equality whenever the ideal in question is 'controversial within the community', because a basic canon of liberalism 'prohibits a government from relying on a claim that certain forms of life are inherently more valuable than others.'[24]

On a first impression, Dworkin observes, utilitarian policy arguments appear secure from liberal objections because they treat the wishes of every member of the community equally; no one is given a bonus or discount because he is more or less worthy than another or his views more or less deserving of respect.[25]

[20] 'What Rights Do We Have?' (first published in *Taking Rights Seriously*); 'Reverse Discrimination' (first published in 1976 in the *New York Review of Books* and later in *Taking Rights Seriously*); 'Social Sciences and Constitutional Rights—the Consequences of Uncertainty' (1977) 6 *Journal of Law and Education* 1; 'Bakke's Case: Are Quotas Unfair?' (first published in 1977 in the New York Review of Books and later in *A Matter of Principle* (Cambridge, Mass, Harvard University Press, 1985)). The filtered-preference theory is also relied on in 'Liberalism' (first published in Stuart Hampshire (ed), *Public and Private Morality* (Cambridge, Cambridge University Press, 1978) and later in *A Matter of Principle*).

[21] *Taking Rights Seriously* 274. See also 232.

[22] ibid 274.

[23] ibid.

[24] ibid.

[25] ibid 275. See also 234.

But this appearance of egalitarianism can be illusory because utilitarianism counts both personal and external preferences in its calculations of the general welfare.[26] Personal preferences are for the assignment of goods and opportunities to oneself.[27] External preferences are for how goods and opportunities are to be assigned to others.[28] If someone morally disapproves of certain conduct and seeks on that basis to constrain another person's liberty to engage in it, this is counted as a preference in the general utilitarian calculation.[29] Though the liberal conception of equality barred moral judgments at the front door, utilitarianism might let them in through the back door, in the form of a 'moralistic' preference for how others should live. Dworkin concludes that utilitarian calculations must be based only on personal preferences if they are to figure in arguments that legitimately constrain liberty; justifications based on racist, moralistic, or other external preferences are inconsistent with equality.[30] Conceived in this way, utilitarianism does not threaten the liberal thesis that 'government has no right to enforce popular morality by law'; indeed if 'utilitarianism is suitably reconstituted so as to count only personal preferences, then the liberal thesis is a consequence, not an enemy, of that theory'.[31]

Although Dworkin implies that moralistic or racist prejudice would be illegitimate in any political setting, the trumping force of rights in the filtered-preference theory is not directed toward the content of external preferences. Instead, Dworkin argues that to count any external preference makes utilitarianism self-defeating. He cites Bentham for the proposition that under utilitarianism everyone is to count for one and not more than one.[32] The racist counts as more than one because he has preferences for both the distribution of goods to himself and the denial of goods to others. This results in double counting, and the resulting distribution is not 'utilitarian at all'—at least in the sense of each person counting as one.[33] Dworkin excludes racist and moralistic preferences not because of their content but because they are external, that is, because they are the preferences of one person about another's opportunities or choices. This argument commits Dworkin to the proposition that utilitarian justifications are corrupted even by altruistic preferences,[34] or personal, self-denying preferences 'for less of a certain good … on the proviso that others will have more.'[35] Such preferences 'may no more be

[26] ibid 275.
[27] ibid.
[28] ibid.
[29] ibid 275–76.
[30] ibid 276.
[31] ibid 236.
[32] See ibid 234, 275. In 'What Rights Do We Have?' Dworkin describes the argument about double counting as the summary of a longer version in 'Reverse Discrimination' (Ch 9 of *Taking Rights Seriously*) 231–38.
[33] ibid 235.
[34] ibid 235, 238.
[35] ibid 277. The self-denying preference described here is technically not an external preference but a personal preference that is parasitic on an external preference.

counted in a defensible utilitarian argument than less attractive preferences rooted in prejudice rather than altruism.'[36]

Dworkin refers to personal preferences as those that 'rightly make up the general welfare';[37] they can thus legitimately be relied upon to constrain liberty and ground law-making. He states:

> The vast bulk of the laws which diminish my liberty are justified on utilitarian grounds, as being in the general interest or for the general welfare; if as Bentham supposes, each of these laws diminishes my liberty, they nevertheless do not take away from me anything that I have a right to have.[38]

Dworkin's egalitarian interpretation of utilitarianism is coupled with a theory about the institutions of political democracy. The institutions best suited to identify and achieve utilitarian policies are democratic ones.[39] But democratically elected legislatures are incapable of separating external from personal preferences.[40] The legislature is like a computer that automatically registers all voter preferences and translates them into law.[41] Bringing together the different strands in the argument, Dworkin proposes a 'general theory of rights':

> The concept of an individual political right ... is a response to the philosophical defects of a utilitarianism that counts external preferences and the practical impossibility of a utilitarianism that does not. It allows us to enjoy the institutions of political democracy, which enforce overall or unrefined utilitarianism, and yet protect the fundamental right of citizens to equal concern and respect by prohibiting decisions that seem, antecedently, likely to have been reached by virtue of the external components of the preferences democracy reveals.[42]

The reference in this passage to 'prohibiting decisions' refers to judicial review of legislation to enforce constitutional rights. Independent courts, Dworkin argues, should have the power to overturn decisions based on corrupted utilitarian justifications, because judges are insulated from society's external preferences expressed through electoral politics.[43] The meaning of 'antecedently' in this general theory of rights is explained in a passage discussing the institutional aspects of the theory in 'Social Sciences and Constitutional Rights—The Consequences of Uncertainty', which was published the same year as *Taking Rights Seriously*:

> [A]ny political judgment about what makes the community better as a whole must count the impact on each particular person as having the same importance. As Bentham said, 'Each man [and woman] to count for one and none for more than one.'

36 ibid.

37 'Social Sciences and Constitutional Rights', above n 1, 10.

38 *Taking Rights Seriously* 269.

39 ibid 276.

40 ibid.

41 'Social Sciences and Constitutional Rights', above n 1, 10; *A Matter of Principle*, 366.

42 *Taking Rights Seriously* 277.

43 See *A Matter of Principle* 70 ('Judicial review insures that the most fundamental issues of political morality will finally be set out and debated as issues of principle and not political power alone, a transformation that cannot succeed, in any case not fully, within the legislature itself'.).

> The political process in a democracy is meant to translate that requirement into legislation through the institutions of representative democracy. The welfare economists have worked out a theory to how that is achieved. Each individual, through his votes and other political activity, registers or reveals a preference. The political process is a machine which is calculated, though imperfectly, to reach decisions such that, though some individuals suffer and others gain, the overall preferences of all the people, considered neutrally with the same consideration for the preferences of each, is improved.

This mechanistic view of legislative activity, as a machine in which every individual preference is registered and fed into the output, forms a key part of Dworkin's concept of rights. He continues:

> In a community which has a settled prejudice of one sort or another, however, whether it be prejudice against blacks, against homosexuals, or against particular political views, the machine will inevitably break down because there is no way of excluding these preferences based on prejudice from affecting the process. If prejudicial preferences are counted, then the personal preferences of those against whom the prejudice acts are not counted equally in the balance; they are discounted by the effect of the prejudice. Therefore constitutional rights are needed.
>
> There is a high antecedent probability that the political judgment reached about a particular matter will not fairly reflect the kind of preferences that rightly make up the general welfare, but will give influential expression to preferences based on prejudice. One reason constitutional rights of one sort or another are created is to guard against the influence of prejudice.[44]

Therefore, Dworkin concludes, '[t]he key point of this explanation of constitutional rights is that rights are based on antecedent probabilities.'[45] This refers to the antecedent likelihood that background racial prejudice or other external preferences in society will result in corrupted utilitarian justifications for laws.[46]

III. Constitutional Rights and Statistics

If rights are based on antecedent probabilities, does this mean judges should use empirical data to determine what the probabilities are? Dworkin answers in the negative, arguing that 'there is ample reason to deplore any general dependence of adjudication upon complex judgments of causal social science, particularly when constitutional rights are at stake'.[47] While physics and similar sciences establish 'some notion of the mechanics that translate the cause to the effect', social science 'usually is only able to provide correlations without the mechanics'.[48] Thus, there

[44] 'Social Sciences and Constitutional Rights', above n 1, 10.
[45] ibid.
[46] ibid.
[47] ibid 6.
[48] ibid 5.

is an element of arbitrariness involved when the researcher chooses the categories between which correlation is taken to be significant.[49] Any need to rely on statistics would be problematic for judicial capacity:

> When a mechanical model is lacking, and you make judgments simply on correlation between observed phenomena, the kinds of techniques necessary to provide arguments for and against the hypothesis belong entirely to a very arcane subject, namely, statistics. The mathematical concepts of statistics are much more removed from the ordinary vocabulary of a trial judge than are the concepts of physics or chemistry he might encounter in, for example, a complicated patent case.[50]

I explore this point further in chapter four, section II, which explains differences between the use of general empirical information in constitutional cases, on the one hand, and, on the other, the expert evidence used in ordinary litigation matters such as medical negligence, products liability, or patents. Sometimes the difference lies in the nature of the evidence and the extent of its reliance on statistical methods, but this is not always the case. There are other differences in the purpose for which the evidence is presented, the processes by which it is acquired and assessed, and the consequences of the decision about the evidence with regard to scope (constitutional rights cases apply to society generally rather than just the parties) and the duration of a judgment. Dworkin touches on the last point when he observes that another problem of using statistics in constitutional cases is that '[c]orrelations of social phenomena are fragile in the sense that the data, the behaviour which forms the correlation, can change very quickly'.[51] Dworkin's assessment of the institutional capacity of courts to deal with such information is negative: 'Controversial causal judgments based on statistical theory lie outside the normal competence of courts, because these judgments are anchored in models that contain arbitrary and transient elements'.[52] His conclusion is simple and clear: 'it is wrong to use numbers to adjudicate rights'.[53]

This presents a circumstantial difficulty for Dworkin, because of the US Supreme Court's decision in *Brown v Board of Education*,[54] which used social science findings to ground its holding that racial segregation in schools violates the right to equal protection of laws (for discussion see chapter four, section I). The case confronted the justices with the 'separate but equal' test for public facilities that it had adopted in 1896.[55] Instead of overruling the test explicitly, the Court relied on psychological studies showing that segregated schooling caused feelings of inferiority in black children, concluding that segregation leads to poorer educational performance.[56] The Court held that separate educational facilities

[49] ibid 5.
[50] ibid 6.
[51] ibid 6.
[52] ibid 12.
[53] ibid 8.
[54] *Brown v Board of Education* 347 US 483 (1954).
[55] See *Plessy v Ferguson* 163 US 537 (1896).
[56] Brown, above n 54, at 491–94 and fn 11.

are inherently unequal.[57] In 'Social Sciences and Constitutional Rights', Dworkin defends *Brown* as well as cases that had relied on statistical information to issue injunctions requiring school districts to take affirmative measures, such as bussing students from one part of a city to another, in order to integrate schools. Dworkin argues that *Brown* and these other cases do not need to be interpreted as relying on statistics-based *causal* judgments but rather *interpretive* judgments about the meaning of laws.

Dworkin's complex argument for this can be summarised as follows. An interpretive judgment recognises that there is background racial prejudice in communities with segregated schools, and that 'segregation is, in and of itself, insulting and degrading'.[58] There is no need for evidence to prove that segregation is an insult. And since this kind of external 'preference' is a motivation that corrupts utilitarian justifications for law, courts should, according to the filtered-preference theory described in the last section, hold that the law violates constitutional rights.[59] In a related context, Dworkin relies on the same theory in concluding that it is constitutionally permissible for a person's minority status to count as a positive factor in educational admissions processes. In response to claims that affirmative action programmes violate the right to equal treatment of white applicants, Dworkin argues that there is no antecedent likelihood that such programmes are based on prejudice against members of the majority race and thus no violation of their constitutional right to equality.[60]

Dworkin's justification for the judgment in *Brown* on the basis of the filtered-preference theory is a key move, because it provides a general answer to objections to rights-based judicial review on the ground that courts lack the capacity to assess general facts about society. As Dworkin acknowledges:

> Obviously, on any theory of rights, decisions about rights are better if they are based on more rather than less information about a variety of facts. But I know of no reason why a legislator is more likely to have accurate beliefs about the sort of facts that, under any plausible conception of rights, would be relevant to determining what people's rights are.[61]

Dworkin's argument, however, fails on its own terms. As we have seen above, his shielded-interest theory holds that rights are protected against utilitarian justifications for laws unless the justification is sufficiently weighty to override the right. This has the same logic as the proportionality test and thus invites the same kind of empirical information that chapter two showed is an integral part of the test. Dworkin's filtered-preference theory requires judges to determine whether laws are motivated by certain kinds of background prejudices and preferences. In the next section I show that in later versions of that theory Dworkin switched the focus

[57] ibid.
[58] See 'Social Sciences and Constitutional Rights', above n 1, 5.
[59] ibid 11–12.
[60] See *Taking Rights Seriously*, 'Reverse Discrimination', 237–39; *A Matter of Principle* 301.
[61] *A Matter of Principle* 24.

from the *externality* of preferences to their content (a point on which Dworkin was equivocal in the 'Social Sciences' article), excluding motivations for laws such as racial prejudice or paternalistic moral judgement. In the particular circumstances of the US South in the period Dworkin addresses, it is simple and straightforward to conclude that certain laws were motivated by racial prejudice, without resort to statistical data. But this is by no means an adjudicative method that can be easily transferred to other contexts.

The method is strictly concerned only with the motivations for laws held by citizens in a democracy, and is not directly addressed toward the effects of a law or even its propositional content—though these might be evidence of the inward motivations of citizens that brought the law into being. A judge employing the method must determine: (i) whether citizens hold 'forbidden' motivations; and (ii) whether these motivations are the *causal* explanation for a given law. Forbidden motivations include 'contempt', 'prejudice', and other aspects of the sub-rational psyche. One limitation in this approach is that laws might be enacted on the basis of both forbidden and legitimate motivations, as Dworkin acknowledges.[62] Sometimes the answer is clear, as in *Brown* when the segregated school system was clearly motivated by racial prejudice. But that was over 60 years ago, and so far as I am aware, Dworkin has not argued that any existing laws in the US are motivated by contempt for a group's racial, ethnic, or national characteristics. This is not to say that there are no such laws. Anti-terrorism legislation adopted after 11 September 2001, for example, might be motivated by some combination of the public's legitimate concern for its safety and prejudice against certain national, ethnic, or religious groups. But it is not clear how a reliable determination could be made as to which motivations prevailed in the enactment process. Dworkin would not want courts to use sociological or psychological research, given the limited capacities of courts for statistical analysis and his view that rights should not depend on numbers.[63]

Most of Dworkin's arguments concern not racist or similar motivations but what he calls 'paternalistic' motivations: 'detesting' or 'despising' someone's lifestyle, or reacting to it with 'repulsion' or 'disgust', etc. But searching the democratic background for sub-rational motivations of this type also has its limitations. Consider, for example, why voters might support various types of laws regulating or forbidding the use, possession, or trade of drugs: because they think any use of a mind-altering drug is shameful, or wrong, or harmful to the user; or because legal trade in drugs would increase the number of people whose lives are consumed by addiction. Such a condition might be judged as morally less worthy than other ways of life or as inhibiting a person's ability to direct his life autonomously. The availability of drugs increases crime (which reduces property values in a neighbourhood), and it may reduce the efficiency of the economy or lead to increased

[62] *A Matter of Principle* 356–57.
[63] See 'Social Science and Constitutional Rights', above n 1, 8.

welfare spending. Drug use disproportionately harms the less well-off, who cannot afford expensive treatment for recovery from addictions. These are stylised descriptions, representing a few of the hundreds of possible motivations that in the actual minds of many citizens will be more nuanced and combined in various complex ways. Some of the motivations are paternalistic according to Dworkin's descriptions of forbidden motivations, and some are not. A judge could attempt to sort the legitimate from forbidden motivations and trace the causal relationship between motivation and enactment. But it is difficult to see how such an effort could produce a reliable conclusion, even with the use of statistical information. The judgment would, in any event, be empirical in nature. Thus, Dworkin's filtered-preference theory of rights does not obviate the need to assess whether courts have the capacity to rely on statistical information.

IV. Revision of the Filtered-Preference Theory

Dworkin ultimately abandoned the filtered-preference theory following an exchange with HLA Hart, during which he initially defended a refined version of the theory. But what Dworkin abandoned was only the formal structure of the theory. Some of the underlying ideas of the filtered-preference theory, as well as its core strategy of opposing rights to the general welfare, survive into his later work. It is worth re-tracing Dworkin's exchange with Hart because both his early rhetoric of rights as trumps as well as argumentative moves he made in response to Hart have informed his influential rhetoric of rights as trumps.

Hart argued that double-counting was not inimical to utilitarianism but entailed by its basic premises; he suspected that Dworkin's true concern was the prejudicial content of external preferences, rather than their externality or tendency to double-counting. In response, Dworkin employed a new conception of external preferences. He attacked 'political' preferences in which someone takes the mere popularity of a proposal as itself a reason for adopting it.[64] Dworkin sometimes depicts this bootstrapping as something individuals do (a circular logic in which someone thinks: I support this proposal because it reflects my opinion). More often, Dworkin locates this thought in the political process, depicting legislatures as deciding to enact a proposal simply because the majority favours it instead of on the basis that the proposal promotes justice or is otherwise worthy of choice.[65] Despite his attempt to deflect Hart's criticisms, Dworkin struck a concessionary note, allowing that the double-counting device was 'meant to summarize the argument, not to make it, and I will not press that particular characterization'.[66] In fact,

[64] ibid 368.
[65] ibid.
[66] *A Matter of Principle* 366.

Dworkin never returned to the double-counting approach and ceased depicting rights in the formalistic terms of his early work.

What Dworkin abandoned were the formal structures of refined utilitarianism and the filtered-preference theory: the fixation on utilitarianism as the background justification, and the exclusion of 'external' preferences—first defined to include even altruistic preferences, and later re-defined as supporting a proposal on the basis of its popularity. Dworkin continued to argue that rights exclude political motivations based on racist, moralistic, or similar prejudice. But in his later work he normally directs his arguments against the content of those prejudices rather than their externality (in line with Hart's contention that this was his true concern all along).[67] At key points, however, Dworkin has re-deployed the strategy of depicting legislatures as voting for proposals because the majority favours it. In his later work Dworkin sometimes rejects legislation on the ground that it is based upon 'official or majority disapproval',[68] or is directed against behaviour or opinions that offend 'shared or conventional morality'.[69] He defines the 'majoritarian' or 'statistical' conception of democracy as one 'in which anything a majority or plurality wants is legitimate for that reason',[70] treating this view as if it were a widely held theory of democracy.

This cynical view of political and legislative processes resonates with the principle-policy distinction of Dworkin's early work. Courts, Dworkin had argued, are a forum of principle, while legislatures are a forum of policy. Rights are a matter of principle, and thus the special responsibility of courts.[71] Legislatures are responsible for promoting the general welfare and need not take account of rights.[72] Indeed according to Dworkin's definition of rights as trumps against the general welfare, a legislature would have to choose between either promoting the general welfare or protecting individual rights. While this presents a tragic dilemma for legislatures, the capacity of courts to refine the legislature's actions allows for happy solutions. But rights, on this view, are vindicated only when courts uphold a claim of right against a countervailing consideration regarding the general welfare. After Dworkin abandoned the filtered-preference theory, he also collapsed the distinction between policy and principle, such that the responsibilities of courts and legislatures were not sharply separated as before.[73] But by this time, the language of rights as trumps had taken on a life of its own. And the notion of having one

[67] See HLA Hart, 'Between Utility and Rights' (1979) 29 *Columbia Law Review* 843.

[68] R Dworkin, *Freedom's Law: The Moral Reading of the American Constitution* (New York, Oxford University Press, 1999) 218.

[69] R Dworkin, *Sovereign Virtue: The Theory and Practice of Equality* (Cambridge, Mass, Harvard University Press, 2002) 158.

[70] Dworkin, *Freedom's Law* 209, 364; *Sovereign Virtue* 16.

[71] Dworkin, *Taking Rights Seriously* 90–91; *A Matter of Principle* 70.

[72] See *Taking Rights Seriously* ix, 115.

[73] See R Dworkin, *Law's Empire* (Cambridge, Harvard University Press, 1986) 311–12. For discussion of the changes in Dworkin's theory over the years, see P Yowell, 'A Critical Examination of Dworkin's Theory of Rights' (2007) 52 *American Journal of Jurisprudence* 93.

forum responsible for principle and another for policy had bored deep in the consciousness of some legal and political theorists.

Dworkin's exchange with Hart also served to draw out Dworkin's fundamental strategy of defining rights as being inherently opposed to the general welfare. Hart criticised Dworkin's attempt to find rights in the 'shadow of utilitarianism', pointing out that if the content of rights is logically dependent on the background justification of utilitarianism, then people would hold no rights against a tyrant who did not seek to promote the general welfare. Dworkin conceded Hart's claim. Taking Hart's example of a ruler who bans all religious practice in a community of devout believers, Dworkin says this would be 'insane or wicked' but that the ban is not properly described as a violation of rights.[74] 'We need rights', he says, 'as a distinct element in a political theory, only when some decision that injures some people nevertheless finds prima facie support in the claim that it will make the community as a whole better off on some plausible account of where the community's general welfare lies.'[75] We do not need the idea of rights to condemn the wicked acts of a Nero or Hitler, Dworkin argues, because such tyrants do not even purport to promote the general welfare.

The framers of the Universal Declaration of Human Rights took a different view. In their language, the 'barbarous acts which have outraged the conscience of mankind' of recent regimes violated the human rights that belonged to all persons everywhere.[76] For many years Dworkin resisted speaking of human rights.[77] The reason for this is apparent in his reply to Hart. Hart had argued that the 'core notion' of constitutional rights and extra-legal, moral rights is 'basic or fundamental individual needs.'[78] Discourse at this level of rights treats 'certain freedoms as … essential for the maintenance of the life, the security, the development, and the dignity of the individual.'[79] Dworkin may have had these statements in mind in this response:

> [Hart's] objections … suppose that whatever rights people have are at least in large part timeless rights necessary to protect enduring and important interests fixed by human nature and fundamental to human development, like interests in the choice of sexual partners and acts and choice of religious conviction. That is a familiar theory of what rights are and what they are for, and I said that I would not give my reasons, in this essay, for thinking that it is in the end an inadequate theory of rights.[80]

[74] Dworkin, *A Matter of Principle* 370–71.

[75] ibid 371.

[76] UDHR, Preamble ('Whereas disregard and contempt for human rights have resulted in barbarous acts which have outraged the conscience of mankind …').

[77] Dworkin finally endorsed the language of human rights in 2006. Nevertheless, relying on the same fundamental strategy as before, he defined human rights not as basic aspects of human well-being but the consequence of excluding certain especially vicious motivations for state action: R Dworkin, *Is Democracy Possible Here?: Principles for a New Political Debate* (Princeton, Princeton University Press, 2006) 33–35.

[78] HLA Hart, 'Bentham on Legal Rights' in AWB Simpson (ed), *Oxford Essays in Jurisprudence, Second Series* (Oxford, Oxford University Press, 1973) 201.

[79] ibid 197. At the level of rights in the 'ordinary' law, Hart endorsed the 'choice' theory of rights.

[80] Dworkin, *A Matter of Principle* 369.

Dworkin insists that rights are not 'timeless' or 'fixed by human nature' but are 'relative to the other elements of a political theory'.[81] Rights come in 'complex packages of political theory' which include the background justification and some description of the way rights trump the background theory's conception of the general welfare.[82] The persistent strategy of Dworkin's work on rights has been to locate the essence of rights not in individuals and their needs but in the exclusion of arguments or political justifications opposed to equality. As he has said, 'rights cannot be identified independently of the overall political morality in which they are meant to figure.'[83]

This conception of rights should be rejected in favour of that reflected in the Universal Declaration, which is proclaimed as a 'common standard of achievement for all peoples and all nations'. As John Finnis has pointed out, the Declaration and like instruments sketch the outlines of the common good and assert the responsibility of those with authority for co-ordinating the common life to consider and favour, at all times, 'each and everyone's well-being, in each of its basic aspects'.[84] The Declaration implicitly rejects a conception of the general welfare that can be furthered by sacrificing individual rights, as well as the notion that the proper or presumptive role of the legislature is to promote some collective goal such as calculating overall preference satisfaction, while rights are the special responsibility of courts. Its Preamble calls on 'every organ of society' to promote rights, not just courts. In order to see legislatures as having full responsibility for protecting and promoting human rights, one must see rights as integral, constitutive aspects of the general welfare, and not as trumps against it. In chapter seven, I will elaborate on this approach, discussing ways in which legislatures can specify vague moral rights by implementing them in legislation.

In the next chapter I take up the theme of the capacity of courts to acquire and evaluate general empirical research. My argument reinforces Dworkin's sceptical conclusions about the ability of judges to handle statistical information, providing several examples of misuse. As this chapter has shown, Dworkin's attempt to evade this problem through his theory of rights as trumps against the general welfare, and his account of how judges should adjudicate them, does not succeed. Dworkin propounded two distinct theories of rights as trumps. The shielded-interest theory protects rights against utilitarian justifications for law. But Dworkin acknowledged that this is not by way of excluding utilitarian arguments but by giving rights a heavy weight against such justifications. The end result is that a judge applying this notion of rights must still engage in the same form of reasoning as in standard balancing and proportionality tests, which, as shown in chapter two, are inherently fact-dependent. The filtered-preference theory does exclude utilitarian justifications for law, but only *external* or *political* preferences.

[81] ibid 370.
[82] ibid.
[83] Dworkin, *Sovereign Virtue* 481 fn 9.
[84] J Finnis, *Natural Law and Natural Rights* (Oxford, Oxford University Press, 1980) 214.

This argument was based on the claim that double-counting corrupted utilitarian justifications. Dworkin ultimately abandoned the argument, turning from a focus on the externality of preferences to their content. The new approach tasks the judge with identifying the *motives* that voters act on when supporting laws and striking down laws based on forbidden motives. I have argued that in both his early and later work, Dworkin's theory of rights adjudication is flawed, in part because of the view it entails of legislative action (a theme I will take up again in chapter five, section V). Moreover, Dworkin's demand that courts determine whether forbidden motivations are the cause behind a law requires judges to make complex empirical judgments. In the final analysis, Dworkin's theory of rights as trumps does not provide a way out of analysing the capacities of courts to assess general empirical research. I now turn to that analysis.

4

Judicial Capacity and Empirical Research

In 1897 Oliver Wendell Holmes wrote: 'For the rational study of the law the black letter man may be the man of the present, but the man of the future is the man of statistics and the master of economics'.[1] Since then, empirical research has entered many domains of law, including criminal procedure and forensics, causation in tort, and various areas of statutory interpretation and constitutional law. Each of these raises distinct concerns and problems. The focus in this book is rights-based challenges to the constitutionality of legislation, which are usually adjudicated by the balancing and proportionality tests discussed in chapter two. Contrary to Dworkin's warnings, discussed in chapter three, about the competence of judges in regard to empirical research, in constitutional rights cases courts regularly assess the results of research in economics, psychology, sociology, medicine, and other fields. The most common way in which courts engage with such research is when litigants present it in the form of a 'Brandeis brief'.

In the first section of this chapter I trace the origin of the Brandeis brief—a term used not only in US law but other countries that have adopted the same practice. I find its origin not in the commonly accepted case of *Muller v Oregon* (1908)[2] but in *Lochner v New York* (1905).[3] *Lochner* is also the first major constitutional case to use proportionality or balancing reasoning to strike down legislation. Both conclusions run counter to a standard narrative, which casts *Lochner* as formalistic opinion blind to empirical realities and hails Louis Brandeis as a visionary who introduced scientific realism into constitutional law with the brief he submitted in *Muller*. The chapter also addresses the general use of empirical research by the US Supreme Court (section II); the difference between ordinary adjudicative fact-finding and the use of empirical information in constitutional interpretation (section III); the kinds of empirical sources used in judicial review and the manner in which courts acquire them (section IV); social science methodology and the capacity of courts to understand it (section V); and case studies of courts using empirical research in the US and elsewhere (section VI).

[1] OW Holmes, 'The Path of the Law' (1897) 10 *Harvard Law Review* 457.
[2] *Muller v Oregon* 208 US 412 (1908).
[3] *Lochner v New York* 198 US 45 (1905).

I. Empirical Research and the Origins of Proportionality

The connection between proportionality and empirical research can be traced to the origin of balancing tests in constitutional law. The standard procedural vehicle used by parties to submit empirical evidence regarding the constitutionality of legislation, the Brandeis brief, is thought to derive from *Muller v Oregon* (1908).[4] An Oregon statute that prohibited women from working more than ten hours per day in factories and laundries was challenged on the basis of the freedom of contract, which the Supreme Court had earlier held was implied in the 14th Amendment right to due process of law.[5] Louis Brandeis, a Boston lawyer who was later to become a justice of the Supreme Court, filed an amicus brief on behalf of Oregon in defence of the law. The brief contained only two pages of legal argument but almost 100 pages referencing social science and other factual material.[6] Brandeis advanced empirical data and policy arguments regarding the harmful effects of long working hours (on women and their families and communities), mostly by way of quoting medical opinions, academic studies, and reports of factory inspectors and bureaus of labour statistics, alongside other sources.[7] The Court upheld the Oregon law, and Brandeis's brief has been used as a model in many subsequent cases, both in the US and in other jurisdictions.

Although it has often been said that Brandeis made constitutional law responsive to facts,[8] his strategy in *Muller* is better understood as a reaction to *Lochner v New York* (1905).[9] In *Lochner* the Supreme Court struck down New York's Bakeshop Act, which limited the hours that bakery employees could work to 60 per week. The Court based its ruling on the 14th Amendment and the right to freedom of contract, which was also the basis of the constitutional challenge in *Muller*. Unlike Brandeis, the attorney for the state of New York did not submit detailed empirical evidence to defend its law on bakeries.[10] This contrast has been widely noted, often alongside the claim that Brandeis was the first to use empirical evidence in constitutional litigation. The latter claim, however, is incorrect.

[4] *Muller v Oregon* 208 US 412 (1908).

[5] See *Allgeyer v Louisiana* 165 US 578 (1897).

[6] Brief for Defendant in Error, Muller v Oregon, in PB Kurland and G Casper (eds), *Landmark Briefs and Arguments of the Supreme Court of the United States Constitutional Law*, vol 16 (hereinafter *Landmark Briefs*) (Washington DC, University Publications of America, 1975).

[7] ibid.

[8] This reputation is based both on the brief in *Muller* and on his later judicial career. See, eg, F Frankfurter, 'Mr Justice Brandeis and the Constitution', in F Frankfurter (ed.), *Mr Justice Brandeis* (New Haven, Yale University Press, 1932) 52 ('At a time when our constitutional law was becoming dangerously unresponsive to drastic social changes, when sterile cliches instead of facts were deciding cases, [Brandeis] insisted … that law must be sensitive to life').

[9] *Lochner v New York* 198 US 45 (1905).

[10] See Brief for Defendant in Error, Lochner v New York, in *Landmark Briefs*, above n 6.

The *Lochner* litigation was orchestrated by the New York Master Bakers Association, which hired Henry Weisman to defend Joseph Lochner, the owner of a small bakery in Utica, NY. Lochner had been convicted under the Bakeshop Act after one of his employees worked excessive hours.[11] Weisman filed a brief containing several pages of information regarding working conditions in the baking trade and the causes of ill health and diseases among bakers.[12] Relying on this evidence, Weisman argued that Bakeshop Act was unnecessary and did little to promote the health of bakers. The brief included citations to three comparative mortality studies for occupations and professions, one of which found that bakers had a low mortality rate (18th out of 22 occupations surveyed), while two others placed bakers near the middle.[13] In one study the chart score (where a lower number indicates a lower mortality rate) for bakers was 920, which compared favourably to dock workers (1829) and general labourers (1221); bakers were worse off than clergymen (533) but similar to lawyers (810).[14] Weisman also cited articles from medical journals urging improved ventilation and sanitary reforms but not shorter hours. A *Lancet* article suggested that shorter hours would not alleviate health problems.[15] Though the Court did not cite Weisman's brief, it clearly relied on the evidence it contained. Justice Peckham wrote in the majority opinion:

> We think that there can be no fair doubt that the trade of a baker, in and of itself, is not an unhealthy one to that degree which would authorize the legislature to interfere with the right to labor, and with the right of free contract on the part of the individual, either as employer or employee. *In looking through statistics regarding all trades and occupations*, it may be true that the trade of a baker does not appear to be as healthy as some other trades, and is also vastly more healthy than still others. (emphasis added)[16]

The content of Weisman's brief has eluded many commentators, and this has contributed to the legend that the Brandeis brief was the first of its kind. One of the few scholars to discuss the brief acknowledged that until reading it he had always regarded Peckham's statistical argument above as a 'flight of fancy'.[17]

The Court assessed the empirical evidence pursuant to an incipient balancing or proportionality test. The Court first rejected any 'labour law' rationale for the Bakeshop Act, holding that the right to freedom of contract prevents the state from limiting working hours on the ground that bakers lack bargaining power in

[11] D Bernstein, *Rehabilitating Lochner: Defending Individual Rights against Progressive Reform* (Chicago, University of Chicago Press, 2011) Ch 2; D Bernstein, 'Lochner v. New York: A Centennial Retrospective' (2005) 83 *Washington University Law Quarterly* 1469, 1487–98.

[12] Brief for Plaintiff in Error, Lochner v New York, *Landmark Briefs*, above n 6. Frank Harvey Field was co-counsel with Weisman on the brief.

[13] ibid.

[14] ibid.

[15] ibid.

[16] *Lochner v New York* 198 US 45, 59 (1905).

[17] S Siegel, 'Lochner Era Jurisprudence and the American Constitutional Tradition' (1991) 70 *North Carolina Law Review* 1, 19 fn 77.

negotiations with employers over desirable working hours.[18] The state was permitted to regulate working hours on the basis of the police power to promote health and safety; however, any 'unreasonable, unnecessary, and arbitrary interference with the right of the individual to his personal liberty' would be annulled.[19] The majority opinion continues:

> It is a question of which of two powers or rights shall prevail—the power of the state to legislate or the right of the individual to liberty of person and freedom of contract. The mere assertion that the subject relates, though but in a remote degree, to the public health, does not necessarily render the enactment valid. The act must have a more direct relation, as a means to an end, and the end itself must be appropriate and legitimate, before an act can be held to be valid which interferes with the general right of an individual to be free in his person and in his power to contract in relation to his own labor.[20]

Here we find all the key components of the modern proportionality inquiry: (i) legitimacy of legislative aim (the Court approved the health and safety aim but rejected the 'labour law' rationale); (ii) a necessity or minimal impairment test that looks for an appropriate relationship between the means and ends of legislation; and (iii) balancing of the public welfare against the 'interference' with the individual right. *Lochner* was the first major Supreme Court case to strike down a law using this type of inquiry.

After noting the mid-level mortality rate of bakers, the Court proceeded to consider other facts in applying the above balancing or proportionality standards, and to justify its use of those standards. The Court observed that in large cities 'there are many buildings into which the sun penetrates for but a short time in each day', which are occupied by the employees of many businesses, and that working prolonged hours in such conditions could be argued to be unhealthy.[21] If a law is valid because it promotes health in any degree whatsoever, the Court reasoned, then it would be possible for a law to prohibit lawyers' and bank clerks and other employees from 'contracting to labor for their employers more than eight hours a day'.[22] Thus, in the absence of a necessity or minimal impairment test, no trade or occupation would be safe from the legislature's 'all-pervading power' and 'paternal wisdom'.[23] The Bakeshop Act already required proper furnishing of wash rooms and set building standards on matters such as drainage and plumbing, ceiling height, and flooring; and it provided for inspections by an official with the power to order alterations. 'Adding to all these requirements', the Court concluded, was unnecessary for the health of bakers; the limitation of working hours was not a

[18] 'There is no contention that bakers as a class are not equal in intelligence and capacity to men in other trades or manual occupations, or that they are not able to assert their rights and care for themselves without the protecting arm of the state, interfering with their independence of judgment and of action': *Lochner v New York* 198 US 45, 57 (1905).

[19] ibid 56.

[20] ibid 57–58.

[21] ibid 59.

[22] ibid 60.

[23] ibid.

'proper, reasonable and fair provision' but an unjustifiable interference with the right to 'liberty of person and of free contract'.[24] This result, Justice Peckham claimed, was an objective, rational inference from the evidence: 'This is not a question of substituting the judgment of the court for that of the legislature'.[25]

Brandeis learned the lesson of *Lochner* and shrewdly responded by compiling an extensive record of factual information to defend the law in *Muller*. But he did not invent the technique; he adapted his litigation strategy to the new paradigm of proportionality-based review and consideration of empirical research, a paradigm set in place by *Lochner* itself. The two pages of legal argument in Brandeis's brief focused on *Lochner* and cited its standards regarding minimal impairment of rights and the appropriate relationship between legislative ends and means.[26]

Although the law Brandeis defended in *Muller* survived scrutiny, the Supreme Court later struck down many other laws concerning economic regulation, working conditions, and related matters, including minimum wage legislation for women in *Adkins v Children's Hospital* (1923),[27] as well as laws designed to enable workers to join unions without suffering adverse employment consequences.[28] During the *Lochner* era, which lasted for some thirty years, the Supreme Court and other federal and state courts struck down hundreds of laws. *Lochner* became a byword for excessive judicial activism.[29]

Although these cases employed a variety of constitutional doctrines, many of them turned on empirical assessments of the effects of legislation. Justice Brandeis, who was appointed to the Court in 1916, observed:

> These issues resemble, fundamentally, that of reasonable care in negligence cases, the determination of which is ordinarily left to the verdict of the jury. In every such case the decision, in the first instance, is dependent upon the determination of what in legal parlance is called a fact, as distinguished from the declaration of a rule of law. When the underlying fact has been found, the legal result follows inevitably. The circumstance that the decision of that fact is made by a court, instead of by a jury, should not be allowed to obscure its real character.[30]

The Supreme Court never explicitly overruled *Lochner*, but it changed its approach to the review of economic regulations in the mid-1930s. In *West Coast Hotel Co v Parrish* (1937)[31] the Court overruled *Adkins* and upheld minimum wage legislation for women. In the following years the Court abandoned the right to freedom of contract as a basis for challenging legislation and applied far less scrutiny to laws on employment and similar subjects.

[24] ibid 62.
[25] ibid 56–57.
[26] Brief for Defendant in Error, Muller v Oregon, in *Landmark Briefs*, above n 6.
[27] *Adkins v Children's Hospital* 261 US 525 (1923).
[28] *Adair v United States* 208 US 161 (1908); *Coppage v Kansas* 236 US 1 (1915).
[29] MJ Phillips, *The Lochner Court, Myth and Reality: Substantive Due Process From the 1890s to the 1930s* (Santa Barbara, Praeger, 2001).
[30] *Burnet v Coronado Oil & Gas Co* 285 US 393, 410 (1932).
[31] *West Coast Hotel Co v Parrish* 300 US 379 (1937).

As discussed in chapter two, section III, the Court signalled a new direction in *United States v Carolene Products Co* (1938),[32] shifting its focus from economic activity and relationships and toward areas such as racial equality and freedom of speech, association and religion. Although the Court developed specialised lines of constitutional doctrine regarding the scope of particular rights and the level of scrutiny with which to apply them, the underlying judicial method that was developed during the *Lochner* era prevailed and remains in operation today. The Court resolves many cases by applying constitutional limitations through balancing tests, and by using empirical evidence to determine the necessity of legislation, the strength of the state's interest in it, and its effects on the rights-protected interests of individuals. Felix Frankfurter, writing before his appointment to the Court, described the revolution in judicial technique in the early twentieth century as an advance of the modern age and a victory for the scientific method:[33]

> [Previously] courts decided these issues on a priori theories, on abstract assumptions, because scientific data were not available or at least had not been made available for the use of courts. But all this time scientific data had been accumulating. Organized observation, investigation, and experimentation produced facts, and science could at last speak with rational if tentative authority. There was a growing body of the world's experience and the validated opinions of those competent to have opinions. …
>
> The *Muller* case, in 1908, was the first case presented to our courts on the basis of authoritative data. For the first time the arguments and briefs breathed the air of reality … For there can be no denial that the technique of the brief in the *Muller* case has established itself through a series of decisions within the last few years, which have caused not only change in decisions, but the much more vital change of method of approach to constitutional questions.[34]

Like many later commentators, Frankfurter failed to notice that the 'vital change of method' was already accomplished in *Lochner*. Brandeis skilfully elaborated the technique that Weisman had used in *Lochner*, but Weisman has the better claim to invention of it.

At a deeper level, however, the use of the Brandeis brief and empirical research should be seen not as the product of lawyerly ingenuity, but as intrinsic to balancing tests of every kind. Justice Peckham's reasoning in *Lochner* can be seen to follow the intrinsic logic of proportionality described by the Canadian Supreme Court, which held that '[i]n determining proportionality, [a court] must determine the actual connection between the objective and what the law will in fact achieve,' by reference to 'the facts of the law at issue and the proof offered of its justification, not on abstractions'.[35]

32 *United States v Carolene Products Co* 304 US 144 (1938).
33 F Frankfurter, 'Hours of Labor and Realism in Constitutional Law' (1915) 29 *Harvard Law Review* 353, 363.
34 ibid 364–65.
35 *RJR-MacDonald, Inc v Canada* [1994] 1 SCR 311 [133].

II. Empirical Evidence in the US Supreme Court

In more recent years the US Supreme Court has considered or directly relied on various kinds of factual information and empirical research in many major cases, on issues ranging from the regulation of obscene and indecent material on the internet,[36] to the death penalty[37] to the constitutionality of abortion law. In *Roe v Wade* (1973),[38] which annulled most state laws prohibiting and regulating abortion, the opinion by Justice Blackmun discusses medical aspects of pregnancy and abortion, the development of the foetus and the point of viability,[39] and comparative mortality rates for women in childbirth and abortion procedures.[40] Much of this discussion reflects research that Blackmun conducted at the Mayo Clinic and later described as 'personally and very privately performed';[41] and it informed the Court's holdings about the level of the state's interest in protecting the life of the foetus and mother at various stages in pregnancy, resulting in *Roe's* well-known trimester framework: (i) during the first trimester, states were not allowed to interfere with or regulate an abortion decided upon between a woman and her physician; (ii) during the second trimester, states could issue regulations reasonably related to maternal health, and (iii) during the third trimester, states could (but were not required to) proscribe abortion, except where necessary to preserve the life or health of the mother.[42]

The Court's most well-known use of social science was in *Brown v Board of Education* (1954),[43] which, as discussed in chapter three, section III, held that racially segregated facilities are inherently unequal. This conclusion was based on psychological research showing that segregation generates feelings of inferiority

[36] *Reno v American Civil Liberties Union* 521 US 844 (1997). In striking down the Communications Decency Act of 1996, the Court relied on detailed findings on internet technology.

[37] *Gregg v Georgia* 428 US 153 (1976). In a decision to uphold some capital punishment statutes, the Court stated: 'Although some of the studies suggest that the death penalty may not function as a significantly greater deterrent than lesser penalties, there is no convincing empirical evidence either supporting or refuting this view. We may nevertheless assume safely that there are murderers, such as those who act in passion, for whom the threat of death has little or no deterrent effect. But for many others, the death penalty undoubtedly is a significant deterrent': ibid 185–86.

[38] *Roe v Wade* 410 US 113 (1973).

[39] ibid 163.

[40] ibid 130 ff, 160–61.

[41] 'I spent two full weeks in the medical library of the Mayo Clinic in Rochester, Minnesota. I traced down, as I hoped to be able to do, the attitudes toward abortion of the American Medical Association (it had changed over the years), of the American Public Health Association, and of the American Bar Association. I wished, furthermore, to study the history of our state abortion statutes, and I wished to ascertain the origin and extent of acceptance of the Hippocratic Oath. That research, personally and very privately performed, was, I believe, rewarding': H Blackmun, Remarks, Franco-American Colloquium on Human Rights 14–15 (1979), unpublished transcript on file in Harvard Law School Library.

[42] 410 US 113, 164–65.

[43] *Brown v Board of Education* 347 US 483 (1954).

in black schoolchildren that diminish the motivation to learn and inhibit educational and mental development. The Court cited four psychological studies and two books in support of this finding.[44] It suggested that its earlier decision may have been based on flawed or missing empirical data: 'Whatever may have been the extent of psychological knowledge at the time of *Plessy v Ferguson* this finding is amply supported by modern authority'.[45]

In *Grutter v Bollinger* (2006),[46] the Court upheld the use of affirmative action for minorities in university admissions programmes against a challenge based on the Equal Protection Clause. The Court relied on social science research, expert testimony in the trial court, and amicus briefs from business leaders and military officers, in concluding that such programmes produce beneficial outcomes and that there is a compelling state interest in maintaining them.[47] The Court, however, ventured to predict that in 25 years race-conscious admissions programmes would no longer be necessary because of changed conditions in society.[48] This prediction illustrates the radical dependency of proportionality-based reasoning on factual information. And it suggests that in a future case the Court might strike down, rather than uphold, affirmative action programmes on the basis of updated social science.

III. Adjudicative Facts and Legislative Facts

Fact-finding is, of course, central to adjudication. There are important differences, however, between reviewing evidence presented in Brandeis briefs and fact-finding in ordinary trials. Kenneth Culp Davis introduced the terms 'adjudicative fact' and 'legislative fact' to distinguish two types of information used in judicial decision-making. Adjudicative facts concern the immediate parties in a case, answering the questions 'who did what, where, when, how, and with what motive or intent'.[49] Legislative facts are the general facts about society that inform a court's judgment on questions of law and policy.[50] Like the term 'Brandeis brief', Davis's distinctions and terminology have been widely adopted by courts and theorists both in the US and other jurisdictions.

The difference between adjudicative facts and legislative facts does not necessarily turn on the subject matter or complexity of the evidence. Adjudicative facts usually consist in historical information about what a person did or said,

[44] ibid 494 and fn 11.
[45] ibid 494.
[46] *Grutter v Bollinger* 539 US 306 (2006).
[47] ibid 330–32.
[48] ibid 343.
[49] KC Davis, 'Judicial Notice' (1955) 55 *Columbia Law Review* 945, 952. See also KC Davis, 'Facts in Lawmaking' (1980) 80 *Columbia Law Review* 931.
[50] Davis, 'Judicial Notice' 952.

the contents of documents, physical characteristics of an object or location, and other discrete facts. But adjudicative facts may also involve expert testimony and evidence on complex scientific and medical issues in areas such as patents, medical malpractice, or forensic use of DNA traces. Legislative facts often pertain to empirical research, but they may consist in general knowledge of a subject such as the stock market (which a judge might rely on in interpreting securities laws). The main conceptual distinction concerns the reason for using the evidence: adjudicative facts relate directly to claims between the parties, while legislative facts transcend the instant case and concern the interpretation or constitutional validity of the law itself.[51] Adjudicative fact-finding is usually retrospective; it concerns past events and their bearing upon the parties in a case. Legislative fact-finding is generally prospective; it anticipates what will happen in the future with regard to the consequences of a law or a contemplated interpretation thereof.[52]

The distinction between adjudicative and legislative facts cannot be marked by a bright line, just as the distinction between questions of law and questions of fact is not clear-cut.[53] In some cases it may be unclear whether a judge's reliance on factual information is to inform his understanding of a question of fact in the particular case or a question about the interpretation of a law (or both), but this difficulty need not detain us. Much of the evidence presented in Brandeis briefs and relied on by courts in proportionality tests is clearly in the realm of legislative facts.

Adjudicative facts are admitted to the record in the trial court, through a formal process that is created by law and closely regulated. Legislative facts, on the other hand, need not be admitted into the trial record or undergo any formal scrutiny. Judges regularly seek out legislative facts on their own initiative and conduct their own research.[54] Examples of this will be discussed below in section IV, but the extent of this practice is not known. As Davis explains in relation to the US:

> How much the Supreme Court goes beyond the record for legislative facts to guide the making of law and policy cannot be accurately ascertained from the opinions just because resort to the practice undoubtedly exceeds specific formal acknowledgments of the practice. But the acknowledgments are numerous enough to show that the practice is a commonplace.[55]

In some cases, evidence of legislative facts and related expert testimony is submitted to the trial court. But in many cases parties submit legislative facts for the first time in appellate briefs, as Brandeis did in *Muller*. In the US, it is increasingly common for non-parties to submit Brandeis briefs. High-profile, controversial cases can attract dozens of such amicus filings. There are generally no procedural rules regarding whether or how courts should consider amicus briefs and the factual

[51] ibid.

[52] When applying the proportionality test, a court must determine 'what the law will in fact achieve,' according to the Canadian Supreme Court: *RJR-MacDonald, Inc v Canada* [1994] 1 SCR 311 [133].

[53] See TAO Endicott, 'Questions of Law' (1998) 114 *LQR* 292.

[54] KC Davis, 'Judicial Notice' (1955) 55 *Columbia Law Review* 945, 955–59.

[55] ibid 955.

assertions and evidence contained therein, or whether the parties have a right to reply to such briefs.

The lack of procedural regulation of legislative fact-finding may seem surprising, especially in light of the rigorous control the law imposes on adjudicative fact-finding. It would be difficult and possibly undesirable, however, to impose comprehensive procedures on legislative fact-finding. In reaching a judgment based on the trial record, judges and juries may be called upon to ignore certain evidence or knowledge derived from sources beyond the closed record of the trial—even if that evidence or knowledge is relevant to and probative of a legal issue, and even if that issue relates to a serious crime. In a sense I explain in chapter five, section I, the trial is an artificial world. But when they are considering legislative facts, judges no less than legislators have the real world as their field of vision. This is especially apparent for broad constitutional issues such as determining the degree of public need for legislation (under standards such as 'pressing social need' or 'compelling governmental interest'). It is debatable whether proportionality is an appropriate standard for determining the constitutionality of legislation in adjudicative processes; but, once proportionality has been accepted, it would be unnecessary and probably futile to impose comprehensive controls on the acquisition or disclosure of the information judges use in applying it. Just as legislators call upon their general knowledge in deciding whether to enact legislation, judges should be expected to do the same in reviewing legislation in proportionality inquiries.

IV. Finding Legislative Facts

Although some of the sources cited for legislative facts carry the imprimatur of an academic or government organisation or established research institutes, courts also cite popular magazines and newspaper articles; *Encyclopaedia Britannica* and other general reference works; books published by popular, commercial presses; and a variety of similar sources, which exhibit varying degrees of reliability. Increasingly, judges cite to sources obtained through internet search engines—either directly after conducting their own research, or indirectly by relying on information in Brandeis briefs which was obtained in this way. This can be inferred from, among other things, the growing number of court citations to Wikipedia, the free, online encyclopedia that often tops search results for topics of general interest in Google and other search engines. A search of state and federal cases in the US reveals over 1,600 cases that cited Wikipedia between 2004 and 2017.[56] In many of these cases courts are responding to the parties' citation of Wikipedia in briefs, and in some

[56] A search for 'Wikipedia' on the Westlaw database of all state and federal cases in the US returned 1,602 cases on 26 September 2017. The first such citation was in 2004.

instances the content of Wikipedia entries is related to a material question of fact in the case (for example, parties and witnesses have described their consultation of Wikipedia to explain a decision or action they took). Many of these citations, however, are for background information related to adjudicative facts or for legislative facts relevant to interpreting statutes or constitutional law.[57] This phenomenon is not confined to the US. A 2009 study in Germany found 294 judgments with citations to Wikipedia.[58] Cases in the European Court of Justice,[59] Canada,[60] and elsewhere have similarly cited the online encyclopedia.

What is the problem with relying on Wikipedia for legislative facts? After all, it provides quick, free access to a great deal of information on a massive number of subjects. Articles are often written by amateurs with a particular interest in a topic, and the collaborative nature of the enterprise allows others to make corrections or add information. Richard Posner has described it as a convenient and 'terrific resource' that is often recently updated and 'very accurate' (though he said he would not rely on it for a 'critical issue').[61] A study published in *Nature* analysed Wikipedia's coverage of science and concluded that its accuracy was close to that of *Encyclopaedia Britannica* (though this claim was disputed by the latter).[62] Even if the information cited is accurate, however, judicial citations to Wikipedia are unseemly and troubling. Anyone in the world who registers as a user can create new entries, and to edit an entry one does not even need to go through a sign-in process. Contributions may be, and usually are, anonymous, and generally are not overseen by any formal process. The ability of users to correct mistakes may impart a certain degree of reliability for some entries. The exposure to instantaneous editing, however, can also lead to errors and false claims, whether intentional

[57] In *Bourgeois v Peters* 387 F3d 1303 (11th Cir 2004), the first US case to cite Wikipedia, the court relied on an entry on the Department of Homeland Security for information about its colour-coded threat level system, in the course of rejecting an argument that the yellow ('elevated') threat level constituted an exceptional circumstance that would justify a police search.

[58] R Zosel, 'Im Namen des Volkes—Gerichte zitieren Wikipedia' in H Rüßmann (ed), *Festschrift für Gerhard Käfer* (Saarbrücken, Juris, 2009).

[59] Eg Case C-275/06 *Productores de Musica de España (Promusicae) v Telefonica de España SAU* [2008] 2 CMLR 17, at fn 14 (citing Wikipedia on the possibility and difficulty of concealing a computer's IP (internet protocol) address).

[60] Eg *Gauvin v Vallée* [2006] QCCS 3363, at fn 9.

[61] Posner was interviewed and quoted in Noam Cohen, 'Courts Turn to Wikipedia, but Selectively' *New York Times* (29 January 2007). He said Wikipedia is valuable '[p]artly because it is so convenient, it often has been updated recently and is very accurate', but added that '[i]t wouldn't be right to use it in a critical issue. If the safety of a product is at issue, you wouldn't look it up in Wikipedia': ibid.

[62] *Nature* asked academic reviewers to assess and compare 42 pairs of articles from Wikipedia and the online content of *Encyclopaedia Britannica* and reported this conclusion: 'Only eight serious errors, such as misinterpretations of important concepts, were detected in the pairs of articles reviewed, four from each encyclopaedia. But reviewers also found many factual errors, omissions or misleading statements: 162 and 123 in Wikipedia and Britannica, respectively': J Giles, 'Special Report: Internet Encyclopaedias Go Head to Head' (2005) 438 *Nature* 900. *Encyclopaedia Britannica* published a corporate response: 'Fatally Flawed: Refuting the Recent Study on Encyclopedic Accuracy by the Journal Nature' <http://corporate.britannica.com/britannica_nature_response.pdf> accessed 24 September 2017. *Nature* replied, in turn <www.nature.com/nature/britannica/eb_advert_response_final.pdf> accessed 25 September 2017.

or unintentional. Furthermore, the entry cited has no fixed form; its content can change from day to day.

The underlying problem here is not Wikipedia itself. Rather, the phenomenon of Wikipedia citations demonstrates that many courts are willing to rely on dubious sources, and that legislative fact-finding by courts may be conducted in a haphazard fashion. Judges who are curious about some factual matter relevant to a legal question sometimes do the same thing that many lay persons do when they want information on a topic: they use an internet search engine (perhaps with the assistance of their law clerks).[63] The California Supreme Court, for example, in ruling that defendants cannot be required to wear an electric stun belt while testifying, cited (inter alia) newspaper and magazine articles[64] for information and analysis of the use and medical effects of stun belts. According to a dissenting justice, the Court discovered this information through a search on Google.[65] Information found this way is determined in part by the algorithms that search engines use to generate results; these algorithms are corporate trade secrets, and neither judges nor the public can know exactly how Google, for instance, determines what websites are relevant to a particular search query.[66] Nonetheless, enterprising individuals have discovered methods for manipulating Google's search results, so that consultants now offer their clients advice on how to alter the search ranking of particular information.[67]

In the US Supreme Court case *PGA Tour, Inc v Martin* (2001),[68] a golfer with a circulatory disorder challenged the Professional Golf Association's rule that players must walk the course, claiming that federal disability legislation required the PGA to permit him to use a golf cart. The legislation requires 'reasonable modification' unless it would 'fundamentally alter the nature' of the services or facilities to which a complainant seeks access.[69] Thus the Court undertook to decide whether walking the course is part of the nature of golf (or, more precisely,

[63] Cass Sunstein told the *New York Times* that he suspects 'that law clerks are using Wikipedia a great deal'. Noam Cohen, 'Courts Turn to Wikipedia, but Selectively', *New York Times* (29 January 2007). See also CM Barger, 'On the Internet, Nobody Knows You're a Judge: Appellate Courts' Use of Internet Materials' (2002) 4 *Journal of Appellate Practice and Process* 417; EG Thornburg, 'The Curious Appellate Judge: Ethical Limits on Independent Research' (2008) 28 *Review of Litigation* 131, 163–65, 198.

[64] *People v Mar* 52 P3d 95, 111–13. Publications cited included the *Progressive*, the *Cleveland Plain Dealer*, the *Los Angeles Times*, and the *New York Review of Books*.

[65] Justice Brown stated: 'There is absolutely no evidence in the record bearing on these questions. In the absence of such evidence, we had two choices. We could have deferred to the Legislature, which can make law after hearing from distinguished experts on all sides of controversial issues. Or we could have waited for a case that raised these questions on an adequate record. Instead, the majority, rushing to judgment after conducting an embarrassing Google.com search for information outside the record, has tied the hands of the Legislature, to the likely peril of judges, bailiffs, and ordinary citizens called upon to do their civic duty': ibid 116.

[66] See EB Laidlaw, 'Private Power, Public Interest: An Examination of Search Engine Accountability' (2009) 17 *International Journal of Law and Information Technology* 113, 131–32.

[67] ibid.

[68] *PGA Tour, Inc v Martin* 532 US 661 (2001).

[69] ibid 682–83.

high-level professional golf) and decided that it is not. The Court consulted and relied on *Rules of the Green*, a popular historical book (for the proposition that 'shotmaking' is the essence of golf); the Random House *International Encyclopedia of Golf* and Golf Magazine's *Encyclopedia of Golf* (describing changes in the methods of transporting clubs over the years); and an article in the *Arizona Republic* about a highly unusual hole-in-one that had recently occurred on the PGA tour (in support of the Court's contention that lucky bounces are also part of the game; hence 'it is impossible to guarantee that all competitors will play under exactly the same conditions or that an individual's ability will be the sole determinant of the outcome').[70] Frederick Schauer observes that although these sources were central to the Court's decision, none of them were contained in the record, lower court decisions, or the briefs of the parties or amici.[71] In other words, he says, the Court 'locates these sources itself':

> Seven Justices [ie those who joined the majority], only one of whom is a serious golfer, with the assistance of approximately twenty-eight law clerks, no more than four or five of whom are likely to be serious golfers, and the library staff of the Supreme Court library, again unlikely to have a large number of serious golfers in their midst, are wandering relatively unguided (by golf expertise) through Lexis, Westlaw, the Internet, and various other sources of nonlegal information in order to decide which of the contingent features of golf are actually essential features of golf.[72]

Despite misgivings, however, Schauer argues that this kind of 'muddling through' can be an acceptable way for a court to find legislative facts, though he also suggests alternative methods that deserve consideration. Schauer argues that making general factual and policy judgments is an endemic part of the common law process (including statutory interpretation), and that having multi-member appellate courts, assisted by law clerks and library staffs, increases the range of skills and experience represented on the court and ameliorates the potential for error.[73] Even if Schauer's argument is sound with regard to common law development and statutory interpretation, questions about the constitutional validity of legislation should not depend on 'muddling through'.

V. The Courts and Social Science

Richard Posner acknowledges that in many cases courts will lack the information necessary to perform balancing tests.[74] But this is a contingent problem, he says,

[70] ibid 683–87.

[71] F Schauer, 'The Dilemma of Ignorance: PGA Tour, Inc. v. Casey Martin' (2001) *Supreme Court Review* 267, 283.

[72] ibid.

[73] ibid 288.

[74] ibid 68.

and '[t]he fault, in part anyway, lies with constitutional theory, which claims to offer the courts a data-free method of deciding cases, rather than helping in the discovery and analysis of the relevant data'.[75] Posner urges legal scholars to team with economists and other social scientists in order to generate the data that could be used by courts in cost-benefit analyses.[76]

Judges, however, 'inevitably lack the scientific training that might facilitate the evaluation of scientific claims or the evaluation of expert witnesses', according to US Supreme Court Justice Stephen Breyer.[77] The difficulties associated with scientific evidence and expert testimony are to some extent unavoidable in adjudicative fact-finding in ordinary private law and criminal cases. While some technical issues can be resolved in specialised tribunals, most disputes in western legal systems are decided by judges whose professional competence lies in systematic knowledge of the law and legal processes. Such knowledge is gained through a career and education that leaves little time for mastering the methods of scientific inquiry, or for keeping abreast of scientific developments in various fields. Judges—not scientists—must exercise control over the admission and evaluation of expert testimony on complex factual issues such as the likelihood of matching DNA samples. There has thus been extensive academic discussion of the standards for admitting scientific evidence, the proper role of judges and juries in evaluating such evidence, and ways to improve decision-making in this area.

When a judge relies on empirical research to hold that legislation violates a human right, the decision implies (or claims explicitly) that the legislature failed to make use of the available empirical data or to assess it properly. Thus, in this area, a comparative analysis of institutional capacities is in order. As will be discussed in chapter five, section III, legislatures have facilities to gather evidence, call witnesses, and sponsor studies, all with the assistance of scientifically trained staff. They can use special commissions and inquiries to conduct investigations and in-depth research on certain topics. Some legislatures have established permanent bodies for assistance with fact-finding. Legislatures may not always fully develop fact-finding resources or use them wisely, and, like any other political process, an empirical investigation is subject to misuse or corruption. Nonetheless, legislatures in general have institutional structures and decision-making processes that facilitate broad empirical investigation.

Courts, in contrast, generally lack internal fact-finding resources. Judges may have law clerks and access to library staff, but these individuals usually do not have scientific training. As Justice Scalia has observed in oral argument: 'We can't call witnesses and see what the real problems are … [W]e have only lawyers before us, we have no witnesses, we have no cross-examination, we have no investigative staff'.[78] Constitutional courts in civil law systems generally have

[75] 'Against Constitutional Theory' 18.
[76] ibid 12, 22.
[77] S Breyer, 'The Interdependence of Science and Law' (1998) 82 *Judicature* 24, 25–26.
[78] *Rasul v Bush* 542 US 466 (2004): Transcript of Oral Argument; 46.

original jurisdiction of constitutional complaints, and the German Federal Constitutional Court sometimes appoints expert witnesses to testify on scientific and technical subjects. In common law systems it is possible for trial courts to appoint neutral experts to provide testimony on scientific or technical matters, but this is rarely done.[79] Though evidence of legislative facts is sometimes submitted in trial courts, much legislative fact-finding is the product of Brandeis briefs presented on appeal or of appellate judges engaging in research on their own initiative. A state supreme court in the US has stated that 'when a decision in a case rests upon technical, specialized or scientific knowledge, if we find the record does not make the subject matter sufficiently clear, we will not hesitate to conduct authoritative study on our own'.[80] The court also asserted that most appellate courts do the same, and research by Allison Larsen has tracked the extent of this practice.[81]

In order to understand even basic findings in numbers-driven social sciences, one must have some knowledge of statistics. More complex social science may require a higher level of statistical competence as well as acquaintance with specialised techniques and terminology native to economics, psychology, or other relevant fields. Published judgments that address and rely on statistical studies are replete with errors and often reveal a misunderstanding of basic concepts in statistics.[82] One widely misunderstood concept is statistical significance. A layman or judge is liable to think that when a researcher reports a 'statistically significant' link between X and Y, this suggests that there is substantial evidence of a causal relationship of some importance. Statistical significance, however, is distinct from what we could call practical significance, ie the importance of the study for practical decision-making based on an overall assessment of the substance and magnitude of its findings. Statistical significance is a narrow, technical concept belonging to a particular (though widely used) method known as null hypothesis testing. One common mistake regarding hypothesis testing is to think that the p-value of a study indicates the probability that its results will be repeated in the future.[83] For example, someone might conclude that if the p-value of a result is 0.05, then there is a 95 per cent chance of replicability. A more serious mistake is to think that one can infer from a p-value that the alternative or research hypothesis has a certain probability of being true.[84] Stating what a p-value actually means requires arcane language. According to

[79] Breyer, above n 77, 27.

[80] *Samuels v Mladineo* 608 So2d 1170, 1184–86 (Miss 1992).

[81] ibid; A Larsen, 'Confronting Supreme Court Fact-Finding' (2012) 98 *Virginia Law Review* 1255.

[82] See, eg, DL Faigman, *Constitutional Fictions: A Unified Theory of Constitutional Facts* (New York, Oxford University Press, 2008); DL Faigman, 'Normative Constitutional Fact-Finding: Exploring the Empirical Component of Constitutional Interpretation' (1991) 139 *University of Pennsylvania Law Review* 541; SE Fienberg and ML Straf, 'Statistical Evidence in the US Courts: An Appraisal' (1991) 31 *Journal of the Forensic Science Society* 259; KC Davis, 'Facts in Lawmaking' (1980) 80 *Columbia Law Review* 931.

[83] See RP Carver, 'The Case Against Statistical Significance Testing' (1978) 48 *Harvard Educational Review* 378.

[84] ibid.

the American Statistical Association, a p-value is 'the probability under a specified statistical model that a statistical summary of the data (eg, the sample mean difference between two compared groups) would be equal to or more extreme than its observed value'.[85] This definition was given in a report of the ASA that discussed widespread misunderstanding of p-values not only among the public but also among researchers.[86]

David Kaye, co-author of the chapter on statistics in the Reference Manual for Scientific Evidence used by US federal courts, has identified numerous errors in the use of statistics by courts at all levels in the US, including the US Supreme Court,[87] revealing that many judges have a profound misunderstanding of statistical significance and related concepts. Some opinions refer to the fact that a study has statistical significance as some indication of its overall importance and quality, while others dismiss any study that is not statistically significant, concluding that, ipso facto, it has no evidentiary value whatsoever.[88] Some opinions treat statistical significance and p-values as directly indicating the probability that the research hypothesis is true.[89] Kaye argues that lawyers and expert witnesses should be precluded from describing studies as statistically significant, and required instead to explain the import of statistical concepts in terms less likely to mislead judges and juries.[90]

The difficulty of achieving proper treatment of statistics in court is evidenced by methodological debates among social scientists. A number of scholars have argued that an undue prominence has been given to null hypothesis testing and statistical significance in the social sciences, and that this distorts the way that researchers present their results, how they design studies, and what they choose to investigate. These 'reformers', as I will call them, have set forth these arguments in what is now a substantial literature,[91] which includes contributions from scholars in sociology,[92] economics,[93] psychology,[94] and other fields. John Ioannidis

[85] R Wasserstein and N Lazar, 'The ASA's Statement on p-Values: Context, Process, and Purpose' (2016) 70 *The American Statistician* 129, 131.

[86] ibid.

[87] DH Kaye, 'Is Proof of Statistical Significance Significant?' (1986) 61 *Washington Law Review* 1333.

[88] ibid 6–7.

[89] ibid.

[90] DH Kaye, 'Statistical Significance and the Burden of Persuasion' (1983) 46 *Law & Contemporary Problems* 13.

[91] A collection of representative essays is in LL Harlow et al, *What If There Were No Significance Tests?* (Mahwah, NJ, Lawrence Erlbaum, 1997).

[92] DE Morrison and RE Henkel, *The Significance Test Controversy* (Belmont, CA, Butterworths, 1970).

[93] Deirdre McCloskey and Stephen Ziliak evaluated all of the full-length, empirical articles published in the American Economic Review during the 1980s on the basis of a list of common errors related to the use of statistical significance, and found hundreds of errors and that around 70 per cent of articles failed to distinguish properly between statistical significance and practical significance: ST Ziliak and DN McCloskey, 'The Standard Error of Regressions' (1996) 34 *Journal of Economic Literature* 97.

[94] eg, J Cohen, 'The Earth Is Round ($P<.05$)' (1994) 49(12) *American Psychologist* 997; WW Rozeboom, 'The Fallacy of the Null Hypothesis Significance Test' (1960) 57 *Psychological Bulletin* 416.

has raised similar concerns in the biomedical field, arguing in an article titled, 'Why Most Published Research Findings are False', that 'the high rate of nonreplication (lack of confirmation) of research discoveries is a consequence of the convenient, yet ill-founded strategy of claiming conclusive research findings solely on the basis of a single study assessed by formal statistical significance'.[95]

The reformers advocate changes in teaching, research practice, and publication standards that would diminish the role of statistical significance and emphasise the magnitude of differences and other contextual factors related to practical significance.[96] Some have even urged eliminating null hypothesis significance testing.[97] A common theme of the reformers is that their claims have been known for decades, widely recognised by others in their fields, and not effectively challenged. One states that it is 'extraordinarily difficult to find a statistician who argues explicitly in favour of the retention of significance tests'[98]—yet the emphasis on statistical significance has continued largely unabated.[99] For the purposes of my argument I do not need to endorse the full extent of the reformers' arguments. It is sufficient to note that such discussions are being carried on at high academic levels, and that there is general acknowledgement among the participants that there is widespread misunderstanding of the methodology of null hypothesis testing.

The above overview only scratches the surface of the method of null hypothesis testing and does not touch on other aspects of the complex discipline of statistics. Dworkin's characterisation of the problem of judicial competence, noted in chapter three, section III, is worth recalling:

> When a mechanical model is lacking, and you make judgments simply on correlation between observed phenomena, the kinds of techniques necessary to provide arguments for and against the hypothesis belong entirely to a very arcane subject, namely, statistics. The mathematical concepts of statistics are much more removed from the ordinary vocabulary of a trial judge than are the concepts of physics or chemistry he might encounter in, for example, a complicated patent case.[100]

Judges who approach social science with little or no training in statistics wander into a minefield.

[95] JP Ioannidis, 'Why Most Published Research Findings Are False' (2005) 2 *Plos Medicine* 696.

[96] eg, RE Kirk, 'Practical Significance: A Concept Whose Time Has Come' (1996) 56 *Educational and Psychological Measurement* 746.

[97] eg, PE Meehl, 'Theoretical Risks and Tabular Asterisks: Sir Karl, Sir Ronald, and the Slow Progress of Soft Psychology' (1978) 46 *Journal of Consulting and Clinical Psychology* 806, 817.

[98] MW Oakes, *Statistical Inference: A Commentary for the Social and Behavioural Sciences* (New York, John Wiley & Sons, 1986) 71.

[99] eg, RP Carver, 'The Case Against Statistical Significance Testing, Revisited' (1993) 61(4) *Journal of Experimental Education* 287.

[100] R Dworkin, 'Social Sciences and Constitutional Rights-the Consequences of Uncertainty' (1977) 6 *Journal of Law and Education* 1, 6.

VI. Case Studies

The discussion thus far has focused on the US, because that is where the practice of Brandeis briefs and using empirical research in judicial review of legislation began. It is also where the bulk of relevant judicial experience has been. But the use of empirical research and Brandeis briefs has tended to follow the adoption of proportionality tests in other jurisdictions.

A case from the European Court of Human Rights illustrates the wide range of evidence that courts consider. In *Hatton v United Kingdom* (2003), the Court was asked to decide whether a UK ruling permitting night flights at Heathrow airport[101] violated the right to private and home life (ECHR, art 8) of nearby residents. The court received information about the decibel levels in homes of the noise from planes and the degree to which different levels impair sleep; a statistical study on sleep disturbance and the likelihood of being awakened by aeroplane noise in comparison to other causes; the value of affected homes near Heathrow and the economic feasibility of residents moving elsewhere; economic assessments of the value of night flights at Heathrow to the aviation industry and the UK economy in general; and measures undertaken for the abatement and mitigation of airport noise.[102] The last category included such matters as

> aircraft noise certification to reduce noise at source; the compulsory phasing out of older, noisier jet aircraft; noise preferential routes and minimum climb gradients for aircraft taking off; [and] noise abatement approach procedures (continuous descent and low power/low drag procedures).[103]

In a divided decision by the Grand Chamber, the Court ruled in favour of the UK.[104]

In this section I will analyse selected cases from the US and Canada that illustrate some of the problems regarding judicial capacity to acquire and assess legislative facts.

A. United States

In *American Amusement Machine Ass'n v Kendrick*,[105] the US Court of Appeal (7th Cir) found an Indianapolis city ordinance limiting access by minors to violent

[101] The ruling was issued by the Secretary of State for Transport pursuant to powers under the Civil Aviation Act 1982.

[102] *Hatton v United Kingdom* (2003) 37 EHRR 611.

[103] ibid [74].

[104] The UK had not 'overstepped their margin of appreciation by failing to strike a fair balance between the right of the individuals affected by those regulations to respect for their private life and home and the conflicting interests of others and of the community as a whole': ibid [129].

[105] *American Amusement Machine Ass'n v Kendrick* 244 F3d 572 (7th Cir 2001).

video games to be unconstitutional. The opinion by Judge Richard Posner turned on his analysis of social science evidence. Because Posner is the leading judicial advocate of relying on social science in constitutional cases, and as he is also considered one of the most skilled judges in understanding social science, his analysis is worth considering in detail. The legal question was the application of the First Amendment protection of freedom of speech. Posner held that the ordinance was a content-based restriction on violence, and thus inquired whether the city had produced evidence of a compelling (not merely plausible) state interest.[106] He held that the state's legitimate interest is to prevent the harm that minors might inflict on others—or suffer themselves—as a result of playing violent video games. The city, according to Posner, 'rightly does not rest on "what everyone knows" about the harm inflicted by violent video games', but instead relied on social science evidence.[107]

That evidence consisted primarily in two studies reported in an article by psychologists Craig Anderson and Karen Dill.[108] Posner's analysis begins thus:

> Those studies do not support the ordinance. There is no indication that the games used in the studies are similar to those in the record of this case or to other games likely to be marketed in game arcades in Indianapolis.

This is factually wrong: the two games in the record discussed by Posner, 'The House of the Dead' and 'Ultimate Mortal Kombat 3',[109] resemble games in the studies, which include 'Mortal Kombat' (made by the same developer, in the same series, as the similar game Posner discussed) and 'Wolfenstein 3D', which was selected for use in one of the studies because it had features like those that Posner emphasised in his discussion: human characters, realistic depictions, and a story line.[110]

The opinion continues:

> The studies do not find that video games have ever caused anyone to commit a violent act, as opposed to feeling aggressive, or have caused the average level of violence to increase anywhere. And they do not suggest that it is the interactive character of the games, as opposed to the violence of the images in them, that is the cause of the aggressive feelings. The studies thus are not evidence that violent video games are any more harmful to the consumer or to the public safety than violent movies or other violent, but passive, entertainments.[111]

Posner mischaracterises the two studies and article reporting them, and his claims about causation are puzzling. Though he acknowledges that one study found a link between violent video games and aggressive feelings, he holds that this link

[106] ibid 576.
[107] ibid 578.
[108] CA Anderson and KE Dill, 'Video Games and Aggressive Thoughts, Feelings, and Behavior in the Laboratory and in Life' (2000) 78 *Journal of Personality and Social Psychology* 772.
[109] *Kendrick* 244 F3d 578.
[110] Anderson and Dill, above n 108, 779, 783.
[111] *Kendrick* 244 F3d 578.

matters only if it is due to the 'interactive character' of games, which distinguishes them from movies or other 'passive' entertainment. When courts look to social science evidence to assess the strength of state interest in legislation, it can be difficult to distinguish 'legal' reasoning about what the state's legitimate interest is from 'factual' reasoning about what the evidence shows. Here Posner appears to think the city has a legitimate interest in regulating video games only if they add some additional harm to what might be caused by minor's exposure to unregulated passive entertainment. But he does not clearly explain the legal grounds for this conclusion.[112]

In any event, contrary to Posner's description of the studies, the authors discuss, in a section titled 'Unique Dangers of Video Games', three reasons why the dangers of violent video games are greater than those for violent movies or television. The first two directly concern their *interactive* nature: (i) identification with the aggressor; (ii) active choice of aggressive responses; and (iii) the addictive nature of video games.[113] Posner not only misrepresents the article, he proceeds with a claim that ignores the authors' argument. He states:

> It is highly unlikely that [video games] are more harmful [than movies and television], because 'passive' entertainment aspires to be interactive too and often succeeds. When Dirty Harry or some other avenging hero kills off a string of villains, the audience is expected to identify with him, to revel in his success, to feel their own finger on the trigger. It is conceivable that pushing a button or manipulating a toggle stick engenders an even deeper surge of aggressive joy, but of that there is no evidence at all.[114]

Posner focuses here on identification with a protagonist, but Anderson and Dill contend that video games involve a different kind of interaction, in which the player is the agent who *causes* the violent scenes through his *active* choice. They write:

> In a sense, violent video games provide *a complete learning environment for aggression*, with simultaneous exposure to modeling, reinforcement, and rehearsal of behaviors. This combination of learning strategies has been shown to be more powerful than any of these methods used singly (Barton, 1981; Chambers & Ascione, 1987; Loftus & Loftus, 1983). (emphasis added)[115]

It is unclear what to make of Posner's claim that the studies do not find that video games have 'caused anyone to commit a violent act [or] caused the average level of violence to increase anywhere', in part because this wording does not track the reported results of the studies, which are summarised in the article abstract (but not mentioned by Posner). It states:

> Two studies examined violent video game effects on aggression-related variables. Study 1 found that real-life violent video game play was positively related to aggressive

[112] ibid 579–80.
[113] Anderson and Dill, above n 108, 788.
[114] *Kendrick* 244 F3d at 579.
[115] Anderson and Dill, above n 108, 788.

> behavior and delinquency. The relation was stronger for individuals who are characteristically aggressive and for men. Academic achievement was negatively related to overall amount of time spent playing video games. In Study 2, laboratory exposure to a graphically violent video game increased aggressive thoughts and behavior.[116]

Posner does not directly challenge the accuracy of these results, and he does not distinguish between: (i) aggressive behaviour, which the studies found was linked to violent video games; and (ii) violence, which he says that the studies failed to show is caused by video games. If he thinks that a real-life, observational study such as Study 1 must find a causal link between violent video game play and actual violent acts in order to support the legislation, then he should explain the difference between violent acts and the 'aggressive behavior' found by the studies. (Must a violent act cause actual physical harm to another person?) With regard to a controlled laboratory experiment such as Study 2, it would be unethical to conduct experiments designed to cause subjects of the experiment to commit violent acts that harm another person. Thus, Posner cannot reasonably object to Study 2 on the ground that it was limited to finding aggressive thoughts and behaviour.

If Posner's objection is that the statistical analysis in the studies is not robust enough to show causation, then he fails to indicate the specific ground of his objection. The authors of the article acknowledge that 'causal statements are risky at best' at the current time, since it is possible that aggressive individuals are especially attracted to violent video games, and that more research into the effects of violent video games is needed.[117] But cautionary statements about causation and calls for more research are common features in social science papers. In an earlier case, *Tagatz v Marquette University*, Posner repeats the common saying, 'Correlation is not causation', but goes on to state, 'Correlations can be suggestive of causality; scientific induction means inferring causality from correlation'.[118] This proposition, though it passes over key issues, is more sensible than Posner's statements about causation in *Kendrick*, which hold out a difficult (perhaps impossible) standard for finding empirical data to show that the legislation is constitutional.

Although Posner twice characterised the studies as providing no evidence to support the legislation, this is the very type of social science evidence that he argues in his theoretical work should be used to answer questions of constitutional interpretation (see section V above), and which, in this case, he required the legislature to submit to support a restriction on free speech. While Posner does not permit the city to rely on 'what everyone knows' about harm caused by video games,[119] he nevertheless helps himself to 'common sense', both in the remarks

[116] ibid 772.
[117] ibid 782.
[118] *Tagatz v Marquette University* 861 F2d 1040, 1044 (7th Cir 1988).
[119] *Kendrick* 244 F3d at 578.

quoted above about audiences identifying with characters such as Dirty Harry and in the following:

> Common sense says that the City's claim of harm to its citizens from these games is implausible, at best wildly speculative. Common sense is sometimes another word for prejudice, and the common sense reaction to the Indianapolis ordinance could be overcome by social scientific evidence, but has not been.[120]

Thus Posner's position amounts to this: the legislature cannot rely on common sense to defend a law, but the court can rely on its common sense about factual and policy matters in striking down a law; and the court's common sense prevails unless overcome by social science submitted by the legislature.

Several later court of appeal cases held that laws regulating violent video games violate the right to freedom of speech, each one dismissing the social science submitted by the state as insufficient to establish its interest in the regulation.[121] A number of courts cited Posner's remarks in *Kendrick* on the failure to show that video games cause violence. Some have made more direct, stringent demands regarding proof of causation with regard to violence or psychological harm.[122] The 8th Circuit Court of Appeals held: '[H]aving failed to come forth with *incontrovertible proof of a causal relationship* between the exposure to [video game] violence and subsequent psychological dysfunction, the State has not satisfied its evidentiary burden' (emphasis added).[123] Even in the physical sciences, there are standard theories that lack 'incontrovertible proof of a causal relationship'.[124] In the years since *Kendrick* a number of new studies on violent video games have appeared, and the state of California relied on some of these to defend a law that prohibited selling certain especially violent video games to unaccompanied minors in *Video Software Dealers Ass'n v Schwarzenegger* (2009).[125] The 9th Circuit Court of Appeals concluded that the evidence does not support the state's interest in preventing psychological harm to minors and struck down the law.[126] The general tenor of the court's approach can be seen in these remarks:

> Nearly all of the research is based on *correlation, not evidence of causation, and most of the studies suffer from significant, admitted flaws in methodology* as they relate to the State's claimed interest. None of the research establishes or suggests a causal link between

[120] *Kendrick* 244 F3d at 579.

[121] *Video Software Dealers Ass'n v Schwarzenegger* 556 F3d 950 (2009); *Entertainment Software Ass'n v Swanson* 519 F3d 768 (8th Cir 2008); *Entertainment Software Ass'n v Hatch* 443 FSupp2d 1065 (D Minn 2006); *Entertainment Software Ass'n v Granholm* 426 FSupp2d 646 (ED Mich 2006); *Entertainment Software Ass'n v Blagojevich* 404 FSupp2d 1051 (ND Ill 2005).

[122] See *Blagojevich* 404 FSupp2d at 1073–74; *Granholm* 426 FSupp2d at 653.

[123] *Entertainment Software Ass'n v Swanson* 519 F3d 768, 772 (8th Cir 2008).

[124] See L Smolin, *The Trouble with Physics: The Rise of String Theory, the Fall of a Science, and What Comes Next* (New York, Houghton Mifflin, 2006) 169–71, 237 (discussing theories accepted by many physicists that have not been verified by experiment).

[125] *Video Software Dealers Ass'n v Schwarzenegger* 556 F3d 950 (9th Cir 2009).

[126] See ibid 962–65.

> minors playing violent video games and actual psychological or neurological harm, and inferences to that effect would not be reasonable. In fact, some of the studies caution against inferring causation. Although we do not require the State to demonstrate a 'scientific certainty,' the State must come forward with more than it has. As a result, the State has not met its burden to demonstrate a compelling interest. (emphasis added)[127]

To contrast correlation with causation in this way is to reveal a profound misunderstanding of social science methodology. To the extent that social science can establish a causal relationship, it is inferred (in large part) from correlation.[128] What the court takes to be 'significant, admitted flaws in methodology' are instances of the technical language that social scientists use to discuss the step-by-step nature of their research. The researchers cited in this case make observations about the limits of individual studies, point out where questions lie for further research, and recite standard cautionary language about drawing causal inferences.[129] This is how such research progresses: it was through a series of repeated, limited studies that researchers established links between smoking and lung cancer.[130] But not all smokers get cancer, and researchers are still exploring why smokers are affected in different ways.[131] Thus for some purposes the data show correlation rather than causation. The correlations between smoking and cancer that have been shown in numerous studies may make it reasonable to choose not to smoke on the supposition that there is a causal relationship between smoking and lung cancer. And such studies may lead medical researchers to discover more about the biological mechanisms that cause lung cancer (and how smoking can trigger them); in the meantime, evidence of correlation is valuable even without strict proof of causation.

The Supreme Court granted certiorari in the 9th Circuit case and decided it under the name *Brown v Entertainment Merchants Association*.[132] The Court upheld the decision in a majority opinion by Justice Scalia. On the pivotal issue of whether there was evidence to demonstrate that California had a compelling state interest in the law, Scalia reviewed some of the same studies as the 9th Circuit and repeated its failure to grasp the nature of social science methods:

> These studies have been rejected by every court to consider them, and with good reason: They do not prove that violent video games *cause* minors to *act* aggressively (which would at least be a beginning). Instead, '[n]early all of the research is based on correlation, not evidence of causation, and most of the studies suffer from significant, admitted flaws in methodology.' *Video Software Dealers Assn.* 556 F 3d, at 964.[133]

[127] ibid 965.

[128] See N Barrowman, 'Correlation, Causation, and Confusion' (2014) 43 *The New Atlantis* 23.

[129] *Video Software Dealers Ass'n v Schwarzenegger* 556 F3d 950 (9th Cir 2009) 963–64; *cf* S Nolan and T Heinzen, *Statistics for the Behavioral Sciences* (New York, Worth Publishers, 2008) 206.

[130] J Cornfield et al, 'Smoking and Lung Cancer: Recent Evidence and a Discussion of Some Questions' (2009) 38 *International Journal of Epidemiology* 1175.

[131] ibid.

[132] *Brown v Entertainment Merchants Association* 564 US 786 (2011).

[133] ibid.

Justice Breyer, dissenting, criticised the majority for not showing deference to the legislature and argued that there was substantial evidence in support of California's position.[134] In regard to studies reaching different conclusions he said, 'I, like most judges, lack the social science expertise to say definitively who is right'.[135] He pointed to reports from professional associations of psychologists that, based on review of multiple studies, found support for the conclusion that prolonged exposure to violent video games led to an increase in aggressive behaviour, with more profound effects than passive entertainment.[136] Breyer also prepared an appendix listing over 100 relevant studies, which he said he compiled with the help of a database search conducted by the Supreme Court Library. He categorised these articles 'as either supporting the hypothesis that violent video games are harmful (listed in Appendix A), or not supporting/rejecting the hypothesis that violent video games are harmful (listed in Appendix B)'.[137] He argued that 'there is substantial (though controverted) evidence supporting the expert associations of public health professionals,' which 'help to substantiate the validity of the original judgment of the California Legislature, as well as that judgment's continuing validity'.[138]

Justice Alito's concurring opinion (joined by Roberts), agreeing with the result but not Scalia's treatment of possible effects of video games, gives a glimpse of another way for courts to seek out facts. His detailed, graphic discussion of extreme violence in games reads like first-hand account:

> In some of these games, the violence is astounding. Victims by the dozens are killed with every imaginable implement, including machine guns, shotguns, clubs, hammers, axes, swords, and chainsaws. Victims are dismembered, decapitated, disemboweled, set on fire, and chopped into little pieces. They cry out in agony and beg for mercy.[139]

Though Scalia chides him for doing 'considerable independent research', Alito provides a description of the physical, interactive environment of the games that is mostly missing from the Scalia's opinion. Alito argued that the games may affect behaviour more than books or movies, whereas Scalia argued that the psychological effects of games are on the same level as literature.[140]

Regardless of what the proper conclusion is regarding the conflicting studies, *Brown* is a striking example of the haphazard nature of finding legislative facts, even in the most well-resourced common law supreme court. The majority demands social science proof but misunderstands its methods; Justice Alito resorts to playing video games on his own; and Justice Breyer relies on librarians to compile a list of relevant articles. Breyer's instincts, and willingness to defer to

[134] ibid.
[135] ibid.
[136] ibid.
[137] ibid.
[138] ibid (internal citation omitted).
[139] ibid (internal citation omitted).
[140] ibid.

the legislature, at least go in the right direction. In chapter seven, section II, I will discuss proposals to give courts access to a research service to supply the expertise that Breyer acknowledges judges lack.

B. Canada

In *Chaoulli v Quebec*,[141] the Canadian Supreme Court's review of legislative facts played the decisive role in a constitutional challenge to a key component of Canada's public health care system, Medicare, which is directed and partially funded by the federal government and administered by provincial governments. Since the 1960s the federal government has pursued a policy of a single-tier system of national health insurance,[142] in line with which Quebec and five other provinces prohibited private insurance contracts to cover most of the medical services provided by Medicare.[143] Other provinces take measures to discourage such contracts, making them financially unfeasible in general. Canada has consistently rejected a 'two-tier' system in which some people would receive publicly funded care while others would have access to private care through insurance purchased privately (or provided or subsidised by an employer).[144] Quebec's prohibition was challenged by Jacques Chaoulli, a doctor who was an advocate for the availability of private insurance, and George Zeliotis, a patient who had waited several months for hip replacement surgery. They claimed that Quebec's prohibition violated the rights to life and to liberty in the Canadian Charter of Rights and Freedoms and the Quebec Charter of Human Rights and Freedoms. In a 4-3 decision, the Canadian Supreme Court held that the prohibition was unconstitutional.[145]

The Court[146] found that Quebec's prohibition on private insurance infringed the right to life on the basis of observations about waiting lists and their effects on patient health:

> Some patients die as a result of long waits for treatment in the public system when they could have gained prompt access to care in the private sector. Were it not for [Quebec's prohibitions] they could buy private insurance and receive care in the private sector ... Not only is it common knowledge that health care in Quebec is subject to waiting times, but a number of witnesses acknowledged that the demand for health care is potentially unlimited and that waiting lists are a more or less implicit form of rationing

[141] *Chaoulli v Quebec* [2005] 1 SCR 791.

[142] See Canada Health Act, ss 1–13 (establishing criteria provinces must meet in order to receive federal payments for health insurance plans, including public administration, comprehensiveness, universality, and accessibility).

[143] *Chaoulli v Quebec* [2005] 1 SCR 791 [1] and [77].

[144] ibid [181] and [230] (Binnie and LeBel JJ, dissenting).

[145] Four justices in the majority rested their decision on the Quebec Charter, while three agreed with respect to the Canadian Charter.

[146] I follow the US convention here in referring to the majority opinion as the opinion of the Court.

(report by J.-L. Denis, Un avenir pour le système public de santé (1998), at p. 13; report by Y. Brunelle, Aspects critiques d'un rationnement planifié (1993), at p. 21). Waiting lists are therefore real and intentional. The witnesses also commented on the consequences of waiting times.

Dr. Daniel Doyle, a cardiovascular surgeon, testified that when a person is diagnosed with cardiovascular disease, he or she is [TRANSLATION] 'always sitting on a bomb' and can die at any moment. In such cases, it is inevitable that some patients will die if they have to wait for an operation. Dr. Doyle testified that the risk of mortality rises by 0.45 percent per month. The right to life is therefore affected by the delays that are the necessary result of waiting lists.[147]

The Court was clearly impressed with Doyle's testimony: a concurring opinion also mentioned the phrase 'sitting on a bomb' and added: 'He confirmed, without challenge, that patients die while on waiting lists. Inevitably, where patients have life-threatening conditions, some will die because of undue delay in awaiting surgery'.[148] It is hardly surprising that there was no challenge to this claim, which (as reported) makes no attempt at quantification or contextualisation—we are told only that 'some' will die, not how many. The Court attempts, unconvincingly, to reinforce its conclusion with statistics, by citing Doyle's testimony that the risk of mortality rises by 0.45 per cent per month. The Court does not reference any study on which the testimony is based. Presumably, the claim refers to a study of a group of patients with cardiovascular disease, but there is no information about the age or any other characteristics of this group or the specific nature of the disease (which can include, among other things, congestive heart failure, coronary artery disease, and various post-heart attack conditions). Moreover, the Court does not state the absolute mortality rate of patients with cardiovascular disease. From the information provided, it is impossible to know the meaning and importance of an increase in mortality of 0.45 per cent per month or to be able to compare the mortality rates of patients with cardiovascular disease and other persons of the same age.

Nonetheless, Doyle's testimony is the crucial evidence on which the Court relied to show that Quebec's prohibition on private insurance infringed the right to life; it is the proof given for the Court's general claim that waiting lists cause Canadians to die. The finding that the right to life was infringed did not directly settle the final outcome, but it served to invoke the proportionality test and shift the burden of proof to the government.[149] It remained for the government of Quebec to attempt to prove that this was a justified infringement by providing evidence that the prohibition on private insurance met the tests of rationality, minimal impairment, and balancing.[150]

[147] ibid [37]–[40].
[148] ibid [112] (McLachlin CJ, concurring).
[149] ibid [60].
[150] ibid [45]–[48].

Doyle himself, according to the trial court's summary of his testimony, was 'not at all certain the solution lay with private insurance', and he criticised certain practices of US insurance companies with regard to heart patients.[151] Although 2,000 patients were on waiting lists in Quebec in 1992, he said the situation had since improved considerably, and the government increased facilities in 1997 (the trial was in 1999).[152] He was still concerned about waiting lists, taking the view that 'waiting should not exist in cardiology, that it is often a question of life or death, as cardiac illness is unpredictable'.[153] But he acknowledged that 'waiting lists are everywhere' and observed that the population is growing older and 'it is now necessary to operate on people 85 years old'.[154] He ascribed the waiting lists to various causes, including a lack of nurses and aggressive recruitment of Quebec's cardiovascular physicians, some of whom leave for Ontario or the US.[155] All of this testimony is from the trial court record. The Supreme Court overlooked it and attempted no detailed analysis of the nature and scope of the problem of waiting lists; nor did the Court discuss evidence and reasons for its belief that the availability of private insurance would alleviate the problems of waiting lists. The Court plucked the figure about the mortality rate increase, and the expression 'sitting on a bomb', from their context and made them the keystone of its finding on infringing the right to life.

The federal policy of promoting a single-tier public health programme, and the decision by Quebec and other provinces to implement that policy by prohibiting private insurance, are two important issues within a web of others: funding and taxation, the administrative structure of Medicare and various province-level health providers, federal-provincial relationships, etc. Chaoulli arose in the midst of extensive discussion and political debate about these issues, which was reflected in a major, 400-page report by an independent commission (chaired by Roy Romanow) and by a multi-volume report by the Standing Senate Committee on Social Affairs, Science and Technology (chaired by Michael Kirby). The Romanow Report and the Final Kirby Report (Volume 6: Recommendations and Reform) were issued in 2002, three years after the end of the trial in which Doyle and other experts provided testimony. After discussing alternatives at length, both reports strongly advocated retaining Canada's single-tier public health plan. The Supreme Court considered aspects of these reports alongside the evidence presented at trial. Though its judgment was lengthy, its discussion of the general debate over health care reform and its examination of specific issues were severely truncated, in comparison to the wide-ranging analyses in the Romanow and Kirby reports.[156]

[151] *Chaoulli v Québec* [2000] RJQ 786 [47]. The quotations in the text above are from the English translation of the judgment of the Superior Court of Quebec in CM Flood et al (eds), *Access to Care, Access to Justice* (University of Toronto Press, 2005) Appendix A, 538.

[152] ibid.

[153] ibid.

[154] ibid.

[155] ibid.

[156] The main conclusions and a number of the findings of the reports are summarised in the dissenting opinion by Binnie and LeBel JJ: *Chaoulli v Quebec* [2005] 1 SCR 791, [173]ff.

The pivotal question for the Court was whether Quebec's prohibition on private insurance satisfied the 'minimal impairment' step in the proportionality analysis.[157] The government argued that the availability of private insurance would undermine the effectiveness of the public plan in several ways, including the following: (i) popular support for the public plan would diminish because those with insurance would not see a need for it; (ii) the quality of care would decline because influential people would purchase and rely on private insurance rather than press for improvement in the public plan; (iii) many physicians and other health-care workers would leave the plan out of a motive for profit; (iv) the increase in for-profit health care would lead to a decline in professionalism and ethical standards among doctors; and (v) physicians would have a financial incentive to keep waiting lists on the public plan long in order to divert patients to the private sector.[158] These and related arguments were advanced at trial by six expert witnesses—leading physicians with academic expertise in public health and administrative experience. The Supreme Court noted that these witnesses did not produce studies in the trial court in support of these arguments (though the Court itself was willing to convey Doyle's testimony in conclusory form and cite no study regarding the mortality rate increase); and concluded that their evidence 'carries little weight':[159]

> While it is true that scientific or empirical evidence is not always necessary, witnesses in a case in which the arguments are supposedly based on logic or common sense should be able *to cite specific facts in support of their conclusions*. The human reactions [ie the projected consequences of private insurance] described by the experts, many of whom came from outside Quebec, do not appear to me to be very convincing … I am of the opinion that the reaction some witnesses described is highly unlikely in the Quebec context. (emphasis added)[160]

Contrary to what the Court implies above, the witnesses did cite facts. The trial court's summary of their factual and policy reasoning covered several pages.[161] The Supreme Court's judgment not only fails to address adequately the specific arguments of the government's expert witnesses, it overlooked a number of studies relevant to those arguments that were among the evidence submitted during the appeal.[162]

After considering questions about its institutional role and whether it should defer to the legislature, the Court affirms its own competence:

> 'Courts do not have to define goals, choose means or come up with ideas. They do not have to create social policies; they just have to understand what the other branches have

[157] ibid [48] and [68].
[158] ibid [63] and [65].
[159] ibid [64].
[160] ibid [64] and [66].
[161] *Chaoulli v Québec* [2000] RJQ 786 [71]–[122].
[162] See Factum of Respondent (mis en cause) Attorney General of Canada, [54]ff, <www.law.utoronto.ca/documents/chaoulli/AGCanada_Factum_English.doc>.

> created. No special expertise is required for such an understanding.'[163] In fact, if a court is satisfied that all the evidence has been presented, there is nothing that would justify it in refusing to perform its role on the ground that it should merely defer to the government's position ... The courts have a duty to rise above political debate. They leave it to the legislatures to develop social policy. But when such social policies infringe rights that are protected by the charters, the courts cannot shy away from considering them.[164]

The Court's claim is the same as that of the US Supreme Court in *Lochner*. It is not deciding social policy or substituting its judgment for that of the legislature; it is simply making a determination of whether a constitutional right has been violated on the basis of the available evidence. The Court adds: 'The instant case is a good example of a case in which the courts have all the necessary tools to evaluate the government's measure'.[165] Its reasoning and handling of the evidence, however, suggest otherwise.

The case of *Carter v Canada*,[166] which was discussed in chapter two, is notable for its very extensive record of legislative facts on the question of whether Canada can implement a regulatory scheme to allow physician-assisted suicide without resulting in undue pressure on the vulnerable to end their lives. The trial court answered yes. Justice Smith's careful, detailed discussion of the evidence covered 50 pages in the judgment. Nonetheless the evidence relied on is scanty, with large gaps, and her conclusions were both hesitant and questionable.

Almost every country in the world prohibits physician-assisted suicide, leaving only a handful of places from which to draw evidence. Justice Smith focused on three places where some form of assisted suicide is legal: Belgium, the Netherlands, and the state of Oregon in the US. In Belgium and the Netherlands physicians are permitted actively to assist in the patient's death when there is an explicit request; such 'voluntary euthanasia' is distinguished from 'non-voluntary euthanasia' where there is no such explicit request. In Oregon euthanasia is not allowed; physicians may prescribe lethal doses of self-administered medication to patients who are diagnosed with a terminal illness and have less than six months to live.[167]

For the Netherlands and Oregon, Justice Smith relied heavily on one 2007 study (Battin et al)[168] which, she concluded, showed that the availability of assisted suicide in those jurisdictions 'has not inordinately impacted persons who might be seen as "socially vulnerable"', a category comprising the elderly, women, racial or ethnic minorities, people with low educational status, the poor, the physically disabled or chronically ill, minors, and people with psychiatric illnesses

[163] Here the Court is quoting G Davidov, 'The Paradox of Judicial Deference' (2001) 12 *National Journal of Constitutional Law* 133, 143.

[164] *Chaoulli v Quebec* [2005] 1 SCR 791 [87] and [89].

[165] ibid [96].

[166] *Carter v Canada (Attorney General)* [2015] SCC 5, [2015] 1 SCR 331.

[167] Oregon Death with Dignity Act 1997.

[168] M Battin et al, 'Legal physician-assisted dying in Oregon and the Netherlands: evidence concerning the impact on patients in "vulnerable" groups' (2007) 33 *Journal of Medical Ethics* 591.

including depression.[169] Justice Smith said, however, that 'no conclusion can be drawn' from the Battin study regarding those who are 'situationally vulnerable' due to factors such as 'personality, emotional distress, untreated symptoms, coercion or the desire not to be a burden'.[170] Noting that 'there is some evidence bearing on that question', however, she discussed anecdotal evidence of some patients receiving subtle or overt pressure, or feeling they were a burden on families, but countered this with other anecdotal and observational evidence, concluding that the instances of patients acting under pressure are 'highly isolated'.[171]

Justice Smith's discussion addresses the issue of whether depression is a factor in seeking assisted suicide,[172] showing that there is an overlap between the 'situationally vulnerable' and the 'socially vulnerable' category of persons having psychiatric illness and depression in the Battin study. In that study, the authors said that their finding with regard to this particular category was based on 'inferential or partially contested data'.[173] With regard to Oregon, the key finding in the Battin study is that 20 per cent of those who requested suicide were patients who had been diagnosed with depression, and none of those were permitted to proceed.[174] However, that leaves a question about the possibility of *undiagnosed* depression. Justice Smith acknowledged that only 8.4 per cent of patients who died between 1998 and 2009 were referred to specialists to determine whether they were suffering from depression.[175] The authors of the Battin study acknowledge that evidence from Oregon does not allow for a 'full examination' of the practice there, since there is a lack of 'studies of the complexity, duration and comprehensiveness of the four Dutch nationwide studies'.[176] With regard to Belgium, Justice Smith admitted that 'it is difficult to reach any firm conclusion', noting testimony from Professor Deliens, who 'acknowledged that patients who do not have a psychiatric disorder but who have some level of depression might be vulnerable to being euthanized'.[177] In the end, Justice Smith concluded that taking the experience of Oregon, the Netherlands and Belgium on the whole, the evidence 'permits'[178] the conclusion that 'the predicted abuse and disproportionate impact on vulnerable populations has not materialized'.[179] However, she said that 'inferences for Canada can only be drawn with caution'.[180]

169 *Carter v Canada (Attorney General)* [2012] BCSC 886, 287 CCC (3d) 1, para 662.
170 ibid para 663.
171 ibid paras 668–72.
172 ibid para 669.
173 M Battin et al, 'Legal physician-assisted dying in Oregon and the Netherlands: evidence concerning the impact on patients in "vulnerable" groups' (2007) 33 *Journal of Medical Ethics* 591.
174 *Carter v Canada (Attorney General)* [2012] BCSC 886, 287 CCC (3d) 1, para 630.
175 ibid para 449.
176 M Battin et al., 'Legal physician-assisted dying in Oregon and the Netherlands: evidence concerning the impact on patients in "vulnerable" groups' (2007) 33 *Journal of Medical Ethics* 591.
177 *Carter v Canada (Attorney General)* [2012] BCSC 886, 287 CCC (3d) 1, para 672.
178 ibid para 682.
179 ibid para 684.
180 ibid.

Justice Smith's conclusion is not only given in a hesitant tone, it is also in tension with another conclusion she made regarding the likelihood of attaining strict legal compliance with regulatory scheme of safeguards. This point arose in regard to undisputed evidence that in the Netherlands and Belgium there is a substantial rate of physicians participating in *non-voluntary euthanasia*. In the Netherlands in 2005 (the last year for which data is available) 560 patients who had not given explicit consent were euthanised; this represents 0.4 per cent of all deaths.[181] Rates of non-voluntary euthanasia are also high in Belgium.[182] In response to Canada's argument that this constitutes evidence that a regulatory scheme permitting euthanasia is likely to be abused, Justice Smith responded in two ways. First, she concluded that the formal legalisation of voluntary euthanasia and introduction of legal regulations has led to doctors taking more care with end-of-life decisions, and may have reduced the incidence of non-voluntary euthanasia, in comparison to an earlier period when euthanasia was illegal but a widespread practice.[183] But she acknowledged that compliance is not 'ideal' and that there are high rates of non-reporting.[184] Second, she concluded that with regard to the question of whether a strict regulatory regime is likely to be followed in Canada, one should disregard the experience of Belgium and the Netherlands, where euthanasia was practised before it was legal, and look to Oregon instead. Given cultural similarities between Canada and Oregon, and testimony that physicians in Canada have a stronger disposition to comply with the law than those in Belgium and the Netherlands,[185] Justice Smith found that '[t]he experience of compliance in Oregon is more likely to be predictive of what would happen in Canada if a permissive regime were put in place, *although even there only a weak inference can be drawn*' (emphasis added).[186] The inference appears even weaker in light of the fact that Justice Smith's order mandated that Canada permit voluntary euthanasia,[187] which is permitted in Belgium and the Netherland but forbidden in Oregon (which allows only the prescription of self-administered lethal doses of medication).

A similar—but stronger—tension is reflected in the Supreme Court's judgment upholding Justice Smith's conclusions. The Court considered the affidavit of Etienne Montero, a Belgian professor of law and expert on the practice of euthanasia. The Court acknowledged and did not dispute his findings regarding a 'number of recent, controversial, and high-profile cases of assistance in dying in Belgium which would not fall within the [legal] parameters … such as euthanasia for minors or persons with psychiatric disorders or minor medical conditions'.[188]

[181] *Carter v Canada (Attorney General)* [2012] BCSC 886, 287 CCC (3d) 1, para 379.
[182] ibid para 657.
[183] ibid paras 655–60.
[184] ibid.
[185] ibid paras 679–80.
[186] ibid para 683.
[187] ibid para 1393.
[188] *Carter v Canada (Attorney General)* [2012] BCSC 886, 287 CCC (3d) 1, para 25.

These findings concern more than the narrow question of physicians participating in non-voluntary euthanasia in some cases, and are suggestive of widespread abuse and an inordinate impact on the vulnerable. The Court, however, states (citing the trial court judgment):

> [T]he permissive regime in Belgium is the product of a very different medico-legal culture. Practices of assisted death were 'already prevalent and embedded in the medical culture' prior to legalization (para 660). The regime simply regulates a common pre-existing practice. In the absence of a comparable history in Canada, the trial Justice concluded that it was problematic to draw inferences about the level of physician compliance with legislated safeguards based on the Belgian evidence (para 680).[189]

The Court seems unaware of the tension between: (1) stating (in para 25 of its judgment) that Canada can design effective safeguards on the ground that 'predicted abuse and disproportionate impact on vulnerable populations has not materialized' in Belgium, the Netherlands, and Oregon; and (2) dismissing (in para 112) evidence of abuse from Belgium as the product of a 'very different medico-legal culture'.

The Court reviewed the trial court's findings under a standard that required Canada to show the court's conclusion was 'unsupported, arbitrary, insufficiently precise or otherwise in error', amounting to 'a palpable and overriding error'.[190] The effect of this standard is to entrust an extraordinary amount of power in the hands of a single trial court judge.

The Supreme Court's dismal performance in handling empirical research in both *Chaoulli* and *Carter*[191] vindicates the remarks of Lord Sumption in *Nicklinson v Ministry of Justice*, a case dealing with assisted suicide in the UK:

> [T]he Parliamentary process is a better way of resolving issues involving controversial and complex questions of fact arising out of moral and social dilemmas. The legislature has access to a fuller range or expert judgment and experience than forensic litigation can possibly provide. It is better able to take account of the interests of groups not represented or not sufficiently represented before the court in resolving what is surely a classic 'polycentric problem'.[192]

[189] ibid para 112.

[190] ibid para 109.

[191] For further discussion see B Chan and M Somerville, 'Converting the "Right to Life" to the "Right to Physician-Assisted Suicide and Euthanasia": An Analysis of Carter v Canada (Attorney General), Supreme Court of Canada' (2016) 24 *Medical Law Review* 143. For a critique of the trial court decision see John Keown, 'A Right to Voluntary Euthanasia? Confusion in Canada in Carter?' (2014) 28 *Notre Dame Journal of Law, Ethics and Pub Policy* 1.

[192] *R (on the application of Nicklinson) (AP) v Ministry of Justice* [2014] UKSC 38, para 233.

VII. Conclusion

Oliver Wendell Holmes's prediction in 1897[193] about statistics and economics in law proved accurate for rights-based judicial review of legislation in the century that followed. In *Lochner* the US Supreme Court introduced the proportionality-based, fact-intensive method of judicial review of legislation that now prevails in many constitutional systems worldwide.

I have argued that courts lack institutional capacities to acquire and assess empirical research and that in many cases courts make mistakes in understanding statistical analysis and social science methodology. I have mostly passed over examples of courts performing adequately when dealing with empirical research, and readers might wonder whether my examples are cherry-picked to show courts at their worst. The examples, however, concern several landmark cases that have prominently dealt with empirical research. My aim is not to suggest some quantitative measure of how frequently courts mishandle empirical research, but rather to illustrate basic aspects of the *methods* by which courts acquire and assess legislative facts as well as what this implies about their *capacity*. We should have reason for concern when judges are conducting their own research on internet search engines, when they are willing to cite sources such as Wikipedia for legislative facts, and when they show themselves capable of mangling the evidentiary record as in some of the examples above. Richard Posner is the most seasoned user of social science in the judiciary and its leading advocate, and has published extensively in social science journals. Yet he approves of the use of Wikipedia by courts. In *Kendrick* he not only mischaracterised the studies but had erroneous expectations of what studies can be reasonably expected to show with regard to causation.

My criticism of the use of empirical research in constitutional law is on a level with that of David Faigman, who has done the most extensive research on the US cases in this area,[194] and who is, generally, a defender of rights-based judicial review of legislation. He writes:

> [The Supreme] Court has completely disregarded the procedural aspects of fact-finding, receiving and deciding factual questions in a slapdash manner ... [It] has never sought to impose any systematic order on its reception of facts in constitutional cases. Although facts are a pervasive presence in the Court's opinions, there is no logic or order to their use. The Court treats them as rhetorical devices, to be used or withheld as the normative circumstances dictate ... Much fact-finding in constitutional cases resembles the tradition in many cultures of shooting guns into the air in celebrations.

[193] OW Holmes, 'The Path of the Law' (1897) 10 *Harvard Law Review* 457.

[194] See, in addition to his many articles cataloguing judicial errors regarding legislative facts, D Faigman, *Constitutional Fictions: A Unified Theory of Constitutional Facts* (New York, Oxford University Press, 2008).

> The practice is great show and usually no one is hurt. But often enough, stray bullets fall out of the air and do real damage; it is just impossible to predict exactly where the bodies will be found.[195]

Faigman is nonetheless committed to the institution of judicial review of legislation, including the power of courts to review fact-finding by legislatures. He acknowledges that legislatures have several institutional advantages in fact-finding:

> They have greater resources than courts, for instance, to sponsor research, hold hearings, and call expert witnesses. They have the power to define research questions and the flexibility to follow them up by redefining the scope, direction and size of any inquiries.[196]

He argues that all this is overcome, however, by their majoritarian character. He states, 'Legislatures, of course, are the quintessential voice of the majority and thus, speaking classically, it is their tyranny that the Bill of Rights was intended to block'.[197] When laws infringe liberties, courts must scrutinise their reasons for acting: 'This, by necessity, means that courts must independently assess the empirical bases for legislative action. Otherwise legislatures could avoid judicial holdings simply by finding facts differently than the courts'.[198]

But this is a counsel of despair, saying that we should check a biased institution with one that has never shown competence for the task. It is like arguing that if the professors in a medical school are skewing their results, the administrators in the dean's office must be empowered to review and screen their research outputs. Constitutional design requires more holistic comparative institutional analysis than this, and that is what I take up in the next chapter. I will also argue against the standard account that sees the legislature as given over to the tyranny of the majority.

[195] ibid 167, 181.
[196] ibid 176.
[197] ibid 175.
[198] ibid 176.

5

Comparative Analysis of Institutional Capacities

This chapter analyses courts and legislatures with regard to their reasoning processes, structures for deliberation and decision-making, and institutional capacities. These are vast topics, and any comprehensive examination of them would be beyond the scope of the book. I will focus on salient differences that are important from the point of view of constitutional design, particularly with respect to the decision of whether—and if so, in what form—to adopt a system of rights-based judicial review of legislation. The chapter will consider the law-making capacity of legislatures and courts, and basic differences in their purpose and institutional structure (sections I and II); the legislature's capacity for empirical reasoning, in light of chapter four's discussion of judicial capacity (section III); a comparative analysis of capacity for moral reasoning (section IV); the majoritarian character of the legislature (section V) and the capacity of courts and legislates to protect minorities (section VI); and an historical perspective on issues concerning minorities (section VII).

I. The Basic Structure of Judicial Reasoning

The lack of judicial capacity for finding general empirical facts about society, which was surveyed in chapter four, is not, properly considered, a defect of courts. It is what we should expect of institutions set up primarily to resolve disputes according to law laid down by another institution, in response to claims initiated by litigants and their lawyers. Although legal scholars tend to focus on interpretation and other aspects of adjudication with law-forming effects—including judicial review of legislation—the purpose for which adjudicative systems and institutions is set up is not to make law. Judicial decisions may contribute to determining and settling the content of the law, and this may be anticipated and accepted in a given legal system. Nonetheless, such consequences are incidental to the main activity of hearing cases and rendering judgment according to law.

Consider, first, the position of the traditional common law trial court. The world of the trial is in important ways an artificial world, which makes it unsuited for finding general empirical facts about society and making difficult choices about social policy. This is an important claim, and it is different from making a claim about the individual, personal qualities of judges; and so I will analyse the structure of a trial in some detail. Although major constitutional questions in common law systems are finally decided by supreme courts rather than trial courts, they begin in trial courts and in many cases a substantial part of the evidence is generated there. Moreover, as observed in chapter one, the American model of constitutional rights adjudication presumes the competence of trial judges to decide whether legislation complies with constitutional rights.

The pre-trial and trial process is mainly controlled by the parties (whether plaintiff, prosecutor, or defendant), who set the court's agenda by the decisions they make in filing criminal charges, initiating civil complaints, asserting defences, and making pre-trial motions. Even with regard to the question of which law to apply to the case, the judge may not have a free hand. A legal norm that fits the facts may be left unmentioned by a party or intentionally set aside for strategic reasons—or because of an attorney's negligence. Depending on the rules of pleading, this could place that law beyond the judge's remit, or this could be treated by the judge as sufficient reason not to consider applying it. With regard to ascertaining the relevant law, the judge may or may not have the responsibility or resources to go beyond the legal research presented by the parties. In the UK, there is a general expectation that a judge will not perform legal research beyond what is submitted by the parties. When judges do this in exceptional cases they are expected, before relying on legal authority not previously submitted by the parties, to raise the issue and invite their comment. In the US any expectations in this regard are relaxed; judges are relatively more likely to research legal issues beyond party submissions, but often do not do so.

The parties are chiefly responsible for gathering and submitting evidence, a process governed by many technical rules and routines. Parties have this responsibility in constitutional as well as ordinary cases, despite the tendency observed in chapter four of some judges to conduct their own research into legislative facts. Documents and physical evidence are subject to stringent standards for authentication. Oral testimony is regulated by a system of exclusionary rules. In criminal cases the accused is not required to testify, and evidentiary privileges allow spouses and certain others not to testify. Many sources that would be valuable to ordinary historical investigation of an incident are not considered in the context of a trial. Some of the traditional rules regarding exclusion of hearsay, similar act evidence, and character evidence have been relaxed in England, but most are still rigorously observed in the US and other common law jurisdictions. These rules are part of an intricate system governing the submission of evidence as well as direct and cross examination, touching not only on matters of content but also on the amount of time allotted to the parties. Decisions regarding the admission of evidence depend on the judge's assessment of relevance and appropriate use of limited time. To further efficiency, parties may be permitted to stipulate certain facts.

Certain procedures allow facts to be deemed to be true for the purposes of a case, and this can be so even when the actual truth is not known or is known to be the opposite.[1]

When the evidentiary record has been compiled, the judge assesses it against the particular legal concepts made relevant by the parties' claims ('contract', 'foreseeable risk', 'intent to defraud', etc), in light of the appropriate standard of proof and the law's allocation of the burden of proof. The two most common standards, 'preponderance of the evidence' (or 'balance of probabilities') in civil cases and 'beyond reasonable doubt' in criminal cases, are chosen for the particular purposes of trials and would be unsuited for much of the work of investigators such as historians—or for legislators. The judge's ultimate decision on the legal claim—and the entire trial process—is not only filtered through a legally prescribed standard of proof but also framed by the bivalent nature of Western legal proceedings.[2] A criminal trial ends in conviction or acquittal of the accused. A civil trial ends in a decision as to whether a legal claim or set of claims—usually a question of liability of one party to another—is established. Bivalence affects judicial review proceedings as well, since they must generally conclude in a judgment that a statute is either constitutional or not constitutional. This point will be taken up in chapter seven in a discussion of whether the remedies available to constitutional courts are appropriate.

The fact-finding process of the trial is not simply a search for historical truth. The path to judgment is bounded on every side by procedural and evidentiary rules. A trial is a technical routine centred on giving an answer to a binary legal question, and it is subject to the shifting strategies of parties who manoeuvre for advantage as the process unfolds. I am not arguing that historical truth does not matter or is not important. A system of adjudication is established to test the accuracy of legal claims, including their factual basis. This aim, however, exists in tension with other goals such as efficient use of limited judicial resources, finality, and procedural fairness.[3] Thus, for example, evidence discovered after a final judgment usually cannot be used to challenge it. There are exceptions to this, but without a general rule of finality cases could be perpetually re-litigated. Some rules promote accuracy by causing the court to focus on what is of greater relevance and to exclude that which could cause prejudice, particularly to lay jurors. Other rules and privileges against testifying, however, promote policy goals distinct from truth-finding in an individual case. A rule excluding evidence obtained through

[1] For example, the US federal rules of civil procedure allow parties to make a 'request for admission' in the form of statement regarding factual and legal issues in a case; the opposing party's failure to make a timely denial results in such statements being deemed true, unless the judge permits the admission to be withdrawn or amended. US Federal Rule of Evidence 36.

[2] See T Endicott, *Vagueness in Law* (Oxford, Oxford University Press, 2001) XX.

[3] For an argument that certain rules excluding relevant evidence promote fairness to the parties see HL Ho, *A Philosophy of Evidence Law: Justice in the Search for Truth* (Oxford, Oxford University Press, 2008) Ch 2.

illegal searches, for example, may be designed to deter police misconduct and promote the integrity of the judicial process, at the known and accepted expense of eliminating information that would enhance the accuracy of judgment in an individual case. An historian would never accept a verdict in a criminal trial as necessarily establishing the guilt or innocence of the accused. The verdict could have turned not only on mistake, bribery, or intimidation, but also on contingent factors that legitimately affect the outcome, such as exclusion of relevant but invalidly obtained evidence or the unavailability of a key witness.

Thus far I have focused primarily on the role of the judge in the traditional common law trial. Appellate courts are accorded greater authority in matters of legal interpretation, but their jurisdiction is often limited to determining whether trial courts made errors substantial enough to warrant reversal. They usually focus on questions of law, reviewing the fact-finding of trial courts under deferential standards and without receiving new evidence on adjudicative facts. This is in part because the capacity of appellate court to determine adjudicative facts is inferior to trial courts, which have the ability to observe and engage with witnesses. With regard to legislative facts, appellate courts increasingly consider new evidence not considered at trial, as described in chapter four. Whether trial or appellate courts have better capacities for finding legislative facts is debatable, but I will argue below that both are inferior to legislatures.

Much of what I have said about the adversarial nature and artificiality of common law trials is characteristic of civil law trial processes as well,[4] though judges there have more power to ensure pertinent legal issues are raised and evidence obtained; they are more involved in questioning witnesses,[5] and there are fewer constraints on the admissibility of evidence.[6] The more focused point of comparison, however, is to the Kelsenian constitutional court, which, as discussed in chapter one, generally has a monopoly on questions of constitutional law in civil law systems and is institutionally structured to be different from ordinary legal courts. It exists outside that system rather than at the top of its hierarchy. The Kelsenian court is not set up primarily to settle disputes between parties, but to resolve controversies over constitutional provisions and their application and interpretation. Thus, it is intentionally set up to play a political role and, for Kelsen, to be a 'negative legislator'. This results in some significant differences regarding institutional capacities and structure between Kelsenian constitutional courts and courts in common law systems, which will be touched on here below and discussed further in chapter seven.

[4] See JH Merryman and R Pérez-Perdomo, *The Civil Law Tradition: An Introduction to the Legal Systems of Europe and Latin America* (Stanford, Stanford University Press, 2007) 82, 112.

[5] Civil procedure reforms in the US and the UK have given trial judges certain powers to manage the pre-trial and trial process that are somewhat like those of civil law judges. See J Resnik, 'Managerial Judges' (1982) 96 *Harvard Law Review* 374; Lord Woolf, 'Access to Justice: Final Report to the Lord Chancellor on the Civil Justice System in England and Wales' (London, HMSO, 1996) Chs 1–8.

[6] See M Damaška, 'Evidentiary Barriers to Conviction and Two Models of Criminal Procedure: A Comparative Study' (1972) 121 *University of Pennsylvania Law Review* 506.

One might question whether supreme courts in common law systems have evolved in the direction of Kelsenian constitutional courts. The US Supreme Court now focuses on settling major questions of law—including questions of statutory interpretation but with an emphasis on constitutional law—and the number of cases it decides has been shrinking steadily. In the early 1980s the Court decided over 150 cases per year, and since 2000 it has been around half that number; in 2014, 71 cases were heard.[7] While there seems to be less emphasis now on resolving individual disputes, the fact that the Court's jurisdiction derives from actual cases and its position on top of the federal court system still frames its institutional capacities in important ways. The Court, like the Canadian and Irish supreme courts, still has the basic structure of a common law appellate court, whose function is to hear appeals from cases in lower courts, mainly on questions of law.

Over and beyond the differences between civil and common law systems, both adhere, generally, to the underlying principle that a judge acts in a public capacity. He renders judgment based only on the legally admissible evidence, not on the basis of his private knowledge. That evidence forms a complete, written record, which can be reviewed on appeal and is subject to public scrutiny. The concept of public or official capacity was established well before Aquinas, who described the judge's role as *persona publica*,[8] and illustrated the principle with his argument that even in a trial of a capital offence, a judge should render a verdict only on the basis of legally admitted evidence, even if he is certain of the innocence of the accused from his private knowledge.[9] The principle that Aquinas defended, and that Roman lawyers had earlier developed, is now generally accepted in Western legal systems, though modulated by rules regarding recusal in cases where a judge cannot sufficiently insulate his public role from what he knows or suspects in his private capacity. That principle—in short, that a judge acts in a public capacity and renders judgment only on the basis of legally admitted evidence—gives structure to the forms and procedures of our legal systems and lies at the centre of our conception of a fair trial. That principle, moreover, entails that judicial reasoning is (to a very large extent) autonomous; it is purposefully insulated from—and impervious to—many truths that guide the reasoning of historians, moral philosophers, or legislators.[10]

When the context is shifted to judicial review of legislation, the cases discussed in chapters two and four demonstrate that the judge's public persona cannot be maintained with respect to finding legislative facts. All that a judge knows

[7] See 'Statistics' at ScotusBlog, available at www.scotusblog.com/statistics/.

[8] See *Summa Theologiae* II-II q. 40 a. 1 ad 1; q. 98 a. 4c.

[9] See J Finnis, *Aquinas: Moral, Political, and Legal Theory* (Oxford, Oxford University Press, 1998) 250. In such a case the judge should strive to obtain admissible, exculpatory evidence: ibid, n 158. Aquinas's position is in contrast to that of Lucas de Penna, who argued in the fourteenth century that a judge had but one conscience; he could not convict on the basis of conscience alone, but nor could he convict if he knew that the accused was innocent. See W Ullmann, *The Medieval Idea of Law As Represented by Lucas De Penna* (London, Routledge, 2010) 127–29.

[10] See J Finnis, 'Natural Law and Legal Reasoning' (1990) 38 *Cleveland State Law Review* 1.

(or thinks he knows), whether from Brandeis briefs, independent research conducted during a case, or from past reading, is relevant to empirical questions in a balancing test (as one court put it, 'the *actual* connection between the objective and what the law *will in fact* achieve' (emphasis added)).[11] There is no requirement for a complete and comprehensive record of legislative facts. That would be as difficult to compile as it would be for a judge to separate on-the-record legislative facts from his general knowledge of the world (recall Justice Blackmun's account of his two weeks in the Mayo Clinic archives, research that was 'personally and very privately performed').[12]

The general limitations on judicial reasoning identified in this section are not a defect. Western artists have, for good reason, chosen to represent Justice with a blindfold. Lord Bingham has well described this commonplace but important ideal of adjudication:

> All legal arbiters are bound to apply the law as they understand it to the facts of individual cases as they find them. They must do so without fear or favour, affection, or ill-will, that is, without partiality or prejudice. Justice is portrayed as blind not because she ignores the facts and circumstance of individual cases but because she shuts her eyes to all considerations extraneous to the particular case.[13]

The concept of law implicit in this ideal is a pre-existing, objective standard, rather than one devised in response to the specific circumstances of the case. Finnis has described the idea of judicial power as a way of relating the present case to a past decision:

> The judicial responsibility is to adjudicate between parties who are in dispute about their legal rights and obligations by applying—to facts agreed between them or found by the court after trial—the law that defined those rights and obligations at that time past when the matter of their dispute (the cause in action) arose. The court's judgment identifies and applies the legal commitments the community should be judged to *have made* to each of the parties now before the court, *by the time* they came into conflict with each other about the content or applicability of those commitments: past. The legislature's responsibility is to make new or amended public commitments about private rights (and public powers) for the future.[14]

In contrast to the artificial world of the trial, legislators must deal with the 'real world' or, in other words, everything that is the case. In their efforts to acquire factual knowledge, legislators are like historians or scientists in that they usually have no need to exclude evidence or to filter information through legal standards of proof. Legislators are responsible to make decisions based on current knowledge of the world, and to change laws that do not fit well with existing (and anticipated) states of affairs. To the extent that judges act as lawmakers, their field of vision

[11] *RJR-MacDonald, Inc v Canada* [1994] 1 SCR 311 [133].
[12] See ch 4, section II.
[13] *Locabail v Bayfield Properties* [2000] QB 451 [2].
[14] J Finnis, 'Judicial Power: Past, Present and Future', Lecture at Gray's Inn Hall, 20 October 2015, Oxford Legal Studies Research Paper No 2/2016 <http://dx.doi.org/10.2139/ssrn.2710880>.

and practical orientation resembles that of legislators in some ways, as evidenced by the practice of finding legislative facts considered in chapter four. The scope of their responsibility, however, is usually much narrower than a legislature's, and their ability to respond to changing conditions in society is far more limited. Such considerations led Hart to characterise the law-making power of courts as interstitial:

> It is important to note that the powers I ascribe to judges to regulate cases left partly unregulated by the law are different from those of the legislature: not only are the judge's powers subject to many constraints *narrowing his choice* from which a legislature might be quite free, but since the judge's powers are exercised only to dispose of particular instant cases he cannot use these to institute large-scale reforms or new codes. So his powers are *interstitial* as well as subject to many substantive constraints.[15]

In constitutional rights cases, the features of judging and judicial power identified by Bingham, Finnis, and Hart are inverted. The circumstances of the individual case are not exactly 'extraneous' to decisions about constitutional rights, but are far less important than the question of whether to strike down or uphold a statute, and the general consequences of that for society. That view of the consequences is forward-looking, an effort to make a better future, not an effort to align the present to a past decision. And there is nothing narrow and incremental about the methods of constitutional rights adjudication analysed in chapter two, and their consequences for the shape and content of the law.

II. The Basic Structure of Legislative Reasoning

The legislature, in contrast to the role of courts in ordinary cases, looks forward, anticipating future dangers and opportunities and prospectively considering whether changes in the law are needed for society to avoid harms and realise goods through co-ordinating in particular ways.[16] The possible courses of action available to a legislature are many and open-ended. Some accounts of the legislature, such as Dworkin's discussed in chapter three, depict it as responding to inputs (say, the preferences of constituents) or choosing among the salient options that have been presented to it. The first and distinctive work of the legislature, however, is to *determine what are* the salient options by means of open-ended investigation and inquiry, and creatively forming and deliberating on proposals. Whereas courts respond to claims initiated by others, the legislature acts on its own initiative. The legislature has the capacity to make new law on any subject and to amend or repeal any existing law, while the law-making capacity of courts extends at most to the particular legal issues raised by parties.

[15] *The Concept of Law*, 2nd edn, (Oxford, Oxford University Press, 1994) 'Postscript', 273.
[16] See R Ekins, *The Nature of Legislative Intent* (Oxford, Oxford University Press, 2012) 118–27.

We can define a legislature as a body that has standing authority to create law in canonical linguistic form—that is to say, statutory law—and the power to amend and change existing law.[17] In this book I use *legislature* to refer to the group of officials responsible for formulating, proposing, and enacting legislation, at whatever place they occupy in the political structure. This usage is broader than referring to a specific body such as the UK House of Commons or US House of Representatives. I assume, for the sake of simplicity, a unitary legislature, setting aside particular differences arising from bicameralism and federalism. In this unitary model[18] the legislature consists not only in elected representatives (and their draftsmen, researchers, and other agents), but also officials who are members of the executive (either by belonging to a separate branch or by having an 'executive' or ministerial role while also serving in the legislature). In the UK and other parliamentary systems, the Prime Minister and cabinet ministers often have the main responsibility for drafting, proposing, and overseeing the passage of legislation. The US President can, like some other separately elected heads of the executive branch, initiate legislation and shape its content, through the power to veto laws and other means. Moreover, the officials of regulatory agencies participate in law-making; in addition to implementing legislative decisions through detailed rule-making, they may influence the content of primary legislation or serve as a repository of information for legislators. My focus in this chapter, however, is on primary rather than delegated legislation.

I assume that the members of the legislature are elected representatives, as is largely true in Western legal systems—though not for administrative lawmakers and certain bodies such as the UK House of Lords. The democratic character of the legislature, however, is not central to my comparative analysis of institutional capacities. There is a tendency in the literature on judicial review and separation of powers to characterise the legislature as an institution whose chief, or only, virtue is its ability to ascertain and act on the will of the people. Dworkin and other theorists rely on the majoritarian character of the legislature to disparage its ability to act as a forum of principle (see chapter three, section II). Jeremy Waldron has turned this argument around, offering a powerful defence of legislatures and critique of judicial review as a violation of democracy and the fundamental right of people to participate in law-making.[19] His defence of the legislature and its deliberative powers focuses primarily on its democratic or majoritarian character.

[17] ibid.

[18] The sense of 'unitary' above is different from the sense in which Waldron criticises unitary models of the legislature in *Law and Disagreement* (Oxford, Oxford University Press, 1999) at 42–45. Waldron argues that the legislature should not be conceived as having intentions like an individual person: ibid. For an opposing view see Ekins, *Legislative Intent*, above n 16, Ch 3. This is an important question for understanding the nature of legislative action, but it can be set to one side for purposes of my argument.

[19] Waldron, *Law and Disagreement*, above n 18, Ch 11.

My critique of judicial review is not, like Waldron's, based on the claim that it is undemocratic, and relies only incidentally on the representative nature of legislatures. In section V below, I push back against depictions of the legislature as being in its essence a *majoritarian* institution. While certain aspects of the discussion below connect legislative capacities to democratic representation, many of the capacities I describe would hold true for an aristocratic or non-elected legislature. There are several important deliberative structures and institutional features of the modern legislature that do not depend on being democratic. These include the following capacities: (i) to acquire and evaluate factual information about society as a whole and about technological and scientific matters relevant to legislation; (ii) to take a general and prospective view of society and relate a variety of problems and opportunities to the inter-connected areas of law that affect them; (iii) to bring together a variety of perspectives from individuals with expertise and abilities in different areas; (iv) to deliberate freely about the common good and the actions and standards of conduct needed to achieve it; (v) to alter more than one legal norm at a time; and, perhaps most importantly, (vi) to amend or repeal existing legal rules, freely and openly through regular procedures, in response to changing societal conditions and goals. My account of comparative institutional capacities emphasises these capacities of a legislature.

III. Capacity for Empirical Reasoning

This section focuses on the legislature's capacity for empirical reasoning, which can be compared to the judicial capacity for this that was analysed in chapter four. Today's legislature needs a wide range of information to identify areas where the law needs to be changed, to form intelligent proposals for legislation and evaluate them, and to anticipate the effects of proposed legislation. Its first source of information is its members' own stock of experience, knowledge, and memory. A legislature typically has hundreds of members with experience in various professions and types of government service, and they have a variety of educational backgrounds and personal knowledge of the regions they represent. This diversity of background and expertise provides the legislature with collective knowledge not possessed by a collegial court, much less a lone judge. Although justices of constitutional and supreme courts are highly educated, they are almost all trained as lawyers and are typically drawn from a small set of elite schools and institutions.

My argument proceeds on the intuitive claim that deliberation about questions of political morality is capable of reaching more sound decisions when it includes voices of people with different kinds of knowledge and expertise, and less capable when important areas of social or economic life are excluded from its view or not understood.[20] This is similar to Aristotle's notion of the 'wisdom of the multitude':

> For each individual among the many has a share of excellence and practical wisdom, and when they meet together, just as they become in a manner one man, who has many feet, and hands, and senses, so too with regard to their character and thought. Hence the many are better judges than a single man of music and poetry; for some understand one part, and some another, and among them they understand the whole.[21]

Applying Aristotle's ideal to the legislature, Waldron argues that its diversity of experience provides 'a basis for reciprocal questioning and criticism and enabling a view to emerge which is better than any of the inputs and much more than a mere aggregation or function of those inputs'.[22] The legislature's deliberations are enhanced by having members with first-hand knowledge of law, medicine, science, and business. Legislative reasoning would be diminished if legislators were all lawyers, all doctors, all scientists, or all business managers.

In addition to their background knowledge, legislators acquire policy expertise in particular areas, often serving on committees that build the knowledge base of the legislature in particular areas. Adrian Vermeule has noted that in the US Congress, 'The seniority norm and the proliferation of subcommittees imply that a member of the modern House of Representatives spends many years becoming deeply expert in a narrow slice of public policy.'[23] In legislatures with a different structure and committee system, a similar result will often be achieved through other paths. It would be impossible for every member to master the details on the various Bills proposed in a legislative session, but Aristotle's ideal of group wisdom—that 'some understand one part, and some another, and among them they understand the whole'—is something a legislature can reasonably strive to attain. When representatives defer to those with greater expertise in a given area, the average competence of the legislature increases.[24]

Diversity of education and professional expertise is generally found in democratic legislatures, but mainly because of their size rather than their democratic character. Electoral systems are usually designed to provide for representation by regions or for proportional representation of political parties. They do not aim intentionally to produce diversity of professional or educational background. But in a large body some degree of diversity is a likely side effect.[25] Although the UK

[20] For an argument on how diversity improves political decision-making see T Gyofi, *Against the New Constitutionalism* (Cheltenham, Edward Elgar, 2016) 108–20.

[21] Aristotle, *Politics*, S Everson (ed) (Cambridge, Cambridge University Press, 1996), Book III: 1281a43-b9. For discussion see Waldron, *Law and Disagreement*, above n 18, 82, 85 136–37; J Waldron, *The Dignity of Legislation* (Cambridge, Cambridge University Press, 1999), Ch 5.

[22] *Dignity of Legislation* 106.

[23] A Vermeule, *Law and the Limits of Reason* (Cambridge, Mass, Harvard University Press, 2008) 85 (citing K Krehbiel, *Information and Legislative Organization* (Ann Arbor, Michigan University Press, 1991)).

[24] See Gyofi, *Against the New Constitutionalism*, above n 20, 107.

[25] Lawyers are often over-represented in democratic legislatures, at least in terms of percentage of population. From 1960 to 2004, 45% of US representatives (House and Senate) were lawyers; 13.6%

House of Lords is a non-elected and now mostly appointed institution, it is more diverse with regard to professional background and life experience than the House of Commons.

Elections and representation also matter in another way for empirical reasoning. As Vermeule observes, 'legislators are connected to constituents and thus have better information about the factual components and causal consequences' of decisions than judges; the demands of re-election 'force legislators to leave the halls of government, to travel the land, and to meet constituents, including, now and again, ordinary people. Judges need never leave the cloister, or at least the bubble of professional prestige that surrounds them'.[26] The greater information of legislatures comes at a cost: 'the need to secure re-election can cause distortion of legislators' true views'.[27] The absence of such demands on judges can make them more impartial, but this also has a cost: 'a relative dearth of facts and tacit knowledge'.[28]

Vermeule argues that the trade-off between information and bias ultimately favours the legislature, because biases among legislators are at the individual level where they tend to cancel out in a large, politically diverse group.[29] Judges, Vermeule says, have correlated biases arising from their common background and educational training.[30] On at least some collegial appellate courts, however, biases of judges could also cancel out due to their having different political opinions and to previous participation in political parties. In my view, constituent representation and the electoral process contribute to the legislature's capacity for empirical reasoning, but that contribution is relatively less important than in Vermeule's account. Of at least equal importance are the ways citizens present views and facts to legislators that are not necessarily tied to re-election or representation: through writing letters, working in pressure groups, and expressing views in formal and informal media (such as blogs and social media). Engaging with citizen activity of this kind could give the non-elected, non-representative House of Lords access to factual aspects of a decision that in many contexts would approximate that of the Commons. It is true, however, that elected MPs have more incentive to pay attention to this source of information.

In addition to the sources of information above, legislators rely on knowledge supplied by researchers and experts of various kinds. This will be more important

had a background in business; 2.2% had worked in health care, half of those as physicians; this was a decline from Congress's first century, when about 5% of representatives were physicians. In 2004 there were eight physicians in Congress. C Kraus and T Suarez, 'Is There a Doctor in the House? … Or the Senate?' (2004) 292 *Journal of the American Medical Association* 2125. From 1960 to 2004, representation by occupation, in declining order, was as follows: attorney, business, public service, education (all levels), military, media/entertainment, agriculture, banking and insurance, other/miscellaneous, health care (nonphysician), physician, law enforcement, minister/clergy: ibid, 2126.

[26] Vermeule, *Law and the Limits of Reason*, above n 23, 86.
[27] ibid.
[28] ibid.
[29] ibid 87.
[30] ibid.

in many contexts than background knowledge or facts learned from constituents. Lawmakers need specialised information on myriad topics: technology and applied science; rates of poverty and employment and other demographic data; levels of debt, lending practices, and bank reserves; the efficacy and safety of pharmaceuticals and many other concerns of public health; environmental issues, etc. In recent decades there has been an explosion in information and empirical research, and the internet has reduced the transactions costs of acquiring it. Information is often supplied by universities, non-governmental organisations and think-tanks at no cost to the legislature. Legislators are capable of obtaining information, but they also need assistance: to sift mountains of data, to understand statistical methods used in reporting, to discard faulty research, and generally to judge the reliability of information and its sources. Experts disagree. Indeed, disagreement among experts and researchers is pervasive in most areas relevant to law-making and policy-making.

Social science is an important but fragile foundation for law-making. (Here I use 'social science' broadly to indicate economics, sociology, psychology, criminology, and related fields such as medical research.) It can reveal patterns of interaction of people with each other and their environment; it can identify probabilities of certain events; and sometimes it can point toward the discovery of causal relationships. What is the correlation between raising the speed limit by 10 miles per hour and the number of traffic fatalities? Legislatures need information on many questions like this. Proving actual causation with certainty is another matter, however. Traffic fatalities are caused by many inter-related factors, some of which are likely to change over the course of a single decade: size and weight of vehicles; safety features; road conditions and signage; driver habits and training; and propensity to drive while intoxicated or using mobile phones, etc. Speed limits play their part, but the difficulty of isolating and arguing for the likely causes of traffic fatalities—much less *proving* those causes—is indicative of the general challenge facing researchers.

Lasting and certain conclusions lie largely outside the grasp of social science. Alasdair MacIntyre argues that social science cannot provide 'law-like generalizations' because of the systematic unpredictability of human affairs. We cannot anticipate certain events that seem to be pure contingencies (eg Napoleon catching a cold before Waterloo) and their further consequences,[31] and we cannot predict radical conceptual innovations such as the invention of the wheel or a new mathematical theorem.[32] Consider the economist at the beginning of the twentieth century attempting to predict the future economy without knowledge of the silicon semiconductor. Even at its most certain, social science has temporal limitations. A finding made today, even if replicated, may not be relevant or accurate for the human situation decades from now, or even a few years from now.

[31] A MacIntyre, *After Virtue*, 2nd edn (Duckworth, London, 1985) 100.
[32] ibid 93.

Reading the original Brandeis brief, which quotes reports of researchers reflecting perceptions of the role of women in society in the early twentieth century,[33] is sufficient to show the fragility of social science. Today's Supreme Court would almost certainly strike down the law upheld in *Muller v Oregon* (1908),[34] given its gender-based distinction on permissible work hours.

Social scientists often direct their research toward what they perceive as problems in social life, and what they perceive as problems depends on their moral and political philosophy, even if inchoate or unarticulated or unconsciously held.[35] Daniel Patrick Moynihan, who was a Harvard sociologist before becoming a senator (as a Democrat representing New York), observes that the political orientation of the social sciences is evident in the shifting fashions in research topics.[36] Trade unions, for example, were heavily researched from 1910 to 1950 but later neglected, Moynihan contends, for political reasons: community organisations funded by government and anti-poverty efforts became more favoured subjects.[37] It is not improper for social science—and the researchers themselves—to be motivated or influenced by moral concerns or political considerations. One should, rather, assume that they often are. Neither law-makers engaging with social science nor judges reading Brandeis briefs should, therefore, presume that studies are unaffected by researchers' views on questions of political morality.

In addition to the temporal limitations of social science and possible bias, there is the problem of understanding statistical methods. In chapter four, section V, I considered persistent judicial misunderstandings surrounding 'statistical significance' and related concepts, and the disagreement among statisticians about proper methods for research and reporting data. While judges lack competence for understanding social science, as I have argued, the same will be true for many individual legislators. Some legislators have a background in fields such as medicine or engineering, but even they need help in navigating the statistical minefield.

It is at this crucial juncture of the *interface* between law-makers and researchers that the institutional differences between courts and legislatures are perhaps most pronounced. Courts are largely *passive* recipients of empirical research, which is usually presented by advocates in Brandeis briefs in an adversarial setting designed not for discovering general empirical knowledge about society but for resolving legal disputes between parties and finding the particular facts relevant to that dispute. The exception to this passive reception is when judges conduct their own independent empirical research—a deficient procedure. Legislatures, in contrast, can actively engage with both researchers and intermediates who help to interpret data and statistical methods. Legislatures can hold hearings, examine experts

[33] See A Baron, 'Protective Labor Legislation and the Cult of Domesticity' (1981) 2 *Journal of Family Issues* 25.

[34] *Muller v Oregon* 208 US 412 (1908).

[35] See J Haidt, *The Righteous Mind: Why Good People are Divided by Politics and Religion* (London, Allen Lane, 2012).

[36] DP Moynihan, 'Social Science and the Courts' (1979) 54 *Public Interest* 12, 20.

[37] ibid.

and other witnesses, and commission various sorts of research, investigations and inquiries. Some legislatures, such as the US Congress, assign responsibility to study particular areas to committees, which interact with and provide a degree of oversight to a corresponding executive department. In a Westminster-style Parliament such responsibilities are controlled more directly and extensively by Cabinet ministers, though legislative committees may have important responsibilities as well. In both systems legislators acquire and assess empirical research on a daily basis and gain a level of proficiency superior to that of judges, who handle empirical research on a more occasional basis and in a more detached manner.

The US Congress has three in-house research bodies: the Congressional Budget Office, which provides economic analysis; the Government Accountability Office, which was started to review financial accounting but now also conducts general investigations and in-depth evaluations of government programmes; and the Congressional Research Service (CRS), which provides general research and investigatory services.[38] Together they have about 4,000 employees.[39] The CRS annually responds to about 60,000 specific requests for information from Congress and prepares over 1,000 new full-length reports, on topics ranging from terrorism and national security to water resources.[40] The staff of 600 at the CRS includes reference librarians, economists, lawyers, and social, natural and physical scientists; and its annual budget is about $100 million.[41] In the UK and other parliamentary systems, where government ministries, under a Cabinet minister, have the primary responsibility for drafting and proposing legislation, the fact-finding resources for law-making tend to be concentrated in executive bodies rather than in institutions attached to the legislature such as the CRS. Independent statutory bodies also play a role, such as the UK Statistics Authority, which monitors all official statistics in the UK and provides independent assessment of them, and also oversees its executive arm, the Office for National Statistics. In both presidential and parliamentary systems there is considerable overlap of responsibility for law-making between the 'legislative' and 'executive' branches, particularly in areas that concern technological and scientific information. In both systems the legislature often sets general standards and delegates responsibility for detailed rule-making to executive agencies, which develop their own resources for investigation and building a knowledge base. In Germany, for example, the administration is advised by around 300 permanent scientific advisory councils, and there are about 50 scientific institutes under the auspices of executive departments.[42] The administration receives further advice from para-state institutes such as those in the Max Planck network and the Berlin Science Center.[43]

[38] See I Brudnik, 'The Congressional Research Service and the American Legislative Process' (2008) Congressional Research Service.

[39] ibid.

[40] See Annual Report, Fiscal Year 2015, of the US Congressional Research Service.

[41] ibid.

[42] K von Beyme, *The Legislator: German Parliament as a Centre of Political Decision-making* (Aldershot, Ashgate, 1998) 23.

[43] ibid.

Such institutional structures can, of course, exhibit various forms of incompetence, bias toward the status quo, or corruption. The point of this discussion is not to idealise committees, ministries, or legislative procedure, but to draw a broad sketch of the information-gathering capacities of legislatures, which contrasts with the meagre capacities of courts discussed in chapter four. The key, in keeping with the focus of the book on constitutional design, is *institutional capacity*, not such matters as the specific amount of funding available for research services. Not all legislatures will have—or need—the level of resources of the CRS or other bodies that provide the US Congress with information. But legislatures have the basic capacity to acquire and assess information through the various means discussed above, and to develop those means into structures with appropriate resources. This is a normal outgrowth of their day-to-day activities, and it fits with their future-oriented perspective and their function of having standing authority to change the law on any subject.

It is possible to improve the capacity of courts to investigate legislative facts, and in chapter seven I will consider a proposal for this put forth by Kenneth Davis to add a research service to the US Supreme Court on the model of the CRS. I will argue, however, that such proposals would generally fit better with the Kelsenian model of a constitutional court standing outside the normal system of courts. I will also discuss the German Federal Constitutional Court as an example of a Kelsenian court that has a capacity for active engagement with empirical research, which in certain limited respects resembles the legislative capacities discussed above.

IV. Capacity for Moral Reasoning

In this section I compare the institutional capacities of courts and legislatures to engage in moral reasoning. As this is a vast subject,[44] my discussion focuses on the arguments usually offered in defence of rights-based judicial review. These arguments rarely stress the personal acumen of judges for ethical theory, or the general quality of the reasoning expressed in judicial opinions on moral issues. This should not be surprising, since the educational background and training of judges typically focuses on technical legal learning and reasoning, with no specific component for moral reasoning. No one thinks that lawyers are inherently moral experts, or that they become such by donning a black robe.

Many arguments amount to variations of Dworkin's distinction between principle and policy and his argument that courts are the forum of principle (and hence the forum of rights: see chapter three, section I). These arguments preserve

[44] Several topics within that subject are explored in depth in G Webber, P Yowell et al, *Legislated Rights: Securing Human Rights Through Legislation* (Cambridge, Cambridge University Press, forthcoming).

a sphere for democratic decision-making but cast it as deficient for areas that come within constitutional rights. In Dworkin's summing up, judicial review 'insures that the most fundamental issues of political morality will be finally set out and debated as issues of principle and not political power alone'.[45]

Before proceeding, we should recall the scope of constitutional rights jurisdiction discussed in chapter two. It is not confined to a few of the most fundamental issues. Because of the nature of balancing and proportionality tests along with the conception of prima facie rights they assume, that jurisdiction is almost unlimited. In recent decades, cases on constitutional rights in recent decades have addressed, among many other issues: assisted suicide and euthanasia; abortion; adoption by same-sex couples or by single parents; surrogacy; polygamy; prostitution; pornography; possession of guns; religious education and prayer in schools; single-sex schools; the wearing of headscarves and other religious dress in schools and other public settings; public display of religious symbols; regulation of campaign finance and political advertisement; speech that disparages someone on account of race, sex, or sexual orientation; and affirmative action programmes designed to give advantage based on race or other personal characteristics. Formerly constitutional rights cases dealt also with issues such as slavery, racial segregation, eugenics, and the free expression and political rights of Communists and others belonging to parties considered subversive.

The reasons given for considering courts to have greater capacities to decide such issues usually come down to two related points. First, deliberation and decision-making in the legislature is said to be motivated at a basic level by the interests and will of the electorate; further, it is liable to corruption because of the possibility of legislators' personal self-interest, arbitrary partisan interest, or prejudice against minorities. Second, judicial reasoning is claimed to be reason-based, and thus, at a basic level, rational in a way that legislative reasoning is not.[46] Whereas legislators must concern themselves with political expediency, judges 'can afford to take the long view that moral insight demands'.[47] A contrast is often drawn between the rancorous debate of legislatures and the calm, serene atmosphere of collegial courts, where judges proceed through arguments in an orderly and measured fashion. Many point to the requirement that judges give reasons to justify decisions as a basis to prefer their moral judgment over legislatures.

The contrast between interest-based legislative reasoning and reason-based judicial reasoning is held to be at its strongest when the interests of minorities are at stake. Dworkin argues:

> Legislators who have been elected, and must be reelected, by a political majority are more likely to take that majority's side in any serious argument about the rights of the minority against it; if they oppose the majority's wishes too firmly, it will replace them with those

[45] R Dworkin, *A Matter of Principle* (Cambridge, Mass, Harvard University Press, 1985) 70.

[46] For a critique of this view, see R Ekins, 'Legislation as Reasoned Action' in *Legislated Rights*, above n 44.

[47] M Moore, 'Moral Reality Revisited' (1992) 90 *Michigan Law Review* 2424, 2477.

> who do not. For that reason legislators seem less likely to reach sound decisions about minority rights than officials who are less vulnerable in that way.[48]

Hence judicial review is justified as a counter-majoritarian institution, a modern version of the argument of Madison and Tocqueville about the tyranny of the majority. For some critics of legislatures, the scepticism regarding their capacity to reason morally extends beyond the counter-majoritarian situations. Ronald den Otter, for example, writes:

> [T]he most honest rationale for the practice of judicial review is rooted in pessimism about the likelihood that ordinary citizens or their elected representatives could decide important cases competently … In the end judicial supremacy turns out to be the lesser of two evils: it is a safer bet in an imperfect world where the vast majority of citizens are either incapable of making informed, reflective decisions on basic questions of public morality or unwilling to make the effort to do so.[49]

Even a judicial review sceptic such as Robert Nagel writes:

> Legislators do not always know or articulate moral objectives before enacting programs and frequently rationalize them to their constituents only afterwards … They respond to wildly irrational arguments and even to power unadorned by intellectual argumentation … Compared to the detached, careful evaluation of briefs and evidence in light of an explicit, consistent set of legal values that is the ideal of the judicial process, the legislative process is a nightmare of irrational decision making.[50]

These arguments are exaggerated in two directions. They are unduly critical of the legislature and overly optimistic about the capacity of courts to engage in reasoned deliberation about moral issues. My argument proceeds as follows. In sections IV.A and IV.B, I make some general proposals regarding the proper role of morality in legislative decision-making. My argument is compatible with many different views on moral and political philosophy, as well as differing conclusions about particular issues. I assume that moral truth exists in the sense that right answers are both possible and available regarding the (im)permissibility or otherwise of activities such as those listed above, as well as on the distinct question of whether moral judgment on such issues should be reflected in law.[51] The term, 'question of political morality', which I have used previously, is meant to capture both of these distinct questions. This account of the role of moral reasoning in legislative deliberation is a prelude to analysis of judicial capacity for moral reasoning, which I take up in section IV.C. In section V, I will argue that it is a misconception of legislatures to see their characteristic function or purpose as enacting the will of

[48] R Dworkin, *Law's Empire* (Cambridge, Mass, Harvard University Press, 1986) 375.

[49] R Den Otter, *Judicial Review in an Age of Moral Pluralism* (Cambridge, Cambridge University Press, 2012) 19.

[50] R Nagel, *Constitutional Cultures: The Mentality and Consequences of Judicial Review* (Berkeley, University of California Press, 1989) 119.

[51] I assume moral objectivity without offering a refutation of scepticism, because readers are unlikely to be interested in a comparison of legislative and judicial capacities to engage in moral reasoning unless they think right answers on these questions are available.

the majority or aggregating citizen preferences. In section VI, I will consider the arguments regarding the capacity to protect minority rights, and contend that in certain key historical contexts legislatures have performed better than courts.

A. Utilitarianism

We have seen in chapter three that Dworkin associates legislative reasoning broadly with utilitarianism, and specifically with making a calculation about overall utilitarian preferences. The association has an historical basis, since Bentham and other nineteenth century legal reformers advocated both social reform based on utilitarian principles and legislation as the vehicle for achieving it. That was during the period when statutes were replacing common law on a wide basis.[52] The attraction to utilitarianism remained strong in the first half of the twentieth century. In 1903 the following claim, from the pages of the *Harvard Law Review*, was fairly unremarkable:

> The law is utilitarian. It exists for the realization of the reasonable needs of the community. If the interest of an individual runs counter to the chief object of the law, it must be sacrificed.[53]

Even in 1951 we find Roscoe Pound saying:

> [W]e come to an idea of a maximum satisfaction of human wants or expectations. What we have to do in social control, and so in law, is to reconcile and adjust these desires or wants or expectations, so far as we can, so as to secure as much of the totality of them as we can.[54]

Pound's approach has been eclipsed by the ascendancy of human rights discourse in recent decades. The prevalence of utilitarianism among moral philosophers is now much diminished, in part due to Rawls's argument that it fails to take account of the importance of individuals. While utilitarianism retains a certain allure and a place in popular political discourse, there is no reason to suppose that legislatures are more prone to it than courts. Indeed, as we have seen in chapter two, the conception of prima facie rights assumed in balancing and proportionality tests has a partially utilitarian character. The operation of those tests is consistent with Mills's idea that an individual right is protected only up to the point that 'social expediency' requires it to be overridden (see chapter two, section V).

While I think there is a danger that balancing and proportionality tests could operate in a utilitarian manner, I do not think this is a necessary tendency. We can also conceive of balancing in a non-technical sense, referring to practical deliberation that involves conflicting considerations and reasons of varying strength, and that recognises that there are trade-offs between different values and factors

[52] See T Campbell, *The Legal Theory of Ethical Positivism* (New York, Routledge, 1996) 4–5.
[53] JB Ames, 'Law and Morals' (1908) 22 *Harvard Law Review* 97, 110.
[54] R Pound, *Justice According to Law* (New Haven, Yale University Press, 1951) 31.

relevant to a decision. In this loose sense many of our everyday decisions, and most legislative decisions, involve 'balancing'. In chapter two, section VII I have argued that courts tend to treat balancing tests in this loose, non-technical manner.

B. Value Incommensurability and the Common Good

My argument proceeds by assuming:[55] (i) that the legislature should seek to protect and promote the common good; and (ii) that the common good consists not in an aggregative notion such as overall utility or maximum preference-satisfaction, but in the realisation of multiple basic human values or goods. More specifically, the common good is a set of conditions that enable each and every member of the community to realise his or her well-being (consisting in multiple goods or values), in community with others, and in particular with regard to those subjects that concern personal interaction and co-operation. Instruments such as the Universal Declaration of Human Rights point to a range of basic human goods (as well as instrumental ones, such as fair procedure), and I have argued elsewhere that the UDHR can and should be considered as a guide to legislative deliberation and action.[56]

The assumptions in the last paragraph about value incommensurability and the legislature's responsibility to promote human good are embraced by a range of approaches to political morality, including Joseph Raz's liberal perfectionism;[57] Martha Nussbaum's capability-based theory of justice;[58] and John Finnis's natural law theory.[59] Value incommensurability entails a rejection of the approach in classical utilitarianism that reduces all value to utility (the net of pleasure over pain), or, in modern variations, to preference-satisfaction, happiness, or—in Posner's normative economic analysis—efficiency or wealth. Proponents of these approaches hold that the value that inheres in our choices is commensurable, that is, calculable in terms of one scale tracking a single value. Proponents of value incommensurability recognise that in much of our practical decision-making more than one basic value is at stake.

Value incommensurability thus supports the rejection of utilitarianism as well as its quantitative version of balancing (compare chapter two, section VII on the formulaic accounts of balancing and proportionality tests). Value incommensurability also helps to show the complexity of legislative deliberation and choice.

[55] For a general defence of incommensurability and application of it to the context of constitutional rights, see F Urbina, *A Critique of Proportionality and Balancing* (Cambridge, Cambridge University Press, 2017) 39–74.

[56] P Yowell, 'From Universal Rights to Legislated Rights' in *Legislated Rights*, above n 44.

[57] J Raz, *The Morality of Freedom* (Oxford, Oxford University Press, 1988).

[58] M Nussbaum, *Sex and Social Justice* (Oxford, Oxford University Press, 1999) 41–42; *The Fragility of Goodness: Luck and Ethics in Greek Tragedy and Philosophy* (Cambridge, Cambridge University Press, revised edn 2001). See also T Nagel, 'The Fragmentation of Value' in *Mortal Questions* (Cambridge, Cambridge University Press, 1979).

[59] J Finnis, *Natural Law and Natural Rights*, 2nd edn (Oxford, Oxford University Press, 2011).

Both Raz and Finnis argue that, given the incommensurable values at stake in legislative choice, it is often rationally under-determined.[60] A legislator, as Finnis states, might have, in some contexts, a 'luxuriant variety of appropriate but competing choices of "means" to "end"'.[61] The legislator's responsibility is not to choose the 'best' law—which may not exist—but to make a choice within the range of reasonable options. Even with regard to prohibiting acts that violate a basic, universal moral norm, Raz points out that the form and content of legal rules 'may rightly vary from place to place and time to time'.[62] As Finnis notes, laws can only rarely be deduced from principle, but many principles require 'due practical acknowledgement in every legislative act'.[63] A legislator must

> … hold in mind the good of autonomous and authentic choice, the evil of hypocrisy, bribery, blackmail, and police corruption, the costliness and scarcity of investigative and prosecutorial resources, the clumsiness of the legal process in analysing and resolving human character and relationships, the dignity of helping others to identify and choose consistently for the worthwhile amongst peddlers of decay, the importance of compulsion to education, the elusiveness of consensus in a pluralistic society, the fragility of allegiance in a society seeming to honour none but formal principles … .[64]

If constitutional framers choose to give judges the power of rights-based judicial review, it must be with a realisation of the complexity of legislative choice, and with an expectation that vaguely formulated rights are likely to lead to broad methods of rights adjudication, including balancing and proportionality tests. If they adopt an enforceable bill of rights, then the reasoning of courts in judicial review should be presumed to be rightly open to the same kinds of moral and empirical reasoning as legislatures, and to embrace its full complexity. The question of what level of *deference* courts should show to legislative judgment is distinct, and will be taken up in chapter seven.

C. Comparing Judicial and Legislative Capacity for Moral Reasoning

The focus of this section is on the capacity of an institution to *deliberate* collectively regarding the important moral issues in constitutional rights cases. Innumerable factors are relevant to whether judges and legislators make correct decisions on moral issues, many involving personal, inward qualities that elude examination from the outside. My argument proceeds on the premise that open-ended, frank deliberation about moral issues generally enhances the ability of a group to make correct decisions. One reason is that it encourages positions to be tested, allowing

[60] See Raz, *Morality of Freedom*, above n 57, 388 ('Choice between incommensurables is undetermined by reason'); Finnis, *Natural Law and Natural Rights*, above n 59, 93, 100, 111–25.

[61] ibid 290.

[62] Raz, *Morality of Freedom* 340.

[63] J Finnis, 'Human Rights and Their Enforcement' in *Human Rights and Common Good: Collected Essays, Volume III* (Oxford, Oxford University Press, 2011).

[64] ibid.

flawed arguments and inconsistencies to be exposed. A second reason arises from the complexity of issues in legislation discussed above. The observations in section III about the wisdom of the multitude are relevant here. It is unlikely that any one individual will be able to see all the moral dimensions of an issue, or to anticipate all the ramifications of a decision to adopt a law—or not to adopt it, or to strike it down. Group deliberation helps us to understand more of the consequences and to see the full picture. A full view sees questions of political morality not in isolation but in relation to questions of fact and to questions about how to implement decisions in the language of law and to make them consistent with existing features of the legal landscape.

The deliberation of legislatures is time-limited and oriented toward practical decision-making regarding whether to change the law. It is presumed that not all legislators will agree either with the premises of a proposed law or its content; thus deliberation will be concluded by voting. So far as can be accommodated within time limits, any legislator may argue for or against a proposal or for amendment, aiming to persuade colleagues. Deliberation is valuable not only because of the possibility of persuading someone to adopt a better view in the present time, but also because the record of it can inform future legislators and other participants in and observers of the political process.

In the democratic legislature deliberation is also valuable because it provides for the many views of citizens to be represented. It is conducive to civic harmony and peace for citizens to know that even if their position has lost, it has been presented in the legislature; and that the legislature remains a forum open for proposals to change the law (see chapter six, section I on legal change). This specifically *democratic* value might contribute to the moral correctness of a decision, but it might also stand in its way (see sections V and VI below). It is, at any rate, a value that is mostly distinct from the present discussion on comparative institutional capacities. A non-elected legislature such as the House of Lords has deliberative capacities similar to those of an elected legislature.

It might be thought that judicial deliberations are not burdened by the kind of practical constraints that legislatures face, and are thus freer to focus on the truth of moral questions in a disinterested fashion. This is in fact true only with respect to the specifically democratic constraint regarding the need to seek re-election, which is only one part of a larger question of political pressure. Judges may not need to seek re-election, but they seek external affirmation. The sources of affirmation are wide, and judges will vary in what they seek. Some will care about how decisions are reported in mass media or highbrow publications;[65] or about the expectations of the politicians who appoint them; or about the approval of legal scholars and criticism in academic journals; or their historical legacy. Perhaps most will care about how fellow members of the elite class of politicians, administrators and educators treat them personally, for judges are social creatures too,

[65] See C Lim, 'Media Influence on Courts: Evidence from Civil Case Adjudication' (2015) 17 *American Law and Economics Review* 87.

who attend cocktail parties and receive dinner invitations. It would be shallow to say such pressures are generally decisive but naïve to ignore them, especially considering the substantial evidence that judicial outcomes in some cases can be predicted by judges' policy preferences.[66] Judges no doubt care directly about the truth of their moral decisions and their potential to change and improve society; but even when they think in this mode, they are not relying on the authority of past legal decisions—the authority that ultimately grounds their legitimate power.

The less that judges are constrained by specific legal sources in their decision-making, the more they are exposed to external pressure.[67] Given the vague and abstract formulations of legal rights, and the tendency of proportionality and balancing tests to focus on overall questions of reasonableness, judges in important constitutional rights cases face public—and indeed political—pressure. This means that the counter-majoritarian question can cut two ways. On the one hand, judges do not have to face the particular kind of pressure of a re-election campaign if they make an unpopular decision regarding, say, a moral issue or a minority interest. On the other hand, when judges make unpopular decisions in the course of applying a vague right or a balancing test, they are more exposed to other kinds of external pressure than they would be if they could attribute their decision squarely to a specific legal text. This is why Justice Black opposed balancing tests, as we saw in chapter two, section III; the interests of minorities can be easily outweighed in a balancing test that pits those interests against the general welfare. Whether or not judges follow the election returns, they anticipate public criticism and often seek to avoid or minimise it.

One instance of this is *Brown v Board of Education* (1954), which, contrary to popular perception, contains very little in the way of overt moral reasoning about the vital issues of racial equality and segregation. Indeed it formally accepts and applies *Plessy v Ferguson* (1896), which established the 'separate but equal' principle. We know from records and correspondence revealed later that some of the justices opposed any segregation on moral grounds and would have liked to overrule *Plessy*.[68] Anticipating a backlash, however, they sought to make a minimal ruling that could command unanimous assent and reduce public controversy.[69] The result was the thin decision discussed in chapter three, section III, which held, as a matter of *fact* rather than moral principle, that segregation disadvantaged black children, on the basis of social science findings.

The point is not that such compromise is wrong, but rather that it calls into question the dichotomy that some have proposed between the interest-based deliberation of legislatures and the reason-based deliberation of courts. It may be objected that courts, nonetheless, are structured around a disciplined practice

[66] J Segal and H Spaeth, *The Supreme Court and the Attitudinal Model Revisited* (Cambridge, Cambridge University Press, 2002).

[67] See Urbina, *A Critique of Proportionality*, above n 55, 179–80.

[68] S Ellmann, 'The Rule of Law and the Achievement of Unanimity in *Brown*' (2004) 49 *New York Law School Law Review* 741.

[69] ibid.

lacking in legislatures, namely that of providing a reasoned basis for their conclusions. This depends on a mistake regarding legislative practice. Legislatures do give reasons for proposed bills and are expected to do so. The reasons come in several forms, including white papers produced by government ministries, committee reports, or preambles to legislation. Most importantly, for purposes of comparison, are legislative debates on bills, where proponents of legislation are called on to give reasons for it and expected to answer arguments of the opposition. It could be objected that the reasons for legislation given in debate are not always sincere. It is true that we usually do not know the full backstory of how a bill came to be proposed, what deals and compromises were made on the way to bringing it to the floor for debate, whether the process has been tainted by corruption, and what truly motivates the representative speaking in a debate.

But by the same token, we usually do not know the backstory on how a constitutional decision comes to be made. There is no reason to assume that a judgment in a constitutional case is a complete and sincere disclosure of the reasoning by which the conclusion was reached. As Justice Frankfurter has said:

> The compromises that an opinion may embody, the collaborative effort that it may represent, the inarticulate considerations that may have influenced the grounds on which the case went off, the shifts in position that may precede final adjudication—these and like factors cannot, contemporaneously at all events, be brought to the surface.[70]

Most judicial deliberation is confidential, and we have limited access at best to records of discussions between justices, or between justices and their law clerks. Richard Posner has said,

> The difficulty outsiders have in understanding judicial behavior is due partly to the fact that judges deliberate in secret, though it would be more accurate to say that the fact that they do not deliberate (by which I mean deliberate *collectively*) very much is the real secret. Judicial deliberation is overrated.

Posner notes, however, that this is a 'pretty open' secret, citing the comments of a federal court of appeal judge who initially 'imagined that conferences [on cases] would be reflective, refining, analytical, dynamic' but discovered that they ordinarily consist in brief discussions that change few minds.[71] Despite the lack of direct access to deliberations, some political scientists have compiled substantial evidence of strategic decision-making by the US Supreme Court; this includes both: (1) the inward strategy of justices anticipating the positions of other justices, and decisions of the Chief Justice in setting the agenda and assigning opinion writing responsibility; and (2) outward strategy that takes into account the positions of other government actors and public opinion.[72]

[70] F Frankfurter, 'The Administrative Side of Chief Justice Hughes' (1949) 63 *Harvard Law Review* 1, 1.

[71] P Wald, 'Some Real-Life Observations about Judging' (1992) 26 *Indiana Law Review* 173, 177.

[72] See L Epstein and J Knight, *The Choices Justices Make* (Washington, DC, Congressional Quarterly Press, 1998). See also W Murphy, *Elements of Judicial Strategy* (Chicago, University of Chicago Press, 1964).

Does the reputation of constitutional courts depend in part on the confidentiality of their deliberations? The nature of the question indicates the difficulty of answering it, but also suggests it is worth inquiring into the basis for confidentiality in constitutional rights cases. There are good reasons for confidentiality of judicial deliberations insofar as they relate to the judicial function of resolving disputes between parties. A Kelsenian court judging the constitutionality of laws in the abstract, outside the context of a party dispute, would have less reason to maintain confidentiality. In chapter seven, I will argue that, from the perspective of constitutional design, framers who choose to adopt rights-based judicial review of legislation would have good reason to adopt an institution that is more open and transparent in its deliberation than a common law supreme court.

The legislature is an institution that is structured to be open to every kind of reason in its deliberation and law-making processes, including moral reasoning.[73] Courts are not structured to be open in the same way. Here we reach a kind of paradox, for in chapters one, two, and four, I have emphasised the extent to which judicial reasoning in constitutional rights cases relies on both moral and empirical reasoning, and that this is invited by vaguely formulated rights and by balancing and proportionality tests. Nonetheless, the structure of judicial decision-making is not well suited to open deliberation on moral issues. This is especially true in common law courts, where deliberation occurs in the context of resolving a dispute between two parties. This has long been personified by blindfolded Justice, who ignores considerations extraneous to the case and the law governing it (see section II above). It would threaten this ideal of the Rule of Law if judges were to engage openly in wide-ranging moral evaluation of a law in deciding whether to uphold it or strike it down. Though judges no doubt engage in personal, internal deliberation on moral issues, the public justification of decisions is weighted toward precedent and other legal sources of authority.[74] In *Roe v Wade* (1973),[75] for example, the question of whether the foetus is a person is treated as an interpretation of the 14th Amendment rather than a subject for moral inquiry, and the holding regarding the permissibility of abortion is reached by a conclusion that it falls within the legal right of privacy and thus admits of only minor limits. Jeremy Waldron has observed that the debate in the UK over the Abortion Act 1967 was far more thorough and robust in its examination of the moral issues than *Roe*.[76] Waldron argues that such disparity should be expected, because the legislative model of deliberation is designed for the airing of all the main arguments in deciding both individual-level moral questions as well as what should be done in the name of the whole society. A more recent example of this

[73] Ekins, *The Nature of Legislative Intent*, above n 16.

[74] See J Waldron, 'Do Judges Reason Morally?' in G Huscroft (ed.), *Expounding the Constitution: Essays in Constitutional Theory* (Cambridge, Cambridge University Press, 2008).

[75] *Roe v Wade* 410 US 113 (1973).

[76] ibid.

kind of contrast can be seen in the UK Parliament's debate over whether to permit physician-assisted suicide.[77] Again, the debate is a substantially more comprehensive examination of the moral issues than, for example, the Canadian Supreme Court's decision in *Carter v Canada*.

In balancing and proportionality cases the discussion of legal authority often takes the form of citing cases to establish what level of general scrutiny to apply, whether to allow for a wide margin of appreciation, or how to weigh an individual or governmental interest of a particular kind. The question of determining where the overall balance lies in a given case is not apt for control by precedent; but it is also not apt for thorough moral reasoning. While judges usually escape the pull toward treating the proportionality test as a utilitarian calculation (see section IV.B), they rarely provide a robust, comprehensive discussion of the values at stake and the moral reasons for favouring the conclusion. It is less problematic, with regard to public perception, for courts to engage in empirical reasoning in balancing cases. But this means that discussion of facts can have the effect of suppressing or concealing moral reasoning. We have seen an example of this in the Supreme Court's decision in *Brown* to rely on sociological data rather than directly engaging the moral issues of segregation. David Faigman has argued with regard to the US Supreme Court:

> The Court treats [facts] as rhetorical devices, to be used or withheld as the normative circumstances of the case dictate ... Holdings premised on hollow empirical propositions are nothing more than pronouncements ... The Court should have to state plainly the true reasons for its decisions. Informed constitutional democracy is not possible without this possibility.[78]

Faigman's prescription—to state reasons plainly—faces formidable obstacles discussed above.

In conclusion, legislatures have better capacities than courts for moral and empirical reasoning, for grasping the interplay between moral and factual questions, and for providing a full and transparent justification for decisions on moral issues. In the next two sections, I take up the question of whether the democratic structure of legislatures prevents legislatures from using their capacities in a way that is neutral between majority and minority groups. It should be noted that even if courts were to have advantages over legislatures in this respect, that is just one factor in the overall choice regarding constitutional design, which must be considered against the disadvantages of courts generally in regard to empirical and moral reasoning.

[77] See HC Debate 11 September 2015, vol 599, cols 655–724.

[78] D Faigman, *Constitutional Fictions: A Unified Theory of Constitutional Facts* (New York, Oxford University Press, 2008) 180.

V. The Tyranny of the Majority?

Dworkin and many other legal and political theorists—including opponents of judicial review such as Waldron—characterise the legislature as a majoritarian institution whose essential function is to enact into law the views or wishes of the majority in society. A related view, sometimes asserted in tandem with the first, is that the legislature *aggregates* preferences of (a majority of) voters into a collective choice. This section argues that the practice of majority voting in democracies is not designed to empower a group designated as 'the majority' or to enact its preferences.

Alexander Hamilton warned that as the result of temporary popular passions inflamed by unscrupulous men, representatives would face pressure from 'whenever momentary inclination happens to lay hold of a majority of their constituents, incompatible with the provisions in the existing Constitution'; in this way the 'major voice of the community' might depart from constitutional rules and instigate 'serious oppressions of the minor party in the community'.[79] James Madison likewise wrote about 'the superior force of an interested and overbearing majority'[80] and Tocqueville later decried the 'tyranny of the majority', with the legislature as its agent:

> The very essence of democratic government consists in the absolute sovereignty of the majority; for there is nothing in democratic states that is capable of resisting it … The legislature is, of all political institutions, the one which is most easily swayed by the will of the majority. The Americans determined that the members of the legislature should be elected by the people directly, and for a very brief term, in order to subject them, not only to the general convictions, but even to the daily passions, of their constituents.[81]

Where Hamilton perceived a transient phenomenon, Madison and de Tocqueville speak more generally of the 'majority' as a collective entity that holds sway in a democracy and imposes its will on others. Following what he characterised as a Madisonian tradition, Alexander Bickel coined the term *counter-majoritarian* to describe the power of courts in judicial review (not long after the first usage for the term *majoritarian* given in the *Oxford English Dictionary* in 1957).[82]

Despite the venerable history of the argument about the tyranny of the majority, the notion of a 'majority' as a coherent group that subsists through time and

[79] *The Federalist* No 78.

[80] *The Federalist* No 10 ('Complaints are everywhere heard … that our governments are too unstable, that the public good is disregarded in the conflicts of rival parties, and that measures are too often decided, not according to the rules of justice and the rights of the minor party, but by the superior force of an interested and overbearing majority').

[81] *Democracy in America* (1839), Henry Reeve (tr) (Cambridge, Sever and Francis, 1862) vol 1, 324 (ch XV). De Tocqueville also refers to 'the omnipotence of the majority', ibid 328, 335, and (quoting a letter from Thomas Jefferson to James Madison) the 'tyranny of the legislature': ibid 345.

[82] In *The Least Dangerous Branch: The Supreme Court at the Bar of Politics* (New Haven, Yale University Press, 1962).

exercises power over legislative outcomes is dubious, and in need of clarification. While it is possible for there to exist in a political society a cohesive, homogenous group whose members act in concert and constitute a numerical majority of the population, the existence of such a group cannot be postulated wherever one finds democratic structures such as majority voting in an elected legislature. The use of majority voting (*majority* here is adjectival) as a method of decision-making must be kept distinct from the question of whether there is a coherent, unified group that constitutes *a* majority (used here as a noun).

GEM Anscombe showed that in a series of votes, each decided by majority vote, a majority of voters can be in the minority on a majority of issues.[83] Her demonstration used a table illustrating a ten-member committee voting on eleven successive motions. Michael Dummett constructed a simplified version of Anscombe's table based on a committee with five members (A–E) voting on three successive motions.[84]

Table 1

	A	B	C	D	E	Result
Motion 1	Pro	Con	Con	Pro	Pro	carried
Motion 2	Con	Pro	Con	Pro	Pro	carried
Motion 3	Con	Con	Pro	Pro	Pro	carried

A, B, and C constitute a majority of the committee, but they are outvoted on two of the three motions. Although it cannot be predicted how frequently such a result will occur, nothing seems unusual about the voting patterns depicted in Dummett's and Anscombe's tables.

Thus, adopting a system of majority voting does not ensure that 'the majority' gets its way in a series of successive votes. Moreover, it should not be assumed that in every society there is 'majority' in the relevant sense. De Tocqueville contemplated a particular kind of majority: a numerically superior class of workers with interests and opinions pitted against a much smaller class of educated property holders. John Stuart Mill perceived a similar demographic imbalance, arguing that the 'pure' idea of democracy is 'government of the whole people, by the whole people, equally represented'.[85] He criticised the democracy practised in his day as 'government of the whole people by a mere majority of the people exclusively

[83] GEM Anscombe, 'On Frustration of the Majority by Fulfilment of the Majority's Will' (1976) 36 *Analysis* 161.

[84] M Dummett, *Voting Procedures* (Oxford, Oxford University Press, 1984) 14; *cf* R Ekins, *The Nature of Legislative Intent*, above n 16, 86–87.

[85] JS Mill, *Representative Government* (1861) J Gray (ed) (Oxford, Oxford University Press, 1998) 302 (Ch VII).

represented'.[86] When each locality has one representative in a national legislature, this exacerbates two dangers to which democracy is prone: 'danger of a low grade of intelligence in the representative body, and in the popular opinion which controls it; and danger of class legislation on the part of the numerical majority, these being all composed of the same class'.[87] Mill proposed a system of proportional representation to enable the minority of educated, cultivated persons to choose representatives of high intelligence, whose powers of persuasion would help compensate for being outnumbered.[88]

The class-based, numerical majorities that worried Mill and Tocqueville are unlikely to form in today's Western democracies, with their diversified economies and social groups. This is seen in the fact that in countries with proportional representation, one typically finds political fragmentation and a multiplicity of parties;[89] hence, the need for coalition governments of the kind found in most European states. In non-proportional systems, there are often two dominant parties that alternate in power, as has traditionally been the case in the US and UK. But closer inspection reveals factions within the parties themselves, and disagreement, compromise, and bargaining even among party loyalists. A two-party system creates a façade of party unity, concealing the underlying fractures that are made visible in systems with proportional representation. The balance of power is often held by a large contingent of independent voters that floats between the two parties. As Richard Bellamy notes, 'majorities' are in fact shifting coalitions of minorities.[90]

Let us turn, then, to the claim that legislatures act by aggregating the preferences of individuals into a collective choice. Dworkin describes the democratic process as a 'utilitarian computer' and a 'giant utilitarian calculation', in which there is a close correspondence between voters' inputs of their preferences and legislative outputs.[91] Dworkin argues that such a system is designed in principle to respect equality and promote fair distribution, but the presence of external preferences (of one person for the distribution of goods to another) corrupts the egalitarian nature of preference-satisfaction utilitarianism, thus necessitating judicial review by independent courts to filter out external preferences (see chapter three, section II).

Social choice theorists, however, hold that there is no simple or automatic correlation between voters' preferences and legislative outcomes; their overall

[86] ibid.

[87] ibid.

[88] ibid 307ff (Ch VII).

[89] D Farrell, *Electoral Systems: A Comparative Introduction* (Palgrave, New York, 2001) 162.

[90] R Bellamy, *Political Constitutionalism* (Cambridge, Cambridge University Press, 2007) 241 ('[M]ost legislation is not the product of a homogeneous majority imposing its will upon a constituent minority, but of a series of compromises brokered by winning coalitions of different minorities').

[91] 'Someone who reports more preferences to the utilitarian computer does not (except trivially) diminish the impact of other preferences he also reports; he rather increases the role of his preferences overall, compared with the role of other people's preferences, in the giant calculation': Dworkin, *A Matter of Principle* 366.

message, as David Miller puts it, is that 'in general there is no fair and rational way of amalgamating voters' preferences to reach a social decision'.[92] Kenneth Arrow's impossibility theorem holds that if there are three or more options and two or more voters who rank the options in order of preference, then no voting system can be designed which meets all of certain conditions assumed to be reasonable requirements of a method of fair voting.[93]

A common phenomenon described by Arrow's theorem is preference cycling, or the intransitive ordering of preferences: the possibility that when voters face a decision among several options, there may be no option that a majority would choose in preference to all of the others, if each option were paired against the others in a series of binary votes. An option that would be chosen by the majority against all alternatives is known in voting theory as a 'Condorcet winner' or, in Dummett's term, a 'top'.[94] In the absence of a top, the majority preference cycles from one option to the next.

Preference cycling can be stopped by decisional rules that differ from traditional majority voting techniques. The Borda count, for example, allows voters to rank options in a list with the first choice receiving the score of n, the second n-1, and so forth. Ranking systems, however, usually violate the condition of fair voting that Arrow called 'independence of irrelevant alternatives'.[95] Moreover, a Condorcet winner will not always win a Borda count, which seems unfair or at least odd.[96] Another way to stop preference cycling is through agenda-setting rules and techniques, which empower a subset of the voting group to decide what will be voted upon and when, and which votes will be conclusive for a given option. Agenda setters can produce majority support for a proposal whether or not it would be a Condorcet winner or win a Borda count. Agenda setters commonly determine the success of proposals in legislatures, often through complex rules governing committee hearings, scheduling of floor debates, and votes on bills and amendments.

Preference cycles can also be broken by tactical voting. The attraction of tactical voting is immense; it is ubiquitous in democracies and may be a sufficient explanation of the existence of political parties. Dummett illustrated the appeal of tactical voting with variations on Table 1 above. The following 'preference satisfaction' table shows how many of the preferences of A—E were satisfied by the votes in Table 1, allotting +1 when a voter has his wishes satisfied on a vote and −1 when the result is contrary to his wishes.

[92] D Miller, 'Deliberative Democracy and Social Choice' in D Estlund (ed.), *Democracy* (Oxford, Blackwell, 2002) 290 and 293.

[93] See KJ Arrow, *Social Choice and Individual Values* (New Haven, Yale University Press, 1970).

[94] M Dummett, *Voting Procedures* (Oxford, Oxford University Press, 1984) 4, fn 1.

[95] ibid 52–56.

[96] In other words, the option that a majority of voters would prefer to all other options in a series of binary votes might lose when taking into account the weighting of preferences assigned by the Borda count.

Table 2

	A	B	C	D	E	Total
Mot. 1 (carried)	+1	−1	−1	+1	+1	+1
Mot. 2 (carried)	−1	+1	−1	+1	+1	+1
Mot. 3 (carried)	−1	−1	+1	+1	+1	+1
Total	−1	−1	−1	+3	+3	+3

On the original voting pattern, the committee's total satisfaction is +3; but A, B, and C each have a satisfaction level of −1. A, B, and C can form a voting bloc, promising that on each motion, each of them will vote in accordance with the wishes of the majority of their party. The ABC party will win all three motions—which will be in their interests overall because each will be more satisfied if all the motions lose—if the committee members vote as follows:

Table 3

	A	B	C	D	E	Result
Motion 1	Con	Con	Con	Pro	Pro	lost
Motion 2	Con	Con	Con	Pro	Pro	lost
Motion 3	Con	Con	Con	Pro	Pro	lost

Now D and E are in the minority on every vote. But note that the ABC party achieved this result only by casting some insincere votes. A voted against motion 1 even though in fact he preferred it, and B and C voted against their preferences on motions 2 and 3 respectively (compare Table 1). This yields the following preference satisfaction table.[97]

Table 4

	A	B	C	D	E	Total
Mot. 1 (lost)	−1	+1	+1	−1	−1	−1
Mot. 1 (lost)	+1	−1	+1	−1	−1	−1
Mot. 3 (lost)	+1	+1	−1	−1	−1	−1
Total	+1	+1	+1	−3	−3	−3

[97] Tables 3 and 4 are taken from Dummett's analysis, ibid 15–16.

Comparing Table 2 to Table 4 we see that each member of the ABC party has improved his total satisfaction level from –1 to +1; but D and E have each gone from +3 to –3. In Table 2 the total preference satisfaction of the committee was +3, but after the ABC party was formed the total is –3.

Dummett argues that the result depicted in Table 4 is endemic: tactical voting always reduces the preference satisfaction of the group as a whole, at least when wins and losses are counted as +1 and –1. It would seem, then, that in order to promote the interests of the whole, individuals should not vote tactically. The sincere, non-strategic voter, however, risks the possibility of consistently being on the losing side. Tactical voting increases his chances of being on the winning side, but at the expense of an overall reduction in preference satisfaction. As Dummett notes, 'Such a satisfaction table should not be taken too seriously; but it provides some intuitive indication of how well the voting procedure has satisfied the wishes of the voters'.[98]

Table 4 does not reflect the possibility that the intensity of the voters' preferences vary across motions 1 to 3. If the five committee members, A to E, were asked not only whether they favour a motion but also how intensely (say, on a scale of 0.1 to 1) then it might be possible to find scenarios in which strategic voting increases the satisfaction level of both individuals and the group as a whole. The pertinent issue, however, is whether the democratic process should be understood as a system for aggregating preferences. If voters are generally willing to trade a loss of satisfaction on many issues that they care about for the sake of a high level of satisfaction on one or a few, then the voting process is not translating their preferences (plural) into outcomes. Contrary to Dworkin's analysis, inputting an additional preference to the utilitarian computer does not necessarily affect output.

Modern election systems contain no *direct* mechanism for inputting such individual preferences, much less for accounting for the intensity of voter preferences across a range of issues. Majority voting is a more complex phenomenon, with less predictable outcomes, than in the theories discussed above.

VI. Capacity to Protect Minorities

The question of the tyranny of the majority is tied to the argument that courts, being unelected, are institutionally better placed to protect the rights of minorities than legislatures. Once we set aside the deterministic accounts of the legislature as responding automatically to preferences of the majority, as I have argued for above, then the question of whether judges or legislators have a better capacity to protect minority interests could rightly be considered in an historical dimension

[98] ibid 15.

that informs our anticipation of likely outcomes. Dworkin, as we have seen in section V strongly predicts the inability of elected legislatures to protect minority rights and the capacity of unelected judges to do so. In this section I will engage in a comparative analysis of legislative and judicial interventions into efforts to promote racial equality, looking in some detail at the US and briefly at the UK. This is the situation that many would consider as providing the strongest argument for judicial review as a counter-majoritarian check on the legislature.

Dworkin goes so far as to argue that in the absence of *Brown v Board of Education* (1954), legal segregation in the US might have endured into the late twentieth century. He makes the claim as part of an argument that courts should take an active, robust approach to constitutional interpretation: 'we would have more to regret if the Court had accepted passivism wholeheartedly: southern schools might still be segregated, for example'.[99] *Brown* is a useful test case for whether we need counter-majoritarian courts to effect social reform that benefits minorities. The black minority in the US has often been the prime example of a 'discrete and insular'[100] minority, lacking in political power. And *Brown* has widely been considered as the paradigm case of courts' ability to produce reform—the 'principal inspiration to others who seek change through litigation'.[101]

Historical and empirical studies of the civil rights movement have forcefully countered this view of *Brown* and reached conclusions about its historical impact nearly opposite to Dworkin's.[102] In 1964, a decade after *Brown*, schools remained almost completely segregated in the 17 southern states whose laws mandated segregation in 1954.[103] Only 1.2 per cent of black school children in those states attended schools with white school children.[104] In the decade after *Brown* the US Congress was mostly inactive with regard to racial equality. Then Congress enacted the 1964 Civil Rights Act, the 1965 Voting Rights Act, and the 1965 Elementary and Secondary Education Act, the last of which provided funding for schools with a high percentage of low-income children. It was at this point that the number of black children attending integrated schools finally began to increase substantially, rising steadily over the next decade. By 1973, over 90 per cent of black children in the South attended integrated schools.[105]

[99] R Dworkin, *Law's Empire* (Cambridge, Mass, Harvard University Press, 1986) 375.

[100] *US v Carolene Products Company* 304 US 144, 152 fn 4 (1938).

[101] J Greenberg, *Litigation for Social Change: Methods, Limits, and Role in Democracy* (Association of the Bar of the City of New York, 1974) 331.

[102] See especially Gerald N Rosenberg, *The Hollow Hope: Can Courts Bring About Social Change?*, 2nd edn (Chicago, University of Chicago Press, 2008); Michael J Klarman, *From Jim Crow to Civil Rights: The Supreme Court and the Struggle for Racial Equality* (Oxford, Oxford University Press, 2004).

[103] Rosenberg, *The Hollow Hope*, above n 102, 52.

[104] ibid.

[105] ibid 52–53.

Gerald Rosenberg attributes this change squarely to Congress and other political actors, and provides data for the view that a similar pattern obtained across other areas regarding racial equality.[106] His conclusion is stark:

> [B]efore Congress and the executive branch acted, courts had virtually no direct effect on ending discrimination in the key fields of education, voting, transportation, accommodations and public places, and housing. Only when Congress and the executive branch acted in tandem with the courts did change occur in these fields ... *Brown* and its progeny stand for the proposition that courts are impotent to produce significant social reform.[107]

Michael Klarman reinforces Rosenberg's conclusions about *Brown*'s lack of direct, causal effect in ending segregation.[108] His research shows that Supreme Court decisions involving racial equality consistently reflected the national consensus, both in several cases that upheld segregation such as *Plessy v Ferguson* (1896) and in the few pre-*Brown* cases that struck down isolated state laws.[109] Where public opinion is evenly divided, Klarman says the Court is apt to move in the direction of the opinion of the elite class from which the justices are drawn. *Brown* was such a case: national opinion polls following the decision found that half of Americans accepted it.[110] What swayed the Court, Klarman argues, is that the justices believed that racial segregation was an immoral institution that should eventually be eliminated throughout the US.[111] This view was increasingly common—particularly among educated elites and the governing class[112]—following World War II, where blacks had fought alongside whites to defend democracy. To deny full equality to blacks was increasingly seen as not only intrinsically unjust, but as harmful to US interests in countering the rise of communist regimes, who highlighted racial segregation in the US to characterise its commitment to democratic equality as a pretence.[113]

Klarman's and Rosenberg's arguments about the inefficacy of *Brown* have been challenged,[114] as has Rosenberg's more general argument about the inability of courts to produce social reform. But for purposes of my argument about the relative capacity of courts and legislatures to protect minorities, I do not need

[106] ibid Ch 2.

[107] ibid 70–71.

[108] Klarman, *From Jim Crow to Civil Rights.*

[109] See ibid 448–50.

[110] ibid 450.

[111] ibid 447–48.

[112] Reflecting the attitude of this class, the US Government filed an amicus brief in *Brown*, which stated: 'The problem of racial discrimination is particularly acute in the District of Columbia, [the] window through which the world looks into our house. ... Foreign officials and visitors naturally judge this country and our people by their experiences and observations in the nation's capital; and the treatment of colored persons here is taken as the measure of our attitude toward minorities generally'. See Peter H Irons, *Jim Crow's Children: The Broken Promise of the Brown Decision* (New York, Penguin, 2004), 135.

[113] Klarman, *From Jim Crow to Civil Rights* 443–45.

[114] But see TM Keck's observation that 'Klarman's insistence on the limited relevance of *Brown* is now approaching scholarly consensus': 'Does the Court Follow the Election Returns?' (2004) 32 *Reviews in American History* 602, 608.

to argue that courts are unable to produce social reform or to claim that *Brown* had no beneficial causal effect on segregation in schools. The points I draw from Rosenberg's and Klarman's work are that legislatures *are capable* of producing social change that benefits minorities, and that courts have a strong tendency to reflect the national consensus on issues relevant to minority interests.

The simplistic view of legislatures as inevitably biased against minorities, as in Dworkin's view, is usually accompanied by an optimistic view of the judiciary's capacity to resist this. Klarman's contrary view can be buttressed with further examples. The most infamous anti-minority decision of the Supreme Court is *Dred Scott v Sandford* (1857),[115] in which the Court attempted to provide a legal, constitutional settlement to the political question of whether slavery would expand westward as US settlers entered territories that were to become new states. Dred Scott was a slave in Missouri, a slave state, who sued for freedom because he had once been held in a territory where slavery was forbidden. The Court denied his claim and issued a wide-ranging opinion on the federal government's power to regulate slavery and on the legal status of black slaves. The Court held that black slaves could not be citizens under the Constitution because, inter alia, the Founders had considered blacks as 'beings of an inferior order, and altogether unfit to associate with the white race, either in social or political relations, and so far inferior that they had no rights which the white man was bound to respect'.[116] Instead, slaves had the legal status of property. In a novel interpretation of the 5th Amendment, the Court held that slaveholders in western territories held property rights in slaves, which would be deprived without due process of law if a territory banned slavery.[117] This had the effect of overturning the 1854 Kansas-Nebraska Act, which Congress had enacted to allow settlers in the territories to vote on whether the territory would become a free state or slave state. The Court effectively ruled that, as a matter of constitutional law, new states admitted to the union must be slave states, so long as slaveholders were present. This prevented political compromise and tilted the balance of power in the Senate to southern states, and the Court's opinion thus took its place among the causes driving the US toward civil war.

After the Civil War, which lasted from 1861 to 1865, Congress proposed the 13th Amendment, which abolished slavery; the 14th Amendment, which provided for equal protection of the law and established civil and political rights on a national basis, prohibiting individual states from denying 'the privileges or immunities of citizens of the United States'; and the 15th Amendment, which provided that the right to vote could not be denied on account of race. They were ratified by the states. Each amendment specifically empowered Congress to enact further appropriate legislation for the enforcement of its provisions, thus adding to the original list of enumerated federal powers in the Constitution.

[115] *Dred Scott v Sandford* 60 US 393 (1857).
[116] ibid 407.
[117] ibid 450.

In pursuance of the new powers granted to it, Congress passed a series of Civil Rights Acts in 1866, 1870, 1871, and 1875.[118] These Acts sought to go beyond the mere abolition of slavery and to establish the full protection of civil and political rights for former slaves.[119] The US Supreme Court struck down the 1875 Civil Rights Act in the *Civil Rights Cases* (1883),[120] and in other cases it adopted a narrow reading of the Reconstruction Amendments that denied Congress the power to enforce against private individuals the full range of rights that the various Acts had sought to protect.[121] The Court held that the Amendments empowered the federal government only to counteract action taken specifically by the state. The larger threat to the rights of former slaves, however, came from private individuals.[122] When the Reconstruction Amendments were being debated, they were understood both by proponents and opponents to grant Congress legislative power to address the subject matter in the manner that it did in the series of Civil Rights Acts between 1866 and 1875, and to make laws applicable to individuals.[123]

In 1890, seven years after the Court struck down the Civil Rights Act 1875, Louisiana enacted a law requiring separation of blacks and whites on railroads—which would have been contrary to the 1875 Act. The Supreme Court upheld the Louisiana law in *Plessy v Ferguson* (1896),[124] which established the 'separate but equal' doctrine that endured until *Brown*. While some historians have argued that *Plessy* led to the expansion of segregation, Klarman argues that there is no direct evidence of this.[125] Rather, *Plessy* reflected the new national consensus and was part of a trend during the 1880s and 1890s departing from the efforts at integration that marked the Reconstruction era.[126] These examples—*Dred Scott*, the *Civil Rights Cases*, and *Plessy*—show that in many key cases involving minorities, the Court has (contrary to the role envisioned for it by Dworkin) failed to take a counter-majoritarian position. As Klarman remarks: '[D]uring the time period covered by this book [ie from the *Plessy* era to *Brown* and its aftermath], not a single Court decision involving race clearly contravened national public opinion'.[127]

Moving forward to the modern era, the main flash point between the Court and legislatures on racial equality in recent decades has been over the constitutionality of affirmative action legislation. Cases on this have repeatedly involved Congress and state governments attempting to promote the interests of minorities through various kinds of affirmative action laws and programmes, while the Supreme Court

[118] 14 Stat. L. 27 (1866); 16 Stat. L. 140 (1870); 17 Stat. L. 13 (1871); 18 Stat. L. 335 (1875).

[119] See E Gressman, 'Unhappy History of Civil Rights Legislation' (1951) 50 *Michigan Law Review* 1323.

[120] *Civil Rights Cases* 109 US 3 (1883).

[121] See especially *The Slaughter-house Cases* 83 US 36 (1873), and discussion in Gressman, 'Unhappy History of Civil Rights Legislation' 1336–38.

[122] ibid 1330.

[123] ibid 1332–36.

[124] *Plessy v Ferguson* 163 US 537 (1896).

[125] Klarman, *From Jim Crow to Civil Rights* 47.

[126] ibid Ch 1.

[127] ibid 450.

and other federal courts have often used the Equal Protection Clause to curtail or strike down those efforts.[128] A similar pattern obtained in *Shelby v Holbrook* (2013),[129] which struck down portions of the Voting Rights Act of 1965.

When the historical record is thus expanded to take account of the century before *Brown* (beginning with *Dred Scott*) and the decades following it, the argument that the Supreme Court was the key institution in bringing about racial equality looks hollow. Cass Sunstein, in an article reviewing scholarship on *Brown*, concisely summarises that historical record:

> Fifty years later, *Brown* does seem increasingly anomalous. Before the Warren Court, the justices were almost never a force for social reform, and they have rarely assumed that role in the past two decades. Most of the time, the judiciary has been an obstacle to racial equality. Before the Civil War, the Supreme Court, in the *Dred Scott* case, interpreted the Constitution so as to entrench slavery. After the Civil War, the Court sharply limited Congress's power to protect the newly freed slaves. During the first half of the twentieth century, the Court did little to promote racial justice (and for much of that time, as Frankfurter and Jackson were painfully aware, it was hostile to legislative attempts to reduce economic inequality); in the last quarter of the century, the Court's most important racial-discrimination decisions struck down affirmative-action programs.[130]

If Sunstein's general claim is correct—'Most of time, the judiciary has been an obstacle to racial equality'—then Dworkin's theory of institutional capabilities must be rejected as applied to the US Congress and the US Supreme Court.

The tragic history of the US with regard to racial equality can be contrasted to the record of the UK. In 1833, 24 years before the *Dred Scott* decision, the UK Parliament ended slavery throughout the Empire. Parliament had earlier abolished the slave trade in 1807, but not slavery itself. As in the US, slavery played a large role in economic activity in the UK. Before 1807, British ships transported around 3.4 million slaves to the Americas (only a small portion of whom were taken to North America).[131] When the Slavery Abolition Act 1833 was enacted, there were 800,000 recognised slaves in the British Empire, most in the West Indies.[132] In the late 1700s and early 1800s, slavery was backed by powerful financial interests in Parliament and tolerated by the majority of people, many of whom directly or indirectly benefited from it economically.[133] Nonetheless, a long, persistent political campaign for abolition, led by William Wilberforce and Thomas Clarkson,[134] eventually persuaded Parliament to adopt the 1807 and 1833 Acts. All this took place without judicial review of legislation.

[128] See KR Johnson, 'The Last Twenty Five Years of Affirmative Action?' (2004) 21 *Constitutional Commentary* 171.

[129] *Shelby v Holbrook* 570 US 2 (2013).

[130] CR Sunstein, 'Did Brown Matter?' *The New Yorker* (3 May 2004).

[131] D Richardson 'The British Empire and the Atlantic Slave Trade, 1660–1807' in PJ Marshall and others (eds), *The Oxford History of the British Empire: The Eighteenth Century* (Oxford, Oxford University Press, 1998) 441.

[132] P Levine, *The British Empire: Sunrise to Sunset* (Harlow, Pearson Education, 2013) 27.

[133] C Hall, *Legacies of British Slave-ownership: Colonial Slavery and the Formation of Victorian Britain* (Cambridge, Cambridge University Press, 2014).

[134] Wilberforce made his first speech on the subject in the House of Commons in 1789.

The argument that we must look to courts to protect minority rights because legislatures are institutionally incapable of doing so has little grounding in the historical record on the issue of racial equality just reviewed—which is often taken to be the case that presents the most compelling need for counter-majoritarian judicial power.

VII. An Historical Perspective

The history reviewed in section VI gives reason for rejecting the common belief that empowering judges to review legislation is necessary for the protection of minorities. The cases also raise a more general issue, which is the propensity of courts to make moral errors in constitutional rights cases. While *Brown v Board of Education* (1954) looms large in constitutional narratives, the unfortunate fact is that for the century before it, beginning with *Dred Scott v Sanford* (1856), the US Reports are replete with cases on constitutional rights that reflect errors in moral reasoning that did lasting damage. Apart from the cases dealing with race in section VI above, these include the many cases in the *Lochner* era where the Court protected the prerogatives of capital and industry and struck down legislation designed to protect workers and improve wages and labour conditions (see chapter four, section I). In a number of cases the Court failed to strike down legislation or executive action under reasoning that was arguably legally correct, but that nonetheless showed (through the Court's rhetoric and what it chose to emphasise) a lack of moral perspicacity or, indeed, hostility to vulnerable groups. In these cases the greater blame should be laid at the door of the legislature or executive, but the Court's failure to intervene nonetheless calls into question its counter-majoritarian capacity.

One such case is *Buck v Bell* (1927),[135] in which the Court upheld a Virginia statute that allowed an order for the sterilisation of Carrie Buck, who as a pregnant 17-year-old was committed to an institution in Virginia called the Colony for Epileptics and Feebleminded. Writing for an 8-1 majority, Oliver Wendell Holmes lent the authority of the Court to eugenic theory and to the classification of some people as 'unfit'. Describing Miss Buck as a 'feebleminded white woman [and] the daughter of a feebleminded white woman [and] the mother of an illegitimate feeble minded child', he wrote:

> It is better for all the world, if instead of waiting to execute degenerate offspring for crime, or to let them starve for their imbecility, society can prevent those who are manifestly unfit from continuing their kind. The principle that sustains compulsory vaccination is broad enough to cover cutting the Fallopian tubes.
>
> Three generations of imbeciles are enough.[136]

[135] *Buck v Bell* 274 US 200 (1927).
[136] ibid.

If a man considered by some to be the greatest Supreme Court justice could write such words about a member of a vulnerable minority, and draw only one dissent, we should question whether the Court is an intrinsically counter-majoritarian institution with the special mission of protecting minorities.

Another theme of this chapter relevant to *Buck v Bell* is the fragility of social science: its susceptibility to mistake, bias, and misuse. The term *eugenics* was coined by Francis Galton, who described it as 'the science which deals with all influences that improve the inborn qualities of a race [and] develop them to the utmost advantage.'[137] Galton was one of the founders of the discipline of statistics, and one of its early applications was to find correlations between 'feeblemindedness' and criminality, prostitution, and other social problems.[138] In eugenic theory, tests were developed to classify people according to their mental age ('idiot', 'moron', and 'imbecile' were technical labels for different kinds of feeblemindedness), and it was concluded that the cause of feeblemindedness was largely or solely hereditary.[139] Environmental factors were dismissed and education considered an ineffectual remedy; many eugenicists advocated mandatory sterilisation of the 'unfit' on a widespread basis. One was Dr Harry Laughlin, who drafted a model law that was the basis for the statute in *Buck v Bell*, and called for sterilising annually 200,000 members of the 'socially inadequate' classes in the US, which included several conditions besides feeblemindedness.[140] He also served as an expert in the case and diagnosed Carrie Buck as feebleminded. Though the theory of hereditary transmission in eugenics is now discredited, it was widely accepted and taught in universities at the time.[141]

While legislatures are more to blame for the uptake of eugenic theory than the judiciary, the Supreme Court's decision in *Buck v Bell* may have had the effect of spurring it on. Holmes's rejection of the challenge to the law under the Equal Protection Clause reasoned that states could promote equal treatment by taking measures to bring the 'multitudes outside' institutions such as Virginia's Colony inside them; and implied they should do this with deliberate speed.[142]

[137] F Galton, 'Eugenics: Its Definition, Scope, and Aims' (1904) 10 *American Journal of Sociology* 1.

[138] D Kevles, *In the Name of Eugenics: Genetics and the Uses of Human Heredity* (Cambridge Mass, Harvard University Press, 1998) 13–19, 46, 71.

[139] ibid 78–79, 110.

[140] 'This model law called for the sterilization, regardless of etiology, of the following inadequate classes: (1) feeble-minded; (2) insane (including the psychopathic); (3) criminalistic (including the delinquent and wayward); (4) epileptic; (5) inebriate (including drug habitues); (6) diseased (including the tuberculous, the syphilitic, the leprous, and others with chronic, infectious, and legally segregable diseases); (7) blind (including those with seriously impaired vision); (8) deaf (including those with seriously impaired hearing); (9) deformed (including the crippled); and (10) dependent (including orphans, ne'er-do-wells, the homeless, tramps, and paupers)': HH Laughlin, *Eugenical Sterilization: 1926* (New York, The American Eugenics Society, 1925) 64.

[141] E Black, *The War against the Weak*, 2nd edn (Washington, DC, Dialog Press, 2012) 75–76.

[142] Holmes wrote: 'But, it is said, however it might be if this reasoning [ie the eugenic theory regarding sterilisation] were applied generally, it fails when it is confined to the small number who are in the institutions named and is not applied to the multitudes outside ... But the answer is that the law does all that is needed when it does all that it can, indicates a policy, applies it to all within the lines, and *seeks to bring within the lines all similarly situated so far and so fast as its means allow*': 274 US 200, 208 (1927).

After *Buck v Bell*, several states adopted laws modelled on Virginia's, and the number of sterilisations in the US increased dramatically.[143]

It might be objected that the cases examined in this and the previous section are from long ago, from one country, and from a regrettable period in that country. It might be thought that we live in a more enlightened, liberal age, and that courts today can avoid the mistakes of the past. That is, of course, precisely how Oliver Wendell Holmes viewed himself: in the vanguard of a progressive movement, at a time when law was burdened by archaic, arbitrary rules and benighted traditions.[144] The historical perspective taken in these sections is the appropriate one for an argument of the kind in this book. Any attempt to gauge the propensity of courts to make correct moral decisions in the context of currently controversial moral issues will be subject to the fact that people disagree widely over decisions made by supreme courts and constitutional courts in recent decades, in cases around the globe. The advantage of looking at the US is that it provides by far the longest history of constitutional rights cases. Focusing on the earlier period provides a perspective relatively free from current political disagreement. Writing in 1949, Robert Jackson, one of the US Supreme Court's most respected justices, observed that

> time has proved that [the Court's] judgment was wrong on the most outstanding issues upon which it has chosen to challenge the popular branches … In no major conflict with the representative branches on any question of social or economic policy has time vindicated the Court.[145]

VIII. Conclusion

This chapter has analysed the institutional capacities of courts and legislatures to engage in empirical and moral reasoning of the kind at issue in constitutional rights cases. It has shown that the capacity of legislatures to acquire and assess general facts about society is far superior to that of courts. By drawing on the diverse background and professional experience of their members, and on information gained through interaction with constituents, legislatures begin with a broader base of collective knowledge than courts. They supplement this through active engagement with experts and with intermediaries who help to interpret studies. Legislatures can commission research, appoint investigators, and question their findings; and they do this on a daily basis. Courts, in contrast, are usually capable

143 Black, *The War against the Weak*, above n 141, Ch 6.

144 See T Leonard, *Liberal Reformers: Race, Eugenics and American Economics in the Progressive Era* (Princeton, Princeton University Press, 2016) 11, Ch 7.

145 R Jackson, *The Struggle for Judicial Supremacy* (New York, Alfred Knopf, 1949) ix–x.

only of passive, occasional engagement with empirical research through Brandeis briefs, without the specialised staff and other resources available to legislatures.

The meagre capacity of courts for empirical research is not a defect, however, when seen in light of the fundamental purpose of courts, which is to resolve disputes between parties in accordance with law laid down in the past. The institutional structures of common law courts, including appellate and supreme courts, are designed for this purpose, leading to the 'artificial world' of the trial in which the rules and general approach to evidence are designed not just for acquiring evidence but for *excluding* evidence not strictly relevant to the case at hand. The Kelsenian constitutional court is not subject to the same strictures as common law courts, because it is not designed for resolving disputes between parties and because of its centralised nature. The advantages of the Kelsenian court are explored in chapter seven, but it still lacks the broad reach of legislatures in empirical reasoning.

With regard to moral reasoning, this chapter has analysed the performance of courts and legislatures respecting the rights of racial minorities in the US and UK. Under the counter-majoritarian theory of judicial review, this should be the area in which courts are most able to correct moral errors of the legislature. But a broad historical perspective shows that the UK Parliament abolished slavery without the help of judicial review, while in the US judicial review was used in support of slavery in *Dred Scott* and since then has often been used to strike down legislation made for the benefit of racial minorities. As Cass Sunstein has observed, *Brown v Board of Education* seems to be an anomalous result against a background in which the Supreme Court has generally been an obstacle to racial equality. The historical perspective on the US shows that the Supreme Court has also made moral errors in cases dealing with the rights of workers, those in mental institutions, and many other vulnerable persons. We have also seen that the background and training of judges does not make them particularly qualified to decide moral issues, and that judicial structures for deliberation of moral issues are not superior to those of legislatures. Independence from elections does not eliminate external pressure or guarantee that deliberation will be guided by reason. Collegial courts decide by majority vote, and decision-making is influenced by strategic considerations.

The need for judges to justify decisions through legal reasons means that judges are less capable than legislatures at engaging in transparent, open-ended deliberation about all the reasons relevant to a decision to adopt or to reject a law. The form and structure of legislative deliberation allows for wide-ranging debate from a variety of perspectives, and the diversity of its membership can reduce the effects of correlated biases. The legislature is better able than courts to see the interplay between moral reasoning and factual considerations, and to adjust the content of law to empirical realities.

Legislatures are, of course, prone to making moral and factual mistakes. From the perspective of constitutional design, however, the question is not simply whether courts or legislatures are more likely to make correct decisions. As we will see in the next chapter, the costs of mistakes in judicial decisions to strike down legislation are high because of the difficulty of reversing those decisions. One of the important issues in institutional capacity is whether an institution can correct its own mistakes, and in this legislatures are clearly superior to courts. Thus, the question for constitutional framers, which is pursued in the next two chapters, is whether we trust courts so much more than legislatures that we are willing to make their judgments part of the enduring—potentially permanent—law of the constitution.

6

The Problem of Entrenchment

A capacity of the legislature that was only touched upon in the last chapter, but is one of its defining features, is the ability to change the law. This chapter discusses, in the context of constitutional law, the value of legal change and of an institution ready to achieve it, and the comparative capacities of legislatures and courts to meet this need. There is a tension between the need for legal change and the entrenchment of constitutional rights. One of the purposes of a constitution is to introduce enduring norms and principles and to limit the ability of the legislature (or other institutions) to change them. Thus, the formal justification for the power of judicial review of legislation, going back to Hamilton and Marshall, is that courts are to enforce the prior commitments of a political community expressed in legal form in its constitution. In other words, courts prevent legislatures from taking their power to create new law and using it to alter more fundamental law. Yet when constitutional principles take the form of abstract moral rights, and when those are joined to the broad methods of adjudication discussed in chapter two, then judicial review of legislation comes to be seen not as a means of preservation of the past, but as a powerful agency for legal reform and social change.

Thus there is a tension between judicial review as *conservation* and judicial review as *reform*. It is further complicated by the fact that the typical tool of judicial review legislation—to strike down or nullify a law—has the effect of changing not only the statute book but also, in effect, the constitution. The latter effect depends both on how venturesome a court is in its reasoning and on the strength of precedent accorded its decision. But it is not uncommon for a landmark constitutional case to take its place alongside the textual constitutional provisions as one of the fixed stars of constitutional law. And it is also not uncommon to regret the decisions of constitutional courts.

Who, then, will guard the guardians?[1] And more pointedly, *how* can this be done? This is a main theme of this chapter, and the need for addressing the question arises from the potential for courts to make moral errors or empirical mistakes when exercising the power of judicial review, which was demonstrated in the last two chapters. In section I, I discuss legal change in general, and in section II, I consider and reject John Rawls's argument that certain constitutional principles should be held to be so fundamental that they are immune to change even from

[1] *Sed quid custodes ipso custodiet?* Juvenal, *Satires*, VI, lines 347–48.

constitutional amendment, and that certain decisions of a supreme court applying constitutional rights should be treated as settling issues and removing them from political controversy 'once and for all'. In sections III and IV I discuss the rarity of constitutional amendment and the structural difficulty of reversing decisions to nullify law either through amendment or other means.

I. Legal Change and the Rule of Law

In *The Concept of Law* Hart invites us to reflect on how and why legal systems arise in human society. A legal system, he says, consists in the union of primary rules, which regulate inter-personal conduct, and secondary rules, which govern the identification, modification, and use of primary rules. His account of how it emerges from a pre-legal system helps to illuminate a main purpose fulfilled by the legislature in a legal system: changing the law.

'It is, of course, possible to imagine'—so Hart begins his account—'a society without a legislature, courts, or officials of any kind'.[2] In the pre-legal order there are primary rules that have some regulative effect within a community, but there is uncertainty about their content, and no recourse to an authoritative text or an official to resolve the question; rules of recognition are a response to this defect.[3] The primary rules also have a static character:

> The only mode of change in the rules known to such a society will be the slow process of growth, whereby courses of conduct once thought optional become first habitual or usual, and then obligatory, and the converse process of decay, when deviations, once severely dealt with, are first tolerated, and then go unnoticed. There is no means, in such a society, of deliberately adapting the rules to changing circumstances, either by eliminating old rules or introducing new ones: for again, the possibility of doing this presupposes the existence of rules of a different type from the primary rules of obligation by which alone the society lives.[4]

The need to change primary rules may arise from new threats to the safety or well-being of a community, or from new opportunities to co-operate in the realisation of some good, say, upon the discovery of a new source of food or energy. Apart from changes in physical circumstances, the need for change may arise from new knowledge or a growing awareness that a particular rule is not (or is no longer) sound or reasonable or well-fitted with other rules. The remedy to the static nature of the pre-legal order is to adopt rules of change that empower an individual or body of persons to change existing primary rules and eliminate old ones.[5] A third defect of the pre-legal order (labelled 'inefficiency' by Hart) is the lack of a

[2] HLA Hart, *The Concept of Law*, 2nd edn (Oxford, Oxford University Press, 1994).
[3] ibid 92, 94.
[4] ibid 92–93.
[5] ibid 95.

co-ordinated and authoritative response to the violation or alleged violation of rules, meaning that apprehending rule-breakers and punishing infractions is left either to individuals or to the unorganised efforts of the group as a whole.[6] This condition is remedied by rules of adjudication.

While Hart's exposition is primarily in terms of rules, he clearly contemplates the establishment of authoritative institutions as a response to the defects of the pre-legal order.[7] He connects rules of change to a legislature and legislation: 'the rules may, besides specifying the persons who are to legislate, define in more or less rigid terms the procedure to be followed in legislation'.[8] The introduction 'of rules enabling legislators to change and add to the rules of duty, and judges to determine when the rules of duty have been broken, is a step forward as important to society as the invention of the wheel'.[9]

A legislature is, moreover, an institution well-suited to attain the Rule of Law desiderata of generality, promulgation, prospectiveness, clarity, and congruence between promulgated law and official action. In common law systems courts have a limited power to make and change the law. But a legal system needs at least one institution that is open to all reasons, able to respond to changing circumstances, and able to introduce comprehensive legal reforms rather than incremental change. The main purpose of courts is to decide legal claims according to existing law, and courts cannot effectively and fairly fulfil that function if they are also the locus for legal change. Changing the law simultaneously with deciding a legal dispute creates tension with—and may violate—the values of prospectiveness and congruence between written law and official action. The *ratio decidendi* of a judgment or a common thread of reasoning in a line of cases may amount to a general norm, and publication of cases is promulgation of a sort. But legislation is needed to fully comply with the values of generality, promulgation, and clarity.[10]

II. Rawls and the Perpetual Constitution

Despite the advantages of an institution capable of introducing deliberate legal change, the Rule of Law also prizes the relative stability of legal rules. In some contexts the need to inhibit, or even prevent, legal change can seem to be acute.

[6] ibid 93, 94.

[7] See ibid 92 ('lack of official agencies'); 97 (rules of adjudication refer to a 'judge or court'). Compare R Summers, *Form and Function in a Legal System: A General Study* (Cambridge, Cambridge University Press, 2006) 72–78 (criticising Hart for claiming that a legal system can be satisfactorily explained as a system of rules).

[8] *Concept of Law* 96.

[9] ibid 41–42. These gains, however, come with 'a certain cost', namely the potential that a centrally organised power can be used to oppress certain segments of society that would have been less vulnerable under a system of primary rules: *Concept of Law* 202.

[10] For further discussion see P Yowell, 'Legislation, Common Law, and the Virtue of Clarity' in R Ekins (ed), *Modern Challenges to the Rule of Law* (Wellington, LexisNexis, 2011).

The making of constitutions is in part a response to that. As Joseph Raz has observed, a constitution

> is, and is meant to be, of long duration: It is meant to serve as a stable framework for the political and legal institutions of the country, to be adjusted and amended from time to time, but basically to preserve stability and continuity in the legal and political structure, and the basic principles that guide its institutions.[11]

John Rawls takes this idea to an extreme. Among his principles of constitutionalism is the proposition that

> by a democratically ratified constitution with a bill of rights, the citizen body fixes once and for all certain constitutional essentials, for example, the equal basic political rights and liberties guaranteeing the security and independence of citizens, such as free movement and choice of occupation, and the protections of the rule of law.[12]

Rawls states that a supreme court, in interpreting rights, should be 'an exemplar of public reason' and provide 'authoritative judgments on fundamental political questions'.[13] The court fulfils this role, Rawls says, 'when it clearly and effectively interprets the constitution in a reasonable way; and when it fails to do this, as ours often has, it stands at the center of political controversy the terms of settlement of which are public values'.[14] Rawls holds that judges, like other public actors addressing 'constitutional essentials and matters of basic justice', must not invoke or rely upon 'the ideals and virtues of morality generally', but must treat them as 'irrelevant' and rely instead on the 'political values of the public conception of justice'.[15] The supreme court's failure to interpret the constitution according to public reason, Rawls says, will land the court in 'controversy'.

Rawls here reflects the tension between the conserving and reforming tendencies of judicial review identified above. In his view the supreme court is simultaneously both (a) the protector of timeless rights (established 'once and for all' in the constitution), enforced in an 'antimajoritarian' way and (b) a tribunal of public reason whose failure to uphold the political conception of justice is evidenced by 'controversy' about its decisions. The tension is not resolved by Rawls's characterisation of the supreme court's power as 'not "antidemocratic"', because it is exercised in opposition to 'transient majorities or, more likely, organized and well-situated narrow interests skilled at getting their way'.[16] Nor is the tension resolved by his claim that the court's power rests on the 'higher authority of the people' expressed in the 'higher law' of the constitution.[17]

[11] See J Raz, 'On the Authority and Interpretation of Constitutions: Some Preliminaries' in *Between Authority and Interpretation* (Oxford, Oxford University Press, 2009) 324.

[12] J Rawls, *Political Liberalism* (New York, Columbia University Press, 2005) 232.

[13] ibid 237.

[14] ibid.

[15] ibid 236.

[16] ibid 233.

[17] '"Higher law" is the expression of the constituent power and has the higher authority of We the People, whereas ordinary legislation has the authority, and is the expression of, the ordinary power and

First, Rawls does not account for the possibility that 'narrow interests skilled at getting their way' can also influence judges and courts; he treats such interests as influencing only legislative decisions. A more central flaw in Rawls's approach appears in his argument that the supreme court is entitled to reject a constitutional amendment if it 'fundamentally contradicts the constitutional tradition' (for example, an amendment to repeal the First Amendment of the US Constitution). An amendment to the US Constitution requires the sustained support of supermajorities over a period of years. It seems that this would indicate that the amendment falls within the 'reasonable overlapping consensus' and thus forms part of the political conception of justice that Rawls ordinarily counts as the appropriate basis for constitutional decision-making.[18] Rawls might answer that the supreme court has a duty to enforce a long-standing historical consensus against a consensus merely of the present era. He implies such an argument in claiming that some amendments might represent a

> constitutional breakdown, or a revolution in the proper sense, and not a valid amendment of the constitution. The successful practise of its ideas and principles over two centuries places restrictions on what can now count as an amendment, whatever was true at the beginning.[19]

But this is mere conservatism—retaining the status quo for its own sake or for political stability—unless 'successful practice' involves some substantive moral idea, by which the court can distinguish (i) constitutional traditions that ought to be upheld even against an amendment supported by a supermajority from (ii) traditions that do not deserve to be so entrenched. The mere fact that a tradition has endured for any length of time is not a legitimate reason for rejecting a constitutional amendment overturning it.

Rawls comes close to acknowledging this in a revealing footnote, where he asserts that it is proper for certain matters to be 'taken off the political agenda' and 'settled once for all'. But he then acknowledges that a society can make mistakes regarding matters of basic justice, as the US did in the past regarding slavery and toleration. He replies as follows:

> Certainly we may have been mistaken, but does anyone doubt for that reason that the principle of toleration may be mistaken or that it is wrong to have abolished slavery? Who seriously thinks so? Is there any real chance of mistake? And surely we don't want to say: we take certain matters off the political agenda for the time being. Or until the next election. Or the next generation. Why isn't 'once and for all' the best way to put it?

authority of Congress and of the electorate. Higher law binds and guides this ordinary power': *Political Liberalism* 231.

[18] Rawls states: 'Thus, a conception of justice may fail because it cannot gain the support of reasonable citizens who affirm reasonable comprehensive doctrines; or as I shall often say, it cannot gain the support of a reasonable overlapping consensus': ibid 36.

[19] *Political Liberalism* 239.

> By using that phrase citizens express to one another a firm commitment about their common status. They express a certain ideal of democratic citizenship.[20]

This reply sidesteps the crucial point, which is that societies can be both certain and mistaken.[21] Rawls's hesitation about 'once and for all' reveals the weakness of his political conception of justice as the foundation for a constitution. The correct reason for regarding the abolition of slavery as settled once and for all is that slavery is always and everywhere an injustice. This is a temporally unqualified moral judgement. If we, as a political society, were to decide to establish unchangeable constitutional provisions on the substantive content of law or the rights of persons, we must be confident that they instantiate true, timeless moral principles. But Rawls's theory of public reason—and of the supreme court as its chief tribunal—rules out such direct appeals to justice and morality:

> I have said that the justices are to appeal to the political values covered by the public political conception of justice, or at least some recognizable variant thereof. The values the justices can invoke are restricted to what is reasonably believed to be covered by that conception or its variants, and not by conception of morality as such, not even political morality.[22]

Rawls's 'political conception of justice' does not provide a legitimate basis for treating any legal or constitutional decision as settled once and for all.

If any example of this needs to be given, we can consider the circumstances in which the anti-slavery principle was finally adopted in the US. The complex figure of Abraham Lincoln provides a window into the political morality of antebellum society. Although he considered slavery to be a grave injustice, in the 1850s he espoused a consensus viewpoint that rejected racial equality and was willing to tolerate slavery. He publicly supported the Fugitive Slave Act 1850. Privately he confessed that he hated to see slaves 'hunted down, and caught, and carried back to their stripes, and unrewarded toils' and that 'the great body of the Northern people do crucify their feelings, in order to maintain their loyalty to the constitution and the Union'.[23] Lincoln argued that the Declaration of Independence embraced blacks in proclaiming that 'all men are created equal' and endowed them with the right to live in freedom, keep the fruits of their toil, and own property. But he said that such equality had limits:

> I will say then that I am not, nor ever have been, in favor of bringing about in any way the social and political equality of the white and black races—that I am not, nor ever have been, in favor of making voters or jurors of Negroes, nor of qualifying them to hold

[20] *Political Liberalism* 152 fn 16.

[21] My point, more carefully formulated, is that it is not reasonable for any society of the present to be trapped perpetually in something perceived now as an error just because it was perceived as true at some distant point in the past.

[22] *Political Liberalism* 237 fn 23.

[23] A Lincoln, Letter to Joshua Speed (24 August 1855), in R Basley (ed), *Collected Works of Abraham Lincoln, Vol 2* (Rutgers University Press, 1953) 321.

> office, nor to intermarry with white people; and I will say in addition to this that there is a physical difference between the white and black races which I believe forever forbid the two races living together on terms of social and political equality. And in as much as they cannot so live, while they do remain together there must be the position of superior and inferior, and I as much as any other man am in favor of having the superior position assigned to the white race.[24]

His first impulse was to free all slaves and 'send them to Liberia—their own native land', but he knew that this would be practically impossible:

> What then? Free them all, and keep them among us as underlings? Is it quite certain that this betters their condition? I think I would not hold one in slavery, at any rate; yet the point is not clear enough for me to denounce people upon. What next? Free them, and make them politically and socially, our equals? My own feelings will not admit of this; and if mine would, we well know that those of the great mass of white people will not. *Whether this feeling accords with justice and sound judgment, is not the sole question, if indeed, it is any part of it.* A universal feeling, whether well or ill-founded, cannot be safely disregarded. We cannot, then, make them equals. It does seem to me that systems of gradual emancipation might be adopted; but for their tardiness in this, I will not undertake to judge our brethren of the south. (emphasis added)[25]

It is worth comparing Lincoln's manner of argument here to Rawls's theory of public reason. His 'feeling' is opposed to the abolitionist doctrine. This is not, strictly speaking, an emotion, but an opinion formed after public and inner debate, and it includes a closely argued distinction regarding different spheres in which equality might be granted. This opinion, Lincoln acknowledges, may not accord with 'justice and sound judgment', but that is not the 'sole question' and perhaps not 'any part of it'. With this Rawls would agree, because in constitutional essentials he holds that 'the ideals and virtues of morality generally', including 'political morality', are 'irrelevant' since they lie outside the 'political values of the public conception of justice'.[26] On similar grounds Lincoln says that he cannot disregard the 'universal feeling' of white people against making slaves their equals.

The abolitionists were a tiny minority, and their espousal of the full equality of human races and demand for an immediate end to slavery were far removed from the 'overlapping consensus' of the day.[27] In the 1830s perhaps no more than one per cent of the population would have endorsed abolitionist demands.[28] The movement grew in the 1840s and 1850s, but still it found its base of support in fringe religious sects such as the Quakers. In many places in the South, and in Washington, DC, it was illegal to distribute abolitionist literature, and the

[24] A Lincoln, Fourth Debate with Stephen Douglas, ibid *Vol 3* pp 146–47.
[25] A Lincoln, Speech at Peoria (16 October 1854) ibid *Vol 3* pp 256–57.
[26] Rawls, *Political Liberalism*, 236.
[27] See TA Upchurch, *Abolition Movement* (Greenwood Publishing, 2011) xii–xvi.
[28] ibid.

public speeches of abolitionists were often met by mobs, in both North and South. The abolitionist editor Eliza Lovejoy was murdered by a mob in Alton, Illinois.[29]

Seeing how deep and pervasive that moral error was during the antebellum period should make us cautious about making perpetual constitutional law. Lincoln's appeals to consensus, over and against 'justice and sound judgment', are suggestive of how precarious of a ground Rawls's theory of public reason would be for such a purpose. Not only those who supported slavery, but also a far-sighted statesman like Lincoln, were blind to basic principles of equality. And on the Supreme Court, the majority in *Dred Scott* in favour of the view that blacks could never become citizens of the US was seven to two.

In *Planned Parenthood v Casey* (1992),[30] decided shortly before the publication of *Political Liberalism*, the Supreme Court announced a doctrine that anticipates Rawls's argument that, with respect to certain issues, the court has a responsibility to settle them 'once for all' and remove them from political controversy. The Court in *Casey* partially overruled *Roe v Wade* (1973)[31] but preserved its 'central holding', which it characterised as a standard of not allowing a state to impose an undue burden on a woman's decision to have an abortion.[32] Although the Court considered whether *Roe* had been wrongly decided initially, and acknowledged this as a possibility, the Court not only affirmed its central holding but announced that the case had a 'rare precedential force'. (emphasis added)[33]

> [When] the Court decides a case in such a way as to resolve the sort of intensely divisive controversy reflected in *Roe* and those rare, comparable cases, its decision has a dimension that the resolution of the normal case does not carry. It is the dimension present whenever the Court's interpretation of the Constitution *calls the contending sides of a national controversy to end their national division by accepting a common mandate rooted in the Constitution.*
>
> The Court is not asked to do this very often, having thus addressed the Nation only twice in our lifetime, in the decisions of *Brown* and *Roe*. But when the Court does act in this way, its decision requires an equally rare precedential force to counter the inevitable efforts to overturn it and to thwart its implementation.[34]

Thus, even if *Roe* had been wrongly decided initially, the circumstances surrounding its settlement and the ongoing controversy over it, lead to the conclusion that it cannot be overturned. The Court in *Casey* averred that only two cases 'in our lifetime' have had such rare precedential force. Five years later, however, in *Washington v Glucksberg*, Justice Souter (a joint author of the *Casey* opinion) said

[29] See DA Richards, 'Public Reason and Abolitionist Dissent' (1993) 69 *Chicago-Kent Law Review* 787, 788.

[30] Planned Parenthood v Casey 505 US 833 (1992).

[31] *Roe v Wade* 410 US 113 (1973).

[32] ibid 838, 874, 901.

[33] *Casey* 505 US 833 (1992).

[34] ibid 867.

that finality attaches generally to decisions regarding constitutional rights that override legislation:

> An unenumerated right should not therefore be recognized, with the effect of displacing the legislative ordering of things, without the assurance that its recognition would prove as durable as the recognition of those other rights differently derived. To recognize a right of lesser promise would simply create a constitutional regime too uncertain to bring with it the expectation of finality that is one of this Court's central obligations in making constitutional decisions. See *Casey*, 505 U.S., at 864–869.[35]

The Court's reasoning in *Casey* and Souter's in *Glucksberg* stand in contrast to a long line of pronouncements by justices in other cases.[36] Justice Brandeis, in an oft-quoted dissent in *Burnet v Coronado Oil & Gas Co*, argued that precedent should have little force in constitutional decisions:

> *Stare decisis* is usually the wise policy, because in most matters it is more important that the applicable rule of law be settled than that it be settled right. This is commonly true even where the error is a matter of serious concern, provided correction can be had by legislation. But in cases involving the Federal Constitution, where correction through legislative action is practically impossible, this court has often overruled its earlier decisions.[37]

In such cases, Brandeis stated, 'the court bows to the lessons of experience and the force of better reasoning'. His dissent was cited by the Court (per Rehnquist J) in *Seminole Tribe v Florida* (1996), which stated: 'Our willingness to reconsider our earlier decisions has been particularly true in constitutional cases, because in such cases correction through legislative action is practically impossible'.[38]

The theory of 'rare precedential force' proposed in *Casey* should be rejected in favour of Brandeis's better reasoned view—above all in cases where questions of fundamental justice are at stake, as with abortion and racial segregation. Here it is more important for a rule of law to be settled right than to be settled. Brandeis's explanation in his *Burnet* dissent of the need to remain open to change is noteworthy in light of the discussion in chapters four and five of the potential for judicial mistake:

> The decision of the court, if, in essence, merely the determination of a fact, is not entitled, in later controversies between other parties, to that sanction which, under the policy of *stare decisis*, is accorded to the decision of a proposition purely of law.
>
> For not only may the decision of the fact have been rendered upon an inadequate presentation of then existing conditions, but the conditions may have changed meanwhile. Moreover, the judgment of the court in the earlier decision may have been influenced by

[35] *Washington v Glucksberg* 521 US 702, 788–89 (1997).

[36] See, eg, *Swift v Tyson* 41 US 1 (1842) 18; *Barden v Northern Pacific R. Co* 154 US 288, 322 (1894) (the only doctrines that endure are those that 'bear the strictest examination and the test of experience') (Field J).

[37] *Burnet v Coronado Oil & Gas Co* 285 US 393, 406–407 (1932).

[38] *Seminole Tribe v Florida* 517 US 44, 63 (1996).

prevailing views as to economic or social policy which have since been abandoned. In cases involving constitutional issues of the character discussed, this court must, in order to reach sound conclusions, feel free to bring its opinions into agreement with experience and with facts newly ascertained.[39]

The view expressed here is a refreshing contrast to Justice Souter's claim in *Glucksberg* that a decision to nullify legislation on rights-based grounds should be accompanied by an expectation of finality.

III. The Rarity of Constitutional Amendment

Although Justice Brandeis and others have rightly identified the need to be able to change constitutional precedents, the practical mechanics of this make it a more arduous task than is suggested by some of the remarks in the last section about overruling prior cases—especially when the precedent is one that has struck down a law. A decision of a supreme court or constitutional court to nullify a statute can be overturned only by: (i) constitutional amendment; or (ii) a process in which the legislature enacts a law that is equivalent or substantially similar to the nullified legislation, and a lawsuit challenging this leads to the court upholding the law and overturning its prior decision. I call (ii) the legislative-judicial method and consider it in section IV below.

Constitutional amendments are uncommon in almost every legal system, and particularly so in federal systems that require ratification by constituent states or regions such as the US and Canada. An amendment to the US Constitution must pass both houses of Congress by a two-thirds majority and then be ratified by three quarters of the states (either in state legislatures or citizen referenda).[40] Since the first ten amendments adopted together as the Bill of Rights, there have been only 17 amendments: about one in every 13 years. In Canada, where the procedural difficulty of amendment procedures is on a par with the US,[41] there have been no major amendments in 34 years since the Constitution Act 1982. The 11 amendments that have been ratified all involved relatively minor issues of provincial laws. The Meech Lake Accord (1987) and Charlottetown Accord (1992), agreements to answer grievances of Quebec, were 'modest' amendments, according to Peter Hogg; but they failed in a manner that led him to conclude that 'significant amendments to the Constitution of Canada are, for the foreseeable future, impossible'.[42] Where the process is less difficult, as in Ireland or

[39] *Burnet v Coronado Oil & Gas Co* 283 US 393 at 412.

[40] US Constitution, art V. Amendments may also be proposed by two thirds of the states.

[41] The amending formula is in sections 38 to 49 of the Constitution Act 1982, and generally requires an amendment to be ratified by two thirds of provinces representing at least 50% of the overall population.

[42] P Hogg, 'Canada: From Privy Council to Supreme Court' in J Goldsworthy (ed), *Interpreting Constitutions: A Comparative Study* (Oxford, Oxford University Press, 2006) 57.

Germany for example, amendments have been relatively more frequent, though still uncommon.

When constitutional amendments have succeeded, most have concerned structural or procedural aspects of constitutions regarding matters such as voting rights and representation. It is very rare for a constitutional amendment to have the purpose of overturning a decision of a constitutional court, and even rarer to overturn a decision that nullifies a law on the ground that its substantive content conflicts with an abstract moral right.[43]

One system that has had repeated occasions of amendments overturning rights-based nullification decisions is India, where constitutional amendment (on most matters) is by a two-thirds majority of Parliament. Some of these amendments were part of a tumultuous period that involved a struggle between the Indian Supreme Court and the political branches over who would have the final say over the content of the Indian Constitution. The Court asserted and reasserted that it has the power to declare amendments to be invalid if they change the 'basic structure' (including major rights provisions) of the Constitution.[44] The power the Court wields is similar to what Rawls says a supreme court should have. But the Court has used it to protect individual property rights and block reforms regarding distribution of land in ways that seem, ironically, to violate Rawls's principles of justice.[45]

Though this survey of amendment practice has been necessarily brief, one may safely conclude that constitutional amendment processes are relatively well-suited for changing structural matters. The resistance to change preserves the stability of state institutions and protects agreements regarding allocation of power reached when groups of people agree to unite politically, while still allowing a society to change its secondary rules when there is widespread agreement. Constitutional amendment, however, is less well suited for creating and changing primary rules, and is almost wholly ineffective as a means for reversing rights-based nullification decisions. One reason for this is that it is difficult to formulate an amendment that

[43] In Ireland, for example, none of the 34 amendments to the 1937 Constitution fall into this category. The proposed 25th Amendment, which failed by a narrow margin in a popular referendum, would have tightened restrictions on abortion in response to *Attorney General v X* (1992) IESC 1, which allowed women to travel to obtain an abortion in certain circumstances. The proposed method was not by precise formulation in the constitution, but by stating that 'the life of the unborn in the womb shall be protected in accordance with the provisions of the Protection of Human Life in Pregnancy Act 2002', with that legislation slated for separate enactment.

Similarly, none of the 60 amendments to the German Basic Law have overturned a decision of the German Federal Constitutional Court. Wojciech Sadurski's 2001 study of decisions by constitutional courts in central and eastern Europe found that only one of those decisions has ever been overturned by constitutional amendment—and this concerned an issue about voting rather than ordinary substantive law. W Sadurski, 'Rights-Based Constitutional Review in Central and Eastern Europe' in Tom Campbell et al (eds), *Skeptical Essays on Human Rights* (Oxford, Oxford University Press, 2001) 319.

[44] See SP Sathe, 'India: From Positivism to Structuralism' in J Goldsworthy (ed), *Interpreting Constitutions: A Comparative Study* (Oxford, Oxford University Press, 2006) 221–25.

[45] See ibid.

is sufficiently general to be appropriate for including in a constitution and at the same time specific enough to overturn the particular result of a case.

Suppose that you wanted to draft a constitutional amendment to overturn *Lochner v New York*.[46] A constitutional case cannot be simply repealed like an ordinary law or abrogated like a textual provision of a constitution, both of which require only a declaration that cancels the existing text. An amendment that declared, '*Lochner v New York* is hereby overturned', would settle nothing regarding constitutional law, because it does not specify what aspect of the decision is rejected. You could draft an amendment to specify that legislatures have the power to set limits to the number of hours worked in bakeries, but it would hardly be worth going through the amendment process for such a narrow principle. You could extend this to all trades and professions, but this would be a narrow specification of legislative power compared to the general areas of competence that constitutions normally address. Moreover, you might meet resistance in the form of a group that is opposed to the legislature regulating hours in certain professions (eg medicine, law, or academic research) and sees this amendment as an invitation for the legislature to do so.

An alternative strategy might be to specify that certain constitutional provisions cannot be used as grounds for nullifying legislation. During the *Lochner* era US courts struck down legislation on the basis of a number of constitutional provisions, including equal protection, freedom of contract, and due process of law (under the theory of 'substantive due process'). This alternative strategy would entail removing procedural protections in order to achieve a substantive result. Even if it were desirable to remove all of these provisions from the grounds for judicial review, it is unlikely that any such amendment could gain the popular support needed for ratification. Finally, you could attempt to delineate the permissible scope or level of scrutiny for judicial review, perhaps along the lines of *United States v Carolene Products Co*,[47] footnote 4, where the Court announced that it would limit strict scrutiny review to cases involving certain core rights and to protect 'discrete and insular' minorities. But such an amendment would be vague and may not achieve the desired result; a court not already inclined to change course (as the *Carolene* Court was) would probably find ways to interpret the amendment to preserve its power of judicial review.

Such difficulties are likely to attend most attempts to reverse a judicial decision through constitutional amendment, especially in cases involving balancing and proportionality. A decision of this kind could be overturned by an amendment that affirms the constitutionality of the specified provisions of the nullified legislation, but amendments such as this could end up cluttering the constitution with specific, substantive legal detail. In sum, it is rare for a constitutional amendment

[46] *Lochner v New York* 198 US 45 (1905).

[47] *United States v Carolene Products Co* 304 US 144 (1938).

to overturn a rights-based judicial nullification decision because of dual obstacles: (i) the difficulty of formulating an amendment to overturn a specific judicial decision; and (ii) the multiple steps and super-majority requirements of the amendment process.[48]

In the US this has never happened at the federal level. The post-Civil War Amendments could be considered to overturn certain aspects of *Dred Scott v Sanford* by abolishing slavery (13th Amendment), according citizenship to former slaves (15th Amendment), and guaranteeing equal protection of the law for all citizens (14th Amendment). They are better considered, however, as part of the global settlement of the Civil War, having been ratified during the Reconstruction era, when the governments of southern states were effectively imposed by the Union. Setting aside the Reconstruction Amendments and the Bill of Rights, all but two of the remaining 14 amendments have dealt with structural matters such as elections, voting rights, term limits, and questions of federal-state relations and competence. The only two amendments regarding the substantive content of law are the 18th Amendment (1919) prohibiting the manufacture, sale, transportation, importation, and exportation of 'intoxicating liquors', and the 21st Amendment, which overturned the 18th in 1933. The Prohibition episode suggests, yet again, the fallibility of attempts to enshrine substantive values in constitutional law.

IV. The Legislative-Judicial Method of Reversing Nullification Decisions

The legislative-judicial method, whereby legislation is re-enacted and upheld by a court that reverses its prior judgment, is better suited than constitutional amendment for reversing nullification decisions in one respect. A later court judgment can fully discuss and describe the reasoning of a prior decision, reject a specified part of its *ratio decidendi*, and articulate a new rule or principle using the prose conventions of judicial opinions. The tersely formulated rules and principles found in Western constitutions are (usually) not fit for this task. The second method, however, is still a difficult and cumbersome process. It involves all the disadvantage of changing the law through common law methods, including retroactive effect for the current parties (and those in like situations), and an appropriate reluctance to change the law without an especially strong reason. This inertia is problematic when lawmaking decisions are based upon empirical assessments that are subject to change, or when the law needs to be capable of regular revision. The cases analysed in chapters four and five show that rights-based nullification decisions may be based on empirical assessments or policy judgments that are

[48] I refer here to decisions that nullify some aspect of the substantive content of law rather than decisions that concern procedural rights.

inherently temporal and subject to revision. Moreover, cases such as *Dred Scott v Sanford* and *Lochner v New York* show that constitutional decisions may well reflect moral error or views of political economy that are seriously flawed or otherwise not worthy of being entrenched in the constitution.

There is another, more fundamental problem with the legislative-judicial method of reversing nullification decisions. In order for a court to reconsider an earlier opinion, generally the legislature must first enact a law that is equivalent or substantially similar to the nullified legislation. This fact not only contributes to the length and difficulty of the second method, it also points to the conceptual and practical difficulties regarding constitutional authority and validity that arise when legislation is enacted contrary to constitutional precedent. In a system of strong judicial review, the supreme court or constitutional court is normally supposed to be the last resort for questions about the interpretation of constitutional rights. It might seem, then, that the legislature lacks legitimate constitutional authority to enact laws contrary to supreme court decisions. But if that were true, there would be a Catch-22 with regard to the legislative-judicial method of reversal. In section II, I argued that supreme courts should consider precedent on the constitutional validity of laws to be freely revisable. Justice Brandeis persuasively argued for this approach to constitutional precedent because, unlike other *stare decisis* contexts, correction of constitutional rulings cannot be made by the legislature. But correction cannot be made by courts, either, unless legislatures are free to enact legislation that is contrary to such precedent; this is (generally) a necessary condition for the case to arise.[49]

It is my view that, even in a strong system of judicial review, legislatures should not consider themselves bound by constitutional precedent in the way that lower courts are bound by higher courts. Such precedent may be treated as persuasive authority, but it is not conclusive with regard to the legislature's duty or legitimate scope of action, whether in relation to factual assessments or judgments on morality, policy, or the appropriateness of legislative means. Two of the reasons for holding this view are that constitutional precedent may be based on: (i) incorrect factual conclusions or errors in moral judgment; or (ii) premises that were tenable at the time of the decision but have since been undermined by changes in society, technology, or growth in human knowledge. Moreover, as I have argued in

[49] I do not consider here the possibility that the constitutional issue in opinion X, which nullifies legislation Y, could arise in a separate area of law, in such a way that the supreme court could alter its doctrine and thereby open a path to restoring legislation Y. I also ignore here complications arising from federalism. A supreme court's decision to nullify a law in state A might leave the constitutional status of a law in state B uncertain, if B's law is similar to A's but distinct in some ways. Litigation regarding the law in B could bring the constitutional issue before the supreme court again. And if that issue bears on several laws in several states, the opportunity for reconsidering, modifying, or clarifying the interpretation of the constitution might arise regularly in the supreme court. Something like this scenario happened in the United States during the *Lochner* era. The Supreme Court upheld a number of challenged economic and other regulations during the *Lochner* era, but it did not substantially restrict the exercise of the kind of power asserted in *Lochner*, or alter the theoretical basis of such exercises, until the 1930s.

chapter five, legislatures have superior institutional capacities for empirical investigation and other reasoning processes that figure in some rights-based nullification decisions, especially when those are based on proportionality inquiries.

If my view is correct, there are nonetheless major practical obstacles to reversing nullification decisions through the legislative-judicial method. Some legislators are likely to reject this view, and argue that it is illegitimate defiance of the supreme (or constitutional) court—or the constitution—to make legislative proposals contrary to constitutional precedent. Some legislators will be reluctant to spend political capital on such controversial proposals, and others will be reluctant to devote scarce legislative resources to try to enact laws of doubtful constitutional validity. And courts themselves are unlikely to reverse their own precedent, especially in the short term. Even if they do not adopt the attitude of the US Supreme Court in *Casey*—of being unwilling to reconsider possible error in prior decisions because that would diminish the reputation of the court and give the appearance of caving in to political pressure—the normal inertia of the common law will predispose courts to uphold their precedent.

Perhaps the most prominent example in US history of reversal of a rights-based nullification decision[50] through the legislative-judicial method is the Supreme Court's decision in the 1930s to discard *Lochner* and to uphold legislation previously ruled unconstitutional. But even this did not result in overruling *Lochner* explicitly. In light of the *Lochner* doctrine's long endurance in the face of scholarly criticism and political circumstances that could hardly have been more propitious for overturning it, one should doubt the efficacy of the legislative-judicial method for constitutional change as well as claims that courts follow the election returns. Thirty years is a long time for such a flawed decision to stand, and it did not fall until the Great Depression was well under way. The Court was under pressure from President Roosevelt's famous court-packing plan, which he put forward to save his popular New Deal proposals from being struck down. This pressure might have led to the 'switch in time that saved nine'.[51]

V. Conclusion

The question of whether to set judges as the guardians of constitutional rights involves more than the issue of whether we consider courts or legislatures to be

[50] In the US, many constitutional precedents that have been discarded involve different categories of case, such as the following: (i) procedural protections for the accused; (ii) federal-state allocations of competence; (iii) compliance with constitutional norms by executive officials and governmental institutions; and (iv) the Supreme Court's initial decision to uphold legislation against a constitutional challenge. These categories do not involve the same kind of structural impediments to reconsideration of earlier decisions as rights-based nullification of a legislative decision.

[51] See WE Leuchtenburg, 'The Origins of Franklin D. Roosevelt's Court-Packing Plan' (1966) *Supreme Court Review* 347, 381–82.

more likely to reach correct decisions about rights. Even if we were to assume that judges have the ability to make better decisions in some (or many) cases, this alone is not sufficient to justify an institutional arrangement in which their decisions have the strongly entrenched character of constitutional law. As Raz states, 'For an authority to be able to pass timelessly valid laws … it must be counted as an expert on morality—that is, as having significantly superior grasp of abstract moral principles than do the people who are bound by its laws'.[52] Decisions to strike down laws are not 'timelessly valid' in precisely this way, but they do have long-lasting and potentially permanent effects. In order to justify judicial review of legislation we would need to be confident not simply that courts are marginally better than legislatures at making decisions about constitutional rights; we would also need to be sure that courts are substantially better and that they are not themselves likely to make significant moral and empirical errors. In chapters four and five, however, we have seen that courts have made many such errors, often causing lasting damage. For the period in US history from 1850 to 1950, time has vindicated not the judicial but the legislative branch, including on the issue of racial equality. The historical perspective taken in chapter five should give constitutional framers strong grounds for hesitating to entrust the fundamental questions of political morality to courts.

[52] See J Raz, 'On the Authority and Interpretation of Constitutions: Some Preliminaries' in *Between Authority and Interpretation*, above n 11, 323, 341.

7

Judicial Review and Constitutional Design

In this concluding chapter, I consider judicial review of legislation from the perspective of constitutional design. Should constitutional framers choose to adopt a system of judicial review of legislation? If so, in what form? The argument, which builds on the analysis of comparative institutional competence in prior chapters, is applicable both to a moment of founding as well as to countries, such as the UK, where there is ongoing debate about whether to adopt judicial review or reform an existing system. The argument can also inform the exercise of judicial review in places where it is unlikely to be abolished or structurally altered, particularly in regard to the question of judicial deference to the legislature.

My argument is at a level of generality that could be compared to an architectural drawing in a design competition (for example, John Raphael Brandon's design for the Royal Courts of Justice depicted on the cover of this book). I sketch the external features, but work would need to be done to fill in the interior elements for any country-specific, practical proposal.

The argument proceeds as follows. In section I, I show that the establishment of rights-based judicial review of legislation has historically progressed with little overt consideration by constitutional framers regarding the institutional capacities of courts to reason about abstract moral rights. In both the American and Kelsenian models, a bill of rights was joined to a judicial model originally devised for another purpose. Before considering *whether* constitutional framers should adopt judicial review, I first discuss in section II the capacities that an institution should have in order to decide constitutional rights cases. I argue that the Kelsenian constitutional court has features that make it a better model for constitutional adjudication than the American model. With regard to the specific task of adjudicating abstract moral rights, I argue that the Kelsenian model is still lacking, and thus I propose additional features. In section III, I consider whether the model proposed in section II is properly called a 'court'. I conclude that the status and character of the institution could be clarified by thinking of its function as that of a 'negative legislator', which is how Kelsen described his constitutional court. I call the model described in section II a 'Council of Revision'. In section IV, I argue that it is legitimate for countries without a system of rights-based judicial review of legislation (which include the UK, Australia, New Zealand, Switzerland, and the Netherlands) to maintain current arrangements. In some contexts, however, constitutional framers might reasonably choose to adopt rights-based judicial review. If so, the Council of Revision sketched in section II provides an appropriate general model, adaptable to local circumstances. Finally, in section V, I consider the import of the arguments above for questions about deference in existing systems of judicial review.

I. The American and Kelsenian Models

The original US Constitution had no bill of rights and made no explicit provision for judicial review of legislation. Most of its limits on the executive and legislative branches were clear and specific, such as the bar on granting any 'title of nobility' or suspending the writ of habeas corpus. The major exception to this, the guarantee to each state of a 'republican form of government', was established in 1849 to be a non-justiciable political question.[1] The 1787 constitutional convention included no direct debate on the scope of judicial review or how it would operate, though statements by delegates reveal a general (albeit not universal) assumption that judges would have certain limited powers to review statutes.[2] The delegates also barely debated a bill of rights. A motion to prepare such a bill was briefly discussed five days before signing the Constitution, and defeated.[3] The delegates did debate at length, however, a topic with relevance for the present discussion, namely the Council of Revision.

The Council of Revision, proposed by the Virginia delegation including James Madison, was to consist of the President and members of the federal judiciary and was to have a general power of veto over laws passed by Congress. The Council was modelled on a body with the same name, and a similar combination of executive and judicial personnel, which was created by the New York Constitution in 1777 and lasted until 1821. The New York Council had the power to reject laws 'inconsistent with the spirit of this Constitution or with the public good', and the proposed federal Council was presumed to have the same power. The debate over the Council assumed a distinction between vetoing laws because they were *unconstitutional* and because they were wrong as a matter of policy. Delegates argued that laws 'may be unjust, may be unwise, may be dangerous, may be destructive …'[4] or 'oppressive or pernicious',[5] and yet not violate any

[1] *Luther v Borden* 48 US 1 (1849).

[2] J Agresto, *The Supreme Court and Constitutional Democracy* (Ithaca, Cornell University Press, 1984) 61.

[3] J Vile, *The Constitutional Convention of 1787: A Comprehensive Encyclopedia of America's Founding, Vol 1* (Santa Barbara, ABC-CLIO, 2005) 59.

[4] J Anderson, 'Learning from the Great Council of Revision Debate' (2006) 68 *Notre Dame Review of Politics* 79.

[5] ibid.

constitutional prohibition or limit.[6] Some delegates supported judges having power to evaluate a law on policy grounds in their role as Council members; but several opposed this, and the proposal for the Council was eventually defeated in a close vote. Most of the statements of the framers regarding judicial review at the convention occurred during the debate over the Council. A recent study shows that, despite disagreement over judges' proper role qua Council members, the delegates unanimously agreed that, *acting in their capacity as judges* they should not review law on policy grounds.[7]

This is consistent with Alexander Hamilton's classic argument for judicial review in *The Federalist* No 78. Hamilton contended that the Constitution is *law* and therefore subject to judicial interpretation and enforcement.[8] He drew an analogy to the situation where one statute contradicts another in specific textual terms, leaving judges no logical choice except to choose one or the other.[9] Ordinarily judges would apply the later-enacted statute. But Hamilton argued that, in the face of such a contradiction (an 'irreconcilable variance' between a statute and the 'manifest tenor' of the Constitution), judges should follow the Constitution as the hierarchically superior law.[10] In *The Federalist* No 84 Hamilton opposed adding a bill of rights to the Constitution in part on the grounds that the existing models, with phrases such as 'liberty of the press', were too vague to have legal meaning or to be capable of legal definition: the 'volumes of those aphorisms which make the principal figure in several of our State bills of rights [would] sound much better in a treatise of ethics than in a constitution of government'.[11]

The Bill of Rights was passed by the first Congress in 1789 and ratified by the states (in the form of the first ten amendments), but it did not become a significant source for constitutional adjudication until much later. Madison, who shepherded the Bill through Congress, had been opposed both to judicial review and a bill of rights during the convention.[12] His decision to support the Bill of Rights in 1789 was 'largely, and perhaps entirely tactical',[13] and did not reflect an embrace of final judicial power to settle questions about rights.[14] In *Marbury v Madison* (1803)[15] John Marshall did not discuss the Bill of Rights. He followed Hamilton's

[6] ibid.

[7] ibid, 96: 'Given the council's opponents' multiple statements opposing judge-made policy, and the absence of even a single statement to the contrary among them, the evidence overwhelmingly suggests that these delegates opposed the idea of justices' playing a policymaking role through their exercise of judicial review.'

[8] *The Federalist* No 84.

[9] ibid.

[10] The higher ranking of the Constitution was owing to the superiority of the permanent constituent power of 'We the People' over the temporal legislature.

[11] ibid.

[12] See S Snowiss, *Judicial Review and the Law of the Constitution* (New Haven, Yale University Press, 1990).

[13] ibid 92.

[14] ibid 91–95.

[15] *Marbury v Madison* 5 US 137 (1803).

argument about the Constitution as hierarchically superior law, in the context of a claimed textual contradiction between a statute and the constitutional provision for the Supreme Court's original jurisdiction.[16] After *Marbury* the Court did not strike down another federal statute until 1857 in *Dred Scott v Sanford*. While the Court in that case relied on the 'due process' clause of the 5th Amendment, the Bill of Rights did not become a significant basis for constitutional adjudication until the twentieth century, following in the wake of the doctrinal developments in the *Lochner* era (see chapter four, section I).

In contrast to the American model, the Kelsenian model of a constitutional court has followed a more intentional course of constitutional design. Kelsen helped to draft the Austrian Constitution in 1919, including provisions on the Constitutional Court, in accord with a memorandum he wrote on the design of the Court.[17] Jurisdiction to enforce the Constitution was confined to the Court, which was separate from ordinary courts. Its members were appointed by Parliament, serving for terms. Kelsen himself was appointed as a justice on the Court and served for ten years. In 'The Nature and Development of Constitutional Adjudication', a 1929 essay offering a general theoretical defence of his model, Kelsen described the Constitutional Court's task as the 'purely juristic work of constitutional interpretation' and said it called for the appointment of 'legal experts'.[18] The constitutional norms the Court enforced would vary according to jurisdiction, but they generally involved the structures of law-making and government and allocation of power between regional and national governments.

Kelsen strongly opposed giving the Court power to enforce principles formulated in abstract moral language, that is, those which make 'an appeal to the ideals of "justice," "freedom", "equality", "equity," "decency", and so on.'[19] As Hamilton had viewed state bills of rights earlier, Kelsen thought that such terms were legally 'vacuous', providing no determinate guidance to judges. Such terms could serve as political norms, directing legislative organs in their creation of law; and law-making could be seen as a process that transforms vague principles by specifying them into positive law.[20] But it would be 'highly dangerous' to make the principles a basis for constitutional adjudication, in particular for review of the constitutionality of statutes.[21]

> What the majority of the judges on the court regard as just may completely contradict what the majority of the state's inhabitants hold to be just, and it undoubtedly contradicts what the majority of the parliament that enacted the statute in question to be just.

[16] ibid.

[17] S Lagi, 'Hans Kelsen and the Austrian Constitutional Court (1918–1929)' (2012) 9 *Revista Co-herencia* 273.

[18] H Kelsen, 'On the Nature and Development of Constitutional Adjudication' in L Vinx (ed), *The Guardian of the Constitution: Hans Kelsen and Carl Schmitt on the Limits of Constitutional Law* (Cambridge, Cambridge University Press, 2015) 48, 76.

[19] ibid 60.

[20] ibid 59.

[21] ibid 60.

> It is self-evident that it cannot be the purpose of a constitution to make every statute enacted by parliament dependent, through the use of an ill-defined and highly ambiguous word like 'justice', or some other equally vacuous term, on the free discretion of a college whose members are as arbitrarily chosen, from a political point of view, as the members of a constitutional court.

The arbitrary character of such an assignment arises from the fact that judges of the Constitutional Court are to be appointed on the basis of legal expertise, not political acumen or wisdom. Kelsen concluded that such a 'shift of power from parliament to an extra-parliamentary institution … is certainly not intended by the constitution'; it would 'concede to the constitutional court a fullness of power that must be regarded as altogether intolerable'.[22] To prevent such transfer of power, Kelsen argued that a constitution must 'abstain from all phraseology of this kind'.[23] In other words, it should not have a bill of rights in the way that they are usually worded.

Despite Kelsen's warnings, nearly all the constitutions that have established constitutional courts on the Kelsenian model have also adopted a bill of rights. One explanation for this is that the framers who established the courts did not have Kelsen's willingness to trust the democratic system. The first wave of constitutional courts came after the fall of fascist regimes in Germany, Italy, and Spain, and the second wave came after the fall of the Berlin Wall and communist regimes in eastern and central Europe. The Kelsenian court was seen as a ready-made model for keeping the legislature within constitutional limits. The addition of the bill of rights was seen as a way of building in a check against a possible lack of popular commitment to the values expressed therein. In joining the bill of rights to an institution designed to operate on the basis of legal expertise, the framers failed to provide constitutional courts with the institutional capacities needed to engage in the moral and empirical reasoning required to make decisions about constitutional rights.

II. Designing a Constitutional Court

In this section I assume that a decision *has been made* by constitutional framers to adopt judicial review, with an enforceable bill of rights, and that the system will be *strong-form* in the sense that a judgment holding that a law is unconstitutional is generally binding on other branches. Given that such a decision has been made, what sort of institution should be entrusted with carrying out the review of legislation? I will discuss some advantages that a Kelsenian constitutional court has over the American model, while arguing that the former model can still be

[22] ibid 61.
[23] ibid.

improved in two key areas. I begin by discussing issues under the broad headings of moral and empirical reasoning, which have guided my analysis of institutional capacities thus far. This analysis assumes that a bill of rights will ordinarily be enforced through balancing and proportionality tests as discussed in chapter two.

A. Empirical Reasoning

Chapter four analysed the weak capacities that courts have for finding legislative facts—general facts about society relevant to decisions about whether a law is needed and how it should function. Chapter five explained the superior capacities of legislatures to acquire and assess empirical research, noting that one key is the ability to interact with experts. Common law trial courts can engage with experts, and can appoint independent experts or special masters for assistance with complex empirical questions. They sometimes do so in constitutional cases. But this capacity is not practically available to courts of appeal and supreme courts, which almost never receive new evidence. It is ultimately the supreme court that must make the decision about constitutionality, mainly in passive reliance on a written record and Brandeis briefs. In contrast, the German Federal Constitutional Court (FCC) has the capacity to interact directly with experts. I will discuss three examples of this.

(1) The *Outright Monetary Transactions Case* involved a constitutional challenge to the programme that Mario Draghi, President of the European Central Bank, announced in September 2012 for buying the bonds of Eurozone member states in crisis situations. Given the importance of the case and the complexities including sovereign bond markets, inflation rates, and money supply, the FCC called witnesses from the ECB, including one of Draghi's assistants, the Bundesbank, economists, and experts in financial markets. In a two-day hearing at the FCC, they gave testimony and responded to questioning from the justices.[24]

(2) In 2009 a German law authorised plea bargaining in criminal cases, a practice that had long been rejected in Germany as contrary to proper procedure.[25] In recent decades, due to increasing dockets, the practice had gradually, and quietly, grown in practice. When a case challenged the constitutionality of the practice, the Court solicited an empirical study. The study, conducted in 2012 ahead of the Court's 2013 decision, surveyed 190 criminal court judges, 68 prosecutors and 76 criminal defence attorneys. It revealed 'a wide chasm between the law on the books and bargaining in practice'.[26]

[24] *Outright Monetary Transactions* Case-I, BVerfGE 134, 366–2 BvR 2728/13 (2014).

[25] See T Weigend and J Iontcheva Turner, 'The Constitutionality of Negotiated Criminal Judgments in Germany' (2014) 15 *German Law Journal* 81. 'Plea bargain' is a rough translation of the German practice.

[26] ibid 92.

(3) In the *Smoking Ban Case*,[27] Baden-Württemberg and Berlin enacted general bans on smoking in public places. Certain establishments were allowed to set up separate smoking rooms. A constitutional complaint was brought by proprietors of establishments without space for a separate room. They alleged violation of their right to occupational freedom and ownership, because the prohibition distorted economic competition in favour of larger establishments. The FCC held that although it would have been constitutional to enact a comprehensive ban, as Bavaria had done in 2007, a non-comprehensive ban must not impose disproportionate costs on the owners of small establishments. The measures in question failed to comply with the principles of consistency and proportionality.[28] The FCC arrived at this conclusion after reviewing studies on mortality and other health effects of passive smoking; analyses of the chemical structure of tobacco smoke and the carcinogens it contains, and the ways in which particulates can harm the body; surveys of smoking habits among the German people and attitudes toward smoking; statistical reports on the current and projected impact of the smoking bans on the revenue of different kinds of establishments; and many other matters. This evidence was submitted by public and private bodies, including the Department for Health, Environment and Consumer Protection; the Federal Statistical Office; the German Society of Occupational and Environmental Medicine; the German Cancer Research Center; the German Hotel and Restaurant Association; two anti-smoking advocacy groups; and a group representing the tobacco industry.[29] Some of these groups presented testimony at an oral hearing, and a medical expert appointed by the Court also testified about the dangers of passive smoking.[30]

In contrast to the system of the FCC, common law systems remain more reliant on Brandeis briefs. It should be recalled that Brandeis briefs were an ad hoc development in the early 1900s, popularised by Louis Brandeis but invented by Henry Weisman in *Lochner* (chapter four, section I). Since that time the practice has spread to other jurisdictions. More than a century later, the use of Brandeis briefs has remained largely untouched by rules of evidence or appellate or trial procedure. Courts have not outlined a systematic framework for it. In the US and Canada, a variety of approaches can be observed. Supreme and appellate courts generally are willing to consider legislative facts submitted for the first time on appeal. Some judges, however, have treated the record of legislative facts compiled in the trial court as a closed record.[31] The Candadian Supreme Court has recently adopted an approach of deferring to the trial court's findings on matters

[27] *Smoking Ban Case*, BVerfGE, 121, 317.

[28] ibid 344.

[29] ibid 350–53.

[30] ibid 353.

[31] S Benjamin, 'Stepping into the Same River Twice: Rapidly Changing Facts and the Appellate Process' (1999) 78 *Texas Law Review* 269, 291–92; *Reno v American Civil Liberties Union* 521 US 844, 855–57 (1997).

of legislative fact.[32] In contrast to the method of the FCC, the common law approach can be seen as splitting up the process of acquiring legislative facts. In a number of cases, trial courts receive both Brandeis briefs and testimony from live witnesses. But in most cases, new evidence is presented at later stages in the appeal process, and it is at the supreme court stage that the Brandeis briefs are generally thought to be definitive.

Regular procedures and standards could help to improve the current system regarding Brandeis briefs, but it does not really address the root issue. Kenneth Davis, the American scholar of administrative law who distinguished legislative and adjudicative facts, has proposed that the US Supreme Court should have a dedicated research bureau along the lines of the Congressional Research Service.[33] He notes that in the first US Congress of 1789, members relied on their own personal knowledge; as industrial economies advanced and society grew more complex, legislatures created new institutional structures to cope with the growing body of scientific and technological knowledge.[34] Similar structures have not been developed for courts, despite the growing reliance on empirical research in adjudication. Since the Supreme Court addresses complex factual questions in applying and interpreting constitutional provisions, Davis argues, it should have a well-resourced research staff with scientific training.

Davis's conclusion is compelling. With the assistance of a research service, a court would be better able to scrutinise Brandeis briefs, and also able to go beyond the parties' presentation of the facts and selection of sources. More to the point, judges in the US, Canada, and elsewhere already conduct their own research into empirical sources, and, as shown in chapter four, sometimes rely on sources of questionable authority and dubious research methods—including on both accounts their use of internet search engines. In the absence of scientific training or concentrated self-study, judges are not well-equipped to comprehend statistical analyses or the results of studies in the social and natural sciences. A research service would eliminate the need for judges to sift through scientific papers on their own while bringing greater transparency to the process. The actual implementation of such a research service would involve a number of questions about its proper role and institutional structure that cannot be addressed here. But it is difficult to resist the conclusion that, in principle, courts should be provided with a research service, if they are meant to consider evidence of the kind discussed in chapter four and in the cases analysed there.

[32] See *Canada (Attorney General) v Bedford*, 2013 SCC 72, [2013] 3 SCR 1101, para 48. The approach in *Bedford*, which was followed in *Carter v Canada* in 2015, contrasts to more vigorous review of the trial court's findings in *Chaoulli v Quebec* [2005] 1 SCR 79. See ibid at para 235 (Binnie J dissenting): 'We note that our colleagues refer to the evidence before the trial judge rather than the view taken of that evidence by the trial judge. The trial judge reached a contrary conclusion on the facts, and deference is due to her view of that evidence'.

[33] KC Davis, 'Judicial, Legislative, and Administrative Lawmaking: A Proposed Research Service for the Supreme Court' (1986) 71 *Minnesota Law Review* 1.

[34] ibid 5.

B. Moral Reasoning

Adrian Vermeule has argued that some justices of the US Supreme Court should be lay justices—individuals with professional qualifications in some field other than law—or lawyers with dual competence in another field.[35] Lay judges are used in a wide variety of contexts in many jurisdictions,[36] and Vermeule argues that they would improve the 'epistemic performance'[37] of the Court. I agree with the proposal, but for slightly different reasons. Vermeule characterises the contributions of lay justices as deriving from their professional expertise and contributing mainly to the empirical side of judicial reasoning. Hence, delicate decisions would be required regarding which subject areas to represent on the Court.[38] A better way to bolster a constitutional court's capacity with regard to empirical reasoning is through the research service discussed above. Any attempt to shore up a court's capacity for empirical reasoning through its core personnel, namely, justices, will necessarily be narrow and limited. A research service allows for comprehensive coverage of disciplines. It is also adaptable as scientific fields change.

Lay justices, though, could make a vital contribution to a court's capacity for moral reasoning.[39] If the jurisdiction of constitutional courts were confined to technical aspects of constitutional law, as envisioned by Hamilton and Kelsen, then there would be no compelling reason to add lay justices. Instead, as Kelsen argued, justices should be appointed on the basis of legal expertise. There are subjects in constitutional law today that exhibit the kind of complex legal reasoning for which legal expertise is needed. The plea bargaining case in Germany mentioned above is an example. It involves the interaction of technical procedural concepts with broad principles such as the presumption of innocence and the integrity of trials. Questions about the competence of a particular organ to make a decision, or about the division of powers in a federal structure, can be the subject of detailed constitutional provisions and nuanced doctrine (as in Canada). In the US, areas of constitutional law that demand expertise include the sovereign immunity of states, habeas corpus law, and other aspects of criminal procedure.

Most constitutional rights cases, however, are not of this complex nature, requiring legal expertise for an appropriate resolution. Instead, as we saw in chapter two, they are usually governed by balancing and proportionality tests. These tests generally amount to the question of whether the legislature has chosen means that unreasonably burden individual interests, in consideration of the value of the aim of the law. There is nothing particularly *legal* about this test, in the sense that having a professional qualification as a lawyer makes one more qualified to

[35] See A Vermeule, 'Should We Have Lay Justices' (2007) 59 *Stanford Law Review* 1569. See also A Vermuele, *Law and the Limits of Reason* (Oxford, Oxford University Press, 2009) 124, 149.

[36] ibid.

[37] ibid 90.

[38] ibid 149.

[39] Vermeule's concept of epistemic performance embraces both moral and empirical reasoning but tends to put emphasis on the latter.

apply a balancing test than someone who does not. Professional ethics courses in, say, medicine or business, often involve balancing varied factors in complex situations. Consider again the range of moral issues to which balancing tests are applied: limits on campaign speech and other aspects of free speech, surrogate parenthood, regulation of guns, affirmative action, abortion, and many more. Moral reasoning about these issues would be poorer if confined to a body comprised of members of a single background (say, doctors or lawyers or corporate executives) in comparison to a more diverse body. Moral reasoning in these areas will be assisted by knowledge of the relevant legal background, for which lawyers can be helpful; but this is true in the same sense that legislators considering moral issues in these areas also need to be aware of existing laws.

If the crucial point in a constitutional rights case is the application of a balancing test, then there is no reason why that decision should be confined to those with law degrees. To the contrary, there are good reasons for expanding the personnel of constitutional courts beyond lawyers. The most interesting model for this is the French *Conseil constitutionnel*, whose members are drawn from a variety of legal, government, and parliamentary backgrounds; often more than half do not have academic degrees in law.[40] A constitutional court with this kind of diverse membership is in a better position for understanding all of the dimensions of the great moral issues that regularly arise in constitutional court cases than a court where all members come from the same narrow—often elite and exclusive—legal background. All current members of the US Supreme Court have law degrees from either Harvard or Yale. The top echelons of the British judiciary are overwhelmingly filled by graduates of Oxford and Cambridge. Similar domination of constitutional courts by law-trained graduates of elite universities is a global phenomenon. There is, perhaps, not much to object about this so long as the cases decided by a constitutional court require legal expertise. We should want complex and important cases to be decided by those with the greatest expertise, and there is some ground for associating that quality with outstanding performance in a selective university. But since the resolution of constitutional rights cases does not demand *legal expertise*, there is no good reason to limit the personnel of constitutional courts to those who have it.

C. Centralised and Separate

The centralised Kelsenian constitutional court structure facilitates the proposals made above for a research service and for lay justices. It should be noted, however, that these particular proposals are in conflict with Kelsen's own more particular vision of what a constitutional court should be. In his view, the court would not enforce a bill of rights but technical matters of constitutional law within the

[40] J Bell, *Judiciaries Within Europe: A Comparative Review* (Cambridge, Cambridge University Press, 2006) 95.

domain of legal expertise. An institution like this would not need lay justices or a research service for empirical facts. In this section, however, I am assuming that the Rubicon has been crossed and a bill of rights has been adopted. Hence the question is what kind of structure and capacities an institution needs to decide constitutional rights cases.

Two features of the Kelsenian model are relevant to the above proposals: constitutional adjudication is centralised in one body, and that body is separate from the rest of the legal system, meaning that it is not required to hear non-constitutional cases. The separateness of the Kelsenian court facilitates the appointment of lay justices. The more a court's docket is filled with cases of statutory interpretation or other cases requiring legal expertise, the more difficult will it be to incorporate lay justices. The need for the centralisation of the court is shown by the proposal for the research service. It would be possible for such a service to be accessible by any judge considering a constitutional rights case on the American model. But a little reflection suggests that this would be practically unworkable, and a little more calls into question the American model of decentralised judicial review.

Judges in general have jurisdiction over constitutional questions in the American model, because of the formal logic—traceable to Hamilton and Marshall—that the constitution is *law* like any other law, except that it is hierarchically superior. But the resolution of a constitutional dispute is not like the resolution of other legal disputes, because it settles an issue that affects a fundamental part of the political order for every person. It would be absurd to assign such a responsibility to make the *final* resolution of such a question to a single judge. Is it any more sensible to allow any duly appointed judge to make a determination of the question in the first instance, pending appeal? Consider that the judge's decision will at least settle the question for a certain geographical region for a period of time, that trial judges in the US sometimes issue nationwide injunctions on the basis of their constitutional rulings, and that when there are multiple cases on the same issue there can be different constitutional settlements applicable in different parts of the country until the Supreme Court provides a final resolution. In light of the basic institutional structure and capacities of trial courts (see chapter five, section I), it seems unreasonable to give them power to decide broad constitutional issues,[41] especially to strike down legislation on the basis of abstract moral rights and balancing tests.

The value of centralised jurisdiction over constitutional rights cases can be seen in its contrast to the fragmentation of the process of acquiring legislative facts in the American model. Often a significant part of the evidence will have been generated at the trial court level, with the judge observing the questioning of the witnesses by the parties. But at the initial stage it cannot be known whether the case will prove to be important, or whether a case in another court might end up before the supreme court. Thus there is uncertainty about what resources to invest

[41] I set aside the question of the application of a constitutional procedural norm in an individual case, and similar questions that are intrinsically single-case focused.

in developing the record of legislative facts, and where. When the case arrives at the supreme court, it may receive new evidence not submitted at the trial court. The supreme court will have not have had the opportunity of questioning experts or even observing their interrogation. My proposal of a research service eliminates this fragmentary, unreliable process and also the temptation for judges to conduct their own personal research into legislative facts. But it can work properly only if attached to a centralised court.

D. Abstract Review

The centralisation of the Kelsenian model is connected to its power to review statutes in the abstract. The American model of judicial review is based on concrete cases, and it is sometimes argued that a court's ability to see the effects of law in a particular case helps to illuminate the overall decision-making process. Concrete review, however, means that in some cases, particular aspects may have an exaggerated impact on judges; and it 'may be difficult for the court to distance itself from those extraordinary cases and adopt a more systematic and nuanced view of the principles and interests at play'.[42] Judges need to be wary to avoid being 'carried away by their spontaneous and passionate reactions to the dramatic circumstances of a case'.[43]

If review is made abstract, then it not only avoids this problem of undue influence, it can also avoid some (not all) contingencies that arise from the nature of litigation. Constitutional adjudication is, like all litigious processes, a time-bound, technical system in which outcomes are influenced by parties' general litigation plan and strategic choices, and by the resources and the skill of the counsel they retain. The question of a law's constitutionality may arise in a case between private parties. More often, the duty to defend the constitutionality of legislation falls to members of the executive branch, whose usual function is to enforce the law rather than to provide theoretical justifications for it or to gather empirical evidence of the kind needed for a law to survive scrutiny under a proportionality inquiry.

Executive officials may have never considered the 'state interest' in legislation, or they may not be in full agreement with the legislature that enacted the law. They might be members of a party that opposed the law at its enactment; they might be privately disposed toward those who are challenging the law. Even if executive officials are keen to defend the law, there may be a mismatch between their resources and those of the law's challengers. In some cases, the challenge to a law is a well-orchestrated campaign by a business lobby (as in *Lochner* and the video game cases in chapter four) or other special interest groups. All of this may lead to imbalances in litigation resources, and it creates the possibility of a law that was made for the benefit of the entire community being struck down because the

[42] VF Comella, *Constitutional Courts and Democratic Values: A European Perspective* (New Haven, Yale University Press, 2014) 69.
[43] ibid.

individuals responsible for its defence made strategic mistakes in legal argument or were unable to muster sufficient empirical evidence to demonstrate the necessity of the law.

To avoid this, constitutional framers should limit the extent to which rights-based judicial review is beholden to some of the usual trappings of adversarial litigation. The research service proposed above would be an important contribution to this, by lessening the advantage one side might have in amassing evidence for a Brandeis brief. Framers might also consider creating a special office whose role is to speak for the public interest in legislation and which is given the full resources needed for that task.

A particular feature of current models of judicial review that should be avoided is the notion that the defenders of legislation should bear the burden of proof after some initial, relatively weak showing by the challengers. An example of this is *Chaoulli v Quebec*, where the Canadian Supreme Court concluded, on the basis of a thin, prima facie showing that the law at issue infringed the right to life, that the burden had shifted to the government to prove that the infringement was justified. Such a burden-shifting manoeuvre is an unhelpful importation from adversarial processes in civil cases, and a prejudicial way of framing questions about the constitutionality of legislation.

Finally, by making judicial review abstract rather than concrete, the process could be made more transparent. The current expectation of confidentiality of judicial deliberation in constitutional rights cases derives from the traditional role of courts deciding disputes between two parties. If the true nature of the dispute concerns the *public* meaning of a constitutional provision broadly affecting the political community, then there seems to be no good reason for the deliberations of those charged with deciding that meaning to be entirely confidential.

E. Remedies

In the major common law jurisdictions with judicial review, formal theory holds that an unconstitutional law is void *ab initio*. This includes the US,[44] Canada,[45] Ireland,[46] and Australia.[47] The reasoning behind this approach can be traced to

[44] See *Norton v Shelby County* (1886) 18 US 425 ('[A]n unconstitutional act is not a law; it confers no rights; it imposes no duties; it is, in legal contemplation, as inoperative as though it had never been passed'). Although later cases have called into question the remedy in *Norton* of imposing invalidity retroactively, the formal void *ab initio* theory has never been overruled.

[45] In Canada, the Constitution Act 1982, s 52(1) provides that laws contrary to it are 'of no force or effect,' and the Supreme Court has clarified that such laws 'are, *and always have been*, invalid and of no force or effect' (emphasis added): *Reference re Manitoba Language Rights* [1985] 1 SCR 721, 767.

[46] The Constitution of Ireland, Art 15, provides that laws repugnant to the constitution are 'invalid'; this has been interpreted by the Supreme Court to mean that an unconstitutional statute 'is to be deemed null and void from the moment of its purported enactment': *Murphy v Attorney General* (1982) IR 241, 309.

[47] *South Australia v Commonwealth* (1942) 65 CLR 373 ('A pretended law made in excess of power is not and never has been a law at all').

Marbury v Madison, where John Marshall held that an unconstitutional law is 'entirely void' and 'not law'.[48] If this theory were applied strictly, it could produce what the Canadian Supreme Court called 'legal chaos' in *Reference re Manitoba Language Rights*.[49]

In that case all the laws of Manitoba were found to be unconstitutional because they were promulgated only in English, contrary to a constitutional requirement that they also be in French. The Court described the chaos that could result from declaring all the laws void *ab initio*, which would render them invalid not only for the present but also the past, meaning that, generally, past decisions made pursuant to them are also invalid.[50] In order to avoid this, the Court relied on an implicit constitutional rule of law principle to deem the laws valid pending translations into French.[51] When the new laws were adopted, they were deemed to have retroactive effect for the period in which they were (formally, officially) void.[52]

The *Manitoba* case shows on a large scale the implications of the void *ab initio* approach that are present in many cases of judicial review of legislation on a smaller scale. To avoid the chaos of retroactive invalidity, courts have resorted to a variety of techniques. In the US courts may, pursuant to a balancing test applied on a case-by-case basis, refuse to impose retroactive effects when a law is annulled.[53] In Canada, the common method following the *Manitoba* case is to issue a suspended declaration of invalidity, allowing Parliament a period of time to reenact a constitutional law before the judgment takes effect.[54] This patchwork approach to evading the problems of the void *ab initio* theory can ameliorate many of the negative effects, but it in turn raises questions about the rule of law and the role of courts.[55]

The efforts of courts to evade the logical implications of the void *ab initio* theory are further evidence of the lack of conscious constitutional design in common law systems of judicial review of legislation. Constitutional framers would act unreasonably if they were to create intentionally a situation in which laws in effect for decades can suddenly be declared unconstitutional, with the effect that all decisions taken under them (taxes collected, criminals convicted[56] etc) are also invalid.

[48] *Marbury v Madison* 5 US 137, 177–78 (1803).

[49] [1985] 1 SCR 721, paras 55, 96.

[50] ibid para 58.

[51] ibid para 107.

[52] See The Re-Enacted Statutes of Manitoba 1987, s 8; B Juratowitch, *Retroactivity and the Common Law* (Oxford, Hart Publishing, 2008) 207.

[53] See *Chicot County Drainage District v Baxter State Bank* (1940) 308 US 371, 374.

[54] See S Choudry and K Roach, 'Putting the Past Behind Us? Prospective Judicial and Legislative Constitutional Remedies' (2003) 21 *Supreme Court Law Review* 2d 205, 228–29.

[55] Ben Juratowitch argues that the remedy of a suspended declaration is similar to the notion of prospective overruling of a law, which has long been thought to be inappropriate for common law courts: *Retroactivity and the Common Law*, above n 52, 207–10. '[I]f a court severs the link between the case before it and the new rule that the court espouses in the course of that case, then the court's function becomes blatantly legislative': ibid 210.

[56] For a case illustrating the problem of retroactive invalidity of criminal law see *A v Governor of Arbour Hill Prison* [2006] 4 IR 88.

Aware of this problem, Kelsen designed the Austrian Constitutional Court so that its declarations of unconstitutionality would take effect prospectively rather than retroactively. The annulled statute 'cease[s] to exist' as soon as the decision comes into force.[57] The decision has retrospective effect for the case in which the declaration is made, but only for that case. Kelsen described the nullification remedy as having 'the same character as a statute which abrogate[s] another statute';[58] in other words, the Court's power is essentially one of repeal. The insight that guided Kelsen is that '[t]he annulment of a law is a legislative function, an act—so to speak—of negative legislation. A court which is competent to abolish laws—individually or generally—functions as a negative legislator'.[59]

The Kelsenian approach is strongly preferable to the void *ab initio* approach with regard to rule of law values, and should be chosen by constitutional framers adopting a system of judicial review. However, framers should also consider whether the blunt remedy of nullification is always appropriate. The current practice of judicial review is, for the most part, fitted to the bivalent nature of judicial decision-making. A constitutional challenge to a law typically results in its either being upheld, or declared to be unconstitutional. Sometimes judges declare specific portions of a law unconstitutional, and sometimes they give signals to the legislature about how to revise a law in order to comply with constitutional rights. It is generally thought, however, that a court cannot itself amend legislation, or order the legislature to produce a law with revisions or particular language specified by the court itself. The *Smoking Ban Case* discussed above, however, is an example of a case in which a court's declaration of a law's unconstitutionality is accompanied by an order that borders on the exercise of legislative power. Here the German FCC specified a time period for legislatures to amend the law on smoking, and in the interim articulated conditions for the applicability of the current law. These consisted in an exception for small, one-room pubs and included specification of details of a legislative nature, such as the exact size of such pubs, warning signs, and restrictions on food service.[60]

Such a remedy is consistent with the premises underlying the use of proportionality inquiries in judicial review. Indeed, those premises support further extension of judicial power to mandate specific revisions to legislation. Nullification is a blunt instrument. It is, in fact, a *disproportionate* remedy for ensuring compliance with the principle of proportionality. It is ironic that the classic illustration of proportionality—using a sledgehammer to crack a nut—is applicable to the remedy of nullifying legislation. It is not always possible to cure a statute by removing one portion that offends against rights. If the German FCC had not

[57] H Kelsen, 'Judicial Review of Legislation: A Comparative Study of the Austrian and the American Constitution' (1942) 4 *Journal of Politics* 183, 186.

[58] ibid.

[59] H Kelsen, *General Theory of Law and the State* (Cambridge, Mass, Harvard University Press, tr A Wedberg, 1945) 268.

[60] *Smoking Ban Case*, BVerfGE, 121, 317.

issued its specified remedy, its reasoning about the law's constitutionality would have compelled its nullification. If a law is unconstitutional and nullification is the only remedy, a statute must be struck down completely.

If courts are presumed competent to engage in proportionality-based review of legislation, then they should also be presumed competent to participate directly in amending legislation. One of the key components of the proportionality inquiry is the question of whether there is a less restrictive alternative, that is, legislation that could effectively instantiate the legislative aim while imposing less of a burden on a constitutional right than the existing legislation. Note that this question does not consider whether the alternative legislation could or would find support in the elected legislature. It is not a question about a politically feasible alternative, but simply whether, in the abstract, there is a less restrictive alternative. There is no guarantee that nullification of existing legislation will be followed by enactment of the less restrictive alternative contemplated by the court. The proportionality inquiry, therefore, does not involve the question of whether the existing legislation, flawed though it may be, is superior to a possible future state of affairs in which that legislation is not replaced by the court's idea of a less restrictive alternative. If constitutional framers presume that courts are competent to determine what the less restrictive alternative is, then a court should be enabled to bring it into being. The alternative is to wait and hope that the legislature (which, *ex hypothesi*, failed the first time) will both possess the acumen and be able to muster the political will to enact the less restrictive alternative. There would be difficulties, which I do not explore here, with regard to whether specific remedial orders would result in constitutionally entrenched law or law that remains subject to change by the legislature. The nullification remedy, however, is far from ideal. By removing the existing law, it creates a legal vacuum in the interim and provides no assurance that, in the future, it will be filled by a law superior to the old one.

III. Council of Revision

The capacities proposed above for an institution exercising the power of rights-based judicial review are presented as an ideal for a country that has committed to adopt that power. Each capacity or feature exists in one or more existing courts, except for the research service. The latter has an analogue in the German FCC's capacity to engage directly with experts and solicit studies. All the capacities together form part of a coherent package that seems to be an attainable ideal. However, is an institution that resolves disputes about the law and constitution rather than between parties, that commissions studies and interrogates experts, that includes non-lawyer members, and that can repeal or revise the text of statutes, properly considered to be a *court*?

For ease of discussion, let us call the model a Council of Revision, in homage to the institution rejected at the Philadelphia convention. This is suggestive of the scope of its powers and avoids any implication of begging the question about its place within a classical separation-of-powers scheme by calling it a court. The name itself is not important, but, from the perspective of constitutional design, thinking about what kind of institution might be needed as a check on potential legislative failures need not be limited to a court in its classical sense. Kelsen acknowledged with regard to the constitutional court he proposed that

> even if it is referred to as a 'court', and even if, by virtue of its 'independence', it is a court from an organizational point of view, [it] is, nevertheless, as a result of its function, engaged in an activity that makes it something more than a *mere court*.[61]

The institution Kelsen conceived was far more limited than existing 'Kelsenian' courts, since his lacked power to enforce a bill of rights.

Each of the structures I have suggested above for the Council of Revision marks a significant departure from the classic adjudicative court described in general terms in chapter five, section I, or from Kelsen's 'mere court'. If one agrees that all or a significant number of the structures are needed for an institution that makes decisions about constitutional rights, then the argument for *judicial* review of legislation is better thought of as an argument for review by a quasi-legislative body that resembles a legislature in all important respects but one: crucially, it is not elected.

IV. Does the Legislature Need a Check?

In considering whether constitutional framers should adopt a Council of Revision as described in section II—or any other means of checking a legislature to protect constitutional rights—it is sensible to begin with the situation of countries that do not have rights-based, strong-form judicial review. These include the United Kingdom, Australia, New Zealand, Switzerland and the Netherlands. The UK has weak-form review under the Human Rights Act 1998, but the Act provides that a declaration of incompatibility does not affect the validity of an Act of Parliament.[62] New Zealand has a codified bill of rights that is an aid to interpretation, but, like the UK, preserves the Westminster tradition of parliamentary sovereignty. Australia has strong-form judicial review, but no bill of rights or rights-based review. The Dutch constitution explicitly prohibits judicial enforcement of the constitution,[63] and the Swiss constitution achieves the same end by providing that courts must apply federal law notwithstanding any constitutional provision.[64] In the Netherlands courts can review legislation for consistency with

[61] H Kelsen, 'On the Nature and Development of Constitutional Adjudication', above n 18, 46.
[62] Human Rights Act 1998, s 6.
[63] Constitution of the Netherlands, art 120.
[64] Constitution of Switzerland, art 190. See H Sniders and S Vogenauer, *Content and Meaning of National Law in the Context of Transnational Law* (Munich, Sellier, 2009) 57.

international law, including certain human rights, but on politically sensitive topics rarely go beyond providing informal declarations.[65]

If the aim of rights-based review is to protect the interests typically expressed in bills of rights and to preserve the healthy functioning of democracy, it would be difficult to find five countries with judicial review that have succeeded as well as the five countries above. If evidence is needed for this, Tamas Gyorfi has charted the performance of countries that lack strong-form judicial review (including the five above) or that exhibit a highly deferential form of review (the Nordic countries of Denmark, Finland, Sweden, and Norway, plus Iceland), and concluded that they consistently rank at the top of indexes that measure for protection of fundamental rights, the rule of law, and the general functioning of democracy.[66]

In any event, the list of countries in which legislatures effectively have the final say on most questions of constitutional rights should make one pause before concluding that rights-based judicial review of legislation is a requirement for legitimate democratic governance. Courts have inferior institutional capacities for empirical reasoning and a poor track record (chapter four), and there are no strong grounds for considering courts to be better at moral reasoning than legislatures (chapter five, section IV) or necessary for the protection of minorities (chapter five, section VI). These are all reasons for caution, and more arise when considering the problems of entrenching judgments that nullify legislative decisions (see chapter six).

Nonetheless, there may be situations in which the anticipation of a poorly functioning legislature or electoral system could justify, all things considered, the adoption of an institution with the power to strike down legislation based on constitutional rights. If so, the considerations analysed in section II above counsel adoption of an institution with the capacities of the Council of Revision analysed there. Otherwise, the body tasked with deciding constitutional rights cases will lack the needed capacities.

[65] J Uzman et al, 'The Dutch Supreme Court: A Reluctant Positive Legislator?' (2010) 14(3) *Electronic Journal of Comparative Law* (December 2010). In Switzerland courts also have direct access to international law, but use it even less than in the Netherlands.

[66] T Gyofi, *Against the New Constitutionalism* (Cheltenham, Edward Elgar, 2016) 146–53. The indexes Gyorfi uses were created by the Economist Intelligence Unit ('Democracy Index 2014'); the Polity IV Project; Freedom House ('Freedom in the world 2015'); the World Justice Project, 'Rule of Law Index 2015'. He also relies on extensive analysis of human rights performance of countries in D Law and M Versteeg, 'Sham Constitutions' (2013) 101 *California Law Review* 863. Gyorfi includes Canada in the list of countries that lack strong-form judicial review, classifying judicial review there as 'penultimate' (*Against the New Constitutionalism*, 220) because of the possibility of an override of Canadian Supreme Court decisions under s 33 of the Canadian Constitution, which allows Parliament to re-enact legislation notwithstanding the Charter of Rights and Freedoms. However, because s 33 has rarely been used at the national level, and is generally disfavoured in Canada, I would classify Canada as, de facto, a strong-form judicial review system. For an argument that s 33 has a more important role to play than is commonly thought, see D Newman, 'Canada's Notwithstanding Clause, Dialogue, and Constitutional Identities' (7 June 2017), available at SSRN: <https://ssrn.com/abstract=3019781>.

V. Deference

While the arguments in this chapter have focused on constitutional design, the book's analysis of institutional capacities of courts and legislatures is also relevant for courts that must decide how much deference to show to legislative judgments. This is a question that can arise in a variety of contexts, including determining the degree of scrutiny to apply in proportionality cases or the allowance of a margin of appreciation in the European Court of Human Rights. Courts should be aware of their relatively weak capacities for finding legislative facts and the legislature's relative strengths. And courts should not be over-confident regarding their capacity to make morally correct decisions. Courts should also take note of the long-lasting effects of nullification decisions, and the difficulty of correcting judicial mistakes. The record of the Nordic countries discussed above by Gyorfi suggests that a consciously deferential approach to rights review is consistent with protection of rights and a health democracy.

VI. Conclusion

Judicial review of legislation arose as a remedial measure against abuse of power by legislatures. At times the abuse was real. At other times it was merely potential. For Mauro Cappelletti the abuses were real. His eloquent argument for judicial review, quoted at the end of the Introduction, is worth revisiting:

> After the sad experiences of the first half of this century, there arose in Europe the need to put a check upon the legislature itself, for it had become evident that even legislation could be the source of great abuses. Hence Europeans, and non-Europeans as well, embarked on the path taken by the Americans so long before. Higher law was to be expressed in constitutions that were difficult to amend. The judiciary, or a part of it, was to be the instrument for assuring conformity to this higher law. The Old World moved from legal to constitutional justice.[67]

If this book has shown nothing else, it has shown that the potential for abuse is not the one-way road that Cappelletti envisions. It is a dual carriageway. Constitutional framers must consider the risks that courts will strike down laws due to errors in moral or empirical reasoning. The risk is greater the more courts exercise power in ways that exceed their institutional capacity. Judicial review of legislation can work injustice to individuals no less than abuse of power by legislatures. And the errors of courts are harder to correct.

Cappelletti characterised judicial review as 'the means by which human aspirations, as expressed in constitutional absolutes, are "concretized" into

[67] M Cappelletti, 'Judicial Review in Comparative Perspective' (1970) *California Law Review* 1017.

a living constitution'.[68] He thought that if constitutional framers forgo this, they 'deprive themselves ... of the sobering and ennobling experience that befalls those who check their acts against their principles and strive in performing the former never to lose sight of the latter'.[69] But this is not the only way to view the relationship between constitutional rights and political decision-making. As Kelsen observed, the broad norms in bills of rights are not yet 'positived': they can guide the legislature and through its work be 'turned into positive law'.[70] In *Carter v Canada* the Canadian Supreme Court struck down the prohibition on assisted suicide on the ground that it disproportionately infringed the right to life. The Canadian Parliament had enacted the law precisely to specify, or 'concretise', the right to life. Among other things, Parliament considered that loosening the prohibition would be a threat to the right to life, especially for the vulnerable.

There is no sound reason, either in the logic of rights or the structure of institutions, to conclude that courts and not legislatures are capable of protecting the right to life and other constitutional rights. The soaring rhetoric about judges as the guardians of rights matches the instinctive associations we make with courts: objectivity, finality, justice for the individual. All this is reinforced with symbolism and high architecture. But when we look behind the façade, we see a set of lawyers with the same elite training and no special competence for deciding the moral and factual issues at the heart of constitutional rights cases. The day to day work of legislatures is conducted in a less august setting, and necessarily described in more prosaic terms. But legislatures are no less capable of protecting and promoting constitutional rights than courts, and arguably more so.[71]

[68] M Cappelletti and JC Adams, 'Judicial Review of Legislation: European Antecedents and Adaptations' (1966) 79 *Harvard Law Review* 1207.

[69] ibid.

[70] Kelsen, 'On the Nature and Development of Constitutional Adjudication', above n 18, 59.

[71] For the argument see G Webber, P Yowell et al, *Legislated Rights: Securing Human Rights Through Legislation* (Cambridge, Cambridge University Press, 2018).

INDEX

www.ingramcontent.com/pod-product-compliance
Ingram Content Group UK Ltd.
Pitfield, Milton Keynes, MK11 3LW, UK
UKHW020820290926
15470UKWH00003B/1271

9 781509 913596